FrH 13

D0485382

Comfortable Cruising

ROMANY
REVISED 2010

Andy and Liza

Comfortable Cruising

Around North and Central America

by
Liza Copeland

Romany Publishing
Revised 2010

Canadian Cataloguing in Publication Data

Copeland, Liza
Comfortable Cruising, Around North and Central America

ISBN 0-9697690-4-0

Copeland, Liza —Journeys. 2. Bagheera (Yacht)
3. Yachting—North America. 4. Yachting—Central America
5. North America—Description and travel. 6. Central America—
Description and travel. I. Title.

GV815.C66 2001   917.04'54   C2001-910546-0

Also by Liza Copeland

Just Cruising, Europe to Australia   ISBN 0-9697690-0-8

Still Cruising Australia, Asia, Africa and America   ISBN 0-9697690-1-6

Cruising for Cowards—Boats, Strategies and   ISBN 0-9697690-3-2

DVD—*Just Cruising*   ISBN 0-9697690-2-4

Romany Publishing
3943 West Broadway
Vancouver, BC, V6R 2C2
Canada
Tel: 1 (604) 228-8712
Fax: 1 (604) 228-8779
Website: http://www.Aboutcruising.com

Cover design by Colin Copeland
Layout and design by Vancouver Desktop Publishing Centre Ltd.
Printed in Canada by Houghton Boston

For
Duncan, Colin and Jamie.
We missed you!

Acknowledgements

As always there are so many people to thank, several of whom have now helped me with all four books. My neighbor, Nancy Garrett has been a tower of strength with her enthusiasm and astute recommendations. Brenda de Roos again critiqued the entire manuscript, as did Lesley Christie. Trevor Jenkins, Graham Kedgley, Christine Chessex and Jean Lee contributed many hours of proofreading and during our recent crossing of the Atlantic Ocean Marc Pessim scrutinized the entire document with a fine toothcomb. I can't thank you all enough for dedicating your time so willingly.

I am also most grateful to Nigel Calder, Margo Wood, George Day and Carol Hasse for their kind endorsements on the back cover and to Margo for the use of Charles' magnificent photograph of Portage Bay.

Particular gratitude goes to my family, for their support and suggestions, and great company during visits to *Bagheera* during this sabbatical year. Colin also gets special merit for designing the front cover and for his expertise with the visual displays. Finally, my heartfelt thanks go to Andy for his great support, contributions, assiduous editing and for insisting that it was time to go cruising again!

Contents

AUTHOR'S NOTE

Imperial Measurements have been used throughout this book in line with U.S. common usage.

Note: 3.28 feet = 1 meter

Distances at sea are measured in nautical miles
1 nautical mile = 1.85 kilometers = 1.15 statute miles
This unit has been used traditionally for ease of navigation because:
   1 minute of latitude = 1 nautical mile
   1 degree of latitude = 60 nautical miles
A knot = one nautical mile an hour

It is useful to know that:
1 imperial gallon = 4.55 liters
1 U.S. gallon   = 3.78 liters

All **prices** are quoted in U.S. dollars

Prologue

Those who have read *Just Cruising* and *Still Cruising* will be familiar with our family cruising adventures when sailing around the world. During visits to eighty-two countries and colonies we absorbed a wealth of cultures, scenery, wild life and cuisine from Europe to the Caribbean, the Galapagos Islands and South Pacific, Australia, Southeast Asia, India and Africa. Our two years turned into six, then it was time to replenish the kitty and for our children to attend regular schools.

The adjustment back to the 'real world' was a shock, far more difficult than making the decision to go cruising! Andy returned to yacht broking. I wrote magazine articles and cruising books, and gave seminars on boating and travel. We sailed locally in the Pacific Northwest and led charter groups to exotic destinations around the world. But the call of the ocean grew stronger and after seven land-based years a one-year cruising sabbatical had been earned. Our first plan was to cross Europe by river and canal. A draft of seven feet and political strife decided us on the second idea, to sail around North and Central America.

After a six-month countdown at home in Vancouver, B.C. we headed out to the Pacific Ocean. Our 12,000 mile sabbatical took our 1985 Beneteau First 38 *Bagheera* down the west coasts of the United States, Mexico and Central America, through the Panama Canal, then up to eastern Canada through Caribbean Central America, Cuba and the American Atlantic seaboard. The eleven countries visited gave an amazing variety of climates and lifestyles, fascinating contrasts between old and new, intriguing histories and ancient sites, and phenomenal 'comfortable' coastal cruising.

For the hundreds who leave San Diego each winter we hope our account will entice many beyond the Sea of Cortez. Those setting out from the Eastern United States and Europe will find uncrowded Central America reminiscent of the eastern Caribbean of the '60s. Cuba offers a world of cruising venues that attracts many nationalities from around the world and the future look bright for Americans to head to its shores. The U.S. east coast provides unexpected cruising diversity, not to mention the seafood, with the mild climate a perfect relief from the summer heat down south. Nova Scotia and the Bras d'Or Lakes have their own unforgettable charm and a trip inland showed the huge cruising potential of the Great Lakes and the numerous waterways.

In contrast to our voyage around the world this coastal trip is far more achievable for less experienced cruisers and for those who do not feel comfortable crossing oceans. It is also feasible for power boaters as well as sail boaters, in fact we motored much of the time, and there are several inexpensive opportunities for leaving the boat for seasonal visits. Those wishing to cruise Alaska and the Pacific Northwest without making the uncomfortable trip up the North American west coast have the option of trucking their boat across the continent from the east coast or Great Lakes. Vancouver and Seattle have excellent marine facilities if required and after a summer of cruising in northern British Columbia and Alaska cruisers can harness the favorable winds and currents to continue to Mexico and the South Pacific.

Our cruise around North and Central America surpassed all expectations. We hope that this combination of practical boating and travel information, along with an account of our adventures, will inspire you to fulfil your dreams.

The
Pacific
Northwest

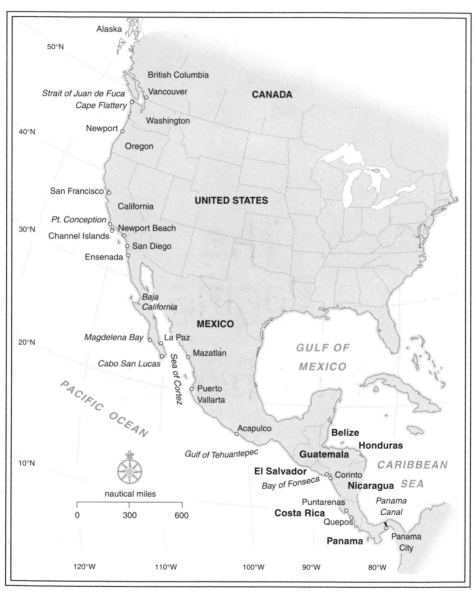

The West Coasts of North and Central America

1. Departure from Vancouver, B.C.

The Gulf Islands, Victoria and The Pacific Ocean

The departure date for our cruising sabbatical was set for August 1st at noon from the Royal Vancouver Yacht Club dock. Friends were to move into our house that same day and our crew to San Francisco had booked his flight from England—so there was no delaying!

The six-month countdown flew by. Our Beneteau 38' *Bagheera* was now thirteen years old and needed a thorough overhaul. New systems were added and gear replaced to make life easier on board, which was necessary due to our aging muscles and no young crew coming along. The house was prepared for renting, those jobs previously ignored now completed, drawers and cupboards packed away, some furniture stored and the basement made self-sufficient for our children. We had to organize two businesses to be left behind, obtain insurance policies (both boat and medical), be immunized for Central America, purchase supplies for the medical chest, provisions, spares, charts, cruising guides . . . The list seemed endless as regular life and work continued; our moods swung from elation to despair as chores were completed then new ones added. With our children staying behind communications took on a new priority. Being able to send e-mail from the boat was a wonderful bonus from modern technology—when we finally got it working!

To our amazement we were ready to greet family and friends on the dock at 10:00am as planned. Two hours flew by as the champagne flowed, then there was a cheer of anticipation as the last cork soared to the spreaders and

Bagheera *ready to go*

Andy started the engine. We cast off the lines right on schedule and excited-ly waved farewell.

As the marina faded astern, I was suddenly struck by a familiar pang. One of the down sides of cruising is saying good-bye to one's secure and comfort-able world. With a lump in my throat, doubts rushed through my mind. Did I really want to leave my children, home, and friends for a year, and go on an ocean passage down the Oregon coast that is renowned for its storms?

I might have succumbed to such dismal thoughts but this was only a tem-porary parting as we were leaving the boat in San Francisco and returning to Vancouver for the month of September. It was also hard to be gloomy on such a spectacular day with friends jubilantly escorting us out. I reminded myself that the offshore voyage should be easy with four on board and it would be great to catch up on sleep. My spirits returned. After all, this was the start of another grand cruising adventure that was to include eleven countries, five of which we'd never explored before.

Vancouver's beauty is often compared to that of Cape Town, Rio and Sydney, but on a sunny summer's day it is hard to rival. Its lush green mountains, still tinged with snow, soared up from the brilliant ocean. Gardens were a blaze of color. The dramatic downtown silhouette danced to the rays of the sun beside the dark green arm of Stanley Park that has a thousand acres of forest, walking paths, lagoons and wildlife.

Bagheera sped by Spanish Banks and out to the Bell Buoy. The log-strewn beaches were covered with sunbathers, volleyball players, kids building sandcastles and joggers, with groups barbecuing in the adjacent parks. The sea was filled with kayakers, fishing boats, daysailers, and racers; we detoured around a group of novice windsurfers who were laughingly spending more time swimming than sailing. Not surprisingly, Vancouver boasts the shortest working hours, lowest stress level, and greatest sales in running shoes, boats and skis in Canada!

Richard, Andy's cousin from England, was joining us for his first passage offshore. "What an incredible place to live," he enthused, "but what about the winter, isn't it very cold?"

"Not really," I replied. "Unlike the rest of Canada the climate is really benign here, not dissimilar to England, and you can cruise almost year round with the right clothing. It does rain a lot in winter but that means more snow for skiing. Whistler is only two hours away and our local mountains are just half an hour. There aren't many places where the discussions in the Yacht Club after winter races are about whether to go cruising, fishing or skiing in the afternoon!"

"It's all amazing," Richard continued as we entered the Straits of Georgia. "And now there are islands in every direction."

"This is one of the most stunning areas in the world for cruising," Andy told him. "It extends for thousands of miles with thousands of islands in mostly protected waters."

I could almost feel Richard thinking, 'Then why are you leaving it?' when Andy explained, "The only problem is I get really gloomy in the winter rains and the water is always cold." Little did we know that we would be away for British Columbia's wettest winter on record!

We moved to British Columbia after leaving the Caribbean in 1973 and are still captivated by its breathtaking vistas, exotic wildlife and the sheer magnitude of the dramatic coast with its soaring mountains and fjords that rank both in size and grandeur with New Zealand, Southern Chile and

Norway. Victoria to Glacier Bay in Alaska is 1000 linear miles but it is so indented with fjords, inlets and islands that it has Over 25,000 miles of coastline. To the south, Puget Sound offers further cruising grounds with the San Juan Islands a particular treasure. Every summer we have cruised the coast to both the popular areas close-by and further afield; the potential is vast, the ultimate cruiser's paradise.

History abounds. The First Nations people are said to have arrived over 10,000 years ago. Europeans started coming in the sixteenth century. Juan de Fuca, a Greek in the service of Spain, reputedly visited in 1592 and is given the credit for discovering the Strait which bears his name located at the southern end of Vancouver Island. Recently there has been speculation that Sir Francis Drake made a voyage up this way in 1579 but was forced to keep the visit a secret as it was believed that he had discovered the Pacific entrance to the vital Northwest passage. The theory is supported by his maps that resemble this coastline far more closely than the southerly location indicated by the latitude on the chart.

Captain Cook's arrival in 1778 stimulated several other intrepid seafarers after whom islands and towns have been named. Manuel Quimper sailed up the Strait of Juan de Fuca and landed at Sooke in 1790, Galiano and Valdes soon followed. Captain George Vancouver came in his war sloop *Discovery* in 1792 and was so taken with the "serenity of the climate, the . . pleasing landscapes" that he explored for the next two years surveying much of the coast, a remarkable feat in view of the reefs and swift currents that surge through the passes in the island chains. He was also looking for the famed Northwest Passage and rivers to link with the interior but Simon Fraser, after whom one of Vancouver's two universities is named, was the first white man to travel the Fraser River to its mouth in 1808.

In 1858 the first gold prospectors swarmed up the coast to the Queen Charlotte Islands, then further through the Inside Passage to Alaska and the Klondike in the Yukon. The salmon that had sustained the native peoples also attracted attention and canneries appeared along the coast. Others saw the potential of the forests, and logging camps and mills sprang up. Soon the primary industries of the coast were thriving with supplies, workers and their families taken in and out by sea.

For centuries boats have plied these waters, from canoes to square riggers, steam ships to cruise ships. Today large numbers of cruisers go north every summer. They are attracted by the tranquility, easy cruising, excellent fishing, abundant wildlife and the great escape from the rat-race of their daily lives.

Just an hour away from our dock lies Howe Sound which, with its many island anchorages, is convenient for weekend venues. Snug Cove on

Bowen Island is our favorite winter destination with its pub on the dock, trails for long walks and small bakery for the perfect cruising breakfast.

The Gulf Islands, to which we were now heading, are a four-hour sail across the Gulf of Georgia. These two hundred and fifty islands stretch fifty miles along Vancouver Island's southeast coast. They have almost a Mediterranean climate and are far drier than the mainland, due to their location in Vancouver Island's rain-shadow. The chain is entered through turbulent passes only possible near slack water: their whirlpools always delighted our boys, making an exciting finish to the end of a passage.

Once through a pass the mass of green conifer and ochre-skinned arbutus-covered islands offer a myriad of attractive anchorages and marine parks. With the flat seas and a good breeze there is wonderful day-sailing down the channels. Vistas vary from the white sands of Sydney spit, to the rocky inlet of Pirates Cove, to large Saltspring Island that is known for its artisan community. Mayne Island bills itself as, 'The Isle of Health and Happiness', a feeling that is reflected in the entire chain. Eight of the larger islands have a substantial permanent resident community and with planning it is easy to replenish supplies en route at one of the friendly stores.

"Everyone is always so energetically enthusiastic, it's a real West Coast trait," was a friend's apt description.

One of Andy's passions in life is wildlife and abundant marine life is one of the fascinations of the Pacific Northwest. We frequently see Dall porpoises, harbor seals and Steller sealions, with Californian sea lions visiting in winter. This area is on the whale migratory route with gray, humpback and finback sighted. Spotting the tall dorsal fins of the distinctive orcas, or killer whales, is a common but always exciting event, especially when they raise their black and white heads and spout close to the boat, or leap up from the sheer joy of being alive. Often a large group of these whales (there are eighteen pods resident in the area) is associated with the five varieties of salmon running to spawn up river.

I still have a vivid memory of being surrounded by killer whales off the Fraser River. It was a particularly awesome experience. Not only were they leaping and spouting as far as the eye could see, I was bringing back our San Juan 24 from a regatta in Bellingham, just south of the U.S. border, with just 15-month old Duncan for crew!

Birdwatchers are also in their element here. Over a million birds use the Pacific flyway for their migration routes. Snow geese visit Siberia for the summer and Rufous hummingbirds travel up from Mexico to hatch their tiny chicks. Typical species that we see from the boat include gulls, murres, murralets, several varieties of duck, swans, vultures, herons and the distinctive bald eagles with their huge nests. On walks ashore we often spot mink, raccoons, river otters and deer; with black bears, skunks, beavers and coyotes prevalent but not often seen.

One of the joys of the Pacific Northwest is that it provides a perfect cruising ground for the less experienced and for families; it is particularly forgiving in the light-wind summer months. Boats often anchor stern-to, with a line tied to a tree or rock ashore. Usually it is calm enough to raft boats together and we have special memories of brightly colored life-jacket clad kids who loved their summers afloat.

"Can I row everyone ashore in the dinghy?" Duncan would frequently ask, as he was often the eldest kid in the group. At other times the children would grab the stern line and pull themselves ashore.

During the long summer evenings while parents enjoyed a sundowner on board with the catch of the day—prawns, clams or oysters, and a mouth-watering salmon, cod or snapper cooked to perfection on a rail-mounted barbecue—the children played contentedly on the beach. They never tired of building forts out of driftwood or discovering fish, crabs, nudibranchs, anemones and starfish in the rocky pools. With such positive experiences there was no hesitation in our boys' response when we told them about our plan to cruise overseas.

"A two-year summer holiday?" they enthused. I quickly added that they would still be doing their schoolwork!

Little did we guess at that time that this would lead to our six-year circumnavigation, which is documented in *Just Cruising* and *Still Cruising*.

By the time we had finished telling Richard about the joys of previous local cruising, *Bagheera* had crossed the Straits of Georgia. After surging through the whirlpools at Porlier Pass, we gave him a quick taste of Gulf Island sailing before stopping for the night at the Yacht Club outstation on Saltspring.

It was a long weekend and full of cruising families. Children lined the docks with their fishing lines, buckets and bait; the water was full of tiny fish with deep purple starfish on the ocean bed. Others were rowing out to pick up their crab traps, buckets of clams already hung from their boats in the water.

"Out for the summer?" was a frequent comment as we chatted to numerous friends.

"Actually, a bit longer," I replied, still finding it hard to believe we weren't as usual part of this scene but instead were heading offshore!

Next day we continued to Victoria, at the southern end of Vancouver Island, and entered the inner harbor. It was bustling with ferry and seaplane traffic while entertaining buskers collected crowds along the wharf. Victoria is an attractive city with its old stone and brick buildings. Not only has it maintained its genteel character it is said to be more English than the English themselves and afternoon tea at the Empress Hotel is an institution.

Peter, a friend from our previous offshore cruising, was waving to us from the dock.

"I've found you a berth," he called out, and gave us directions.

"Thank you so much. I called on the radio but everywhere seemed full," I said to him after we had tied our lines.

"It's the Symphony Splash tomorrow night, "he informed us. "The Victoria Symphony Orchestra plays on a barge in the middle of the harbor. Good timing, it's a great event."

We had a wonderful dinner with Peter and Lydia, and reminisced into the night about our cruising days together. After meeting in Malta, when they were on their catamaran *Blyss II*, we had frequently cruised together in the Mediterranean, had both crossed the Atlantic in the first Atlantic Rally for Cruisers, then sailed through the Caribbean. Their children Anya and Ryan are close to Jamie in age and were his cruising playmates.

"We always watch the Symphony from our canoe," Lydia told us.

"Great, we can go in our dinghy. Can you launch the canoe by *Bagheera* and come for a sundowner first?"

We joined the mass of small boats by the barge in front of the picturesque, floodlit Empress Hotel and Parliament buildings. As Peter fed us superb homemade wine from juice bottles and delicious hors d'oevres we began to feel quite into the 'cruising' mode. It was a lively performance of

Richard and Duncan checking out their lifeharnesses

popular music and a great atmosphere with the boats, lights and appreciative crowds around the harbor.

Meanwhile our eldest son Duncan had arrived and took Richard out 'on the town' with some university friends. "Don't forget we are having a safety check at 9:00am," Andy reminded them.

Bagheera's crew were up but not a lively bunch the next morning. It took an hour to check out the lifeharnesses, equipment and man-overboard procedures and we were all quite relieved that a full gale in the Straits of Juan de Fuca necessitated spending the rest of the day firmly attached to the dock! It gave us time to say more good-byes, sightsee, and refresh our memories of provincial heritage at the Royal British Columbia Museum. We reconnected with the sea by watching whale movies at the IMAX theatre and Richard treated us to a magnificent tour of Victoria and the Saanich Peninsula by floatplane. Not only did this give an extensive perspective of the many island destinations we could also follow the Juan de Fuca Strait out to the Pacific Ocean.

Battling strong head winds up the Strait the following day with *Bagheera* clawing her way past Race Rocks, we decided to pull into Becher Bay for a few hours, hoping that the winds would follow their usual pattern and ease during the night. It was gusting 34 knots, wind against current. By midnight it was down to a steady 12-knot westerly and we set off motor sailing for Cape Flattery. If the weather deteriorated again we could always pull into Neah Bay. By 7:00am the steep 115-foot cliff of Cape Flattery was in sight, its large radar dome prominent above the low cloud, with Tatoosh Island and several dramatic rocks to seaward. The winds were calm as we passed the Cape but *Bagheera* was pounding through short, steep waves.

Looking west Richard voiced with awe, "Four thousand miles of Pacific Ocean before more land."

Visibility was poor as we eased sheets and the big ocean swells lifted the hull. We took deep breaths of both reverence and exhilaration; we were now embarked on another voyage on this, the largest of oceans.

2. Tales of Cruising

Northern British Columbia and Alaska

Although we were not going to visit more of the Pacific Northwest and Alaska on this trip it would be criminal not to mention some of the many other cruising opportunities in this magnificent region. From Seattle north there are numerous choices for anchorages or marinas in Puget Sound and few would give the charming San Juan Islands a miss, particularly as there is so often a sighting of orcas.

Desolation Sound is a destination for those who have more time to spare. Some ninety miles north of Vancouver (250 miles from Seattle) it has the largest marine park in British Columbia and boasts warm waters due to the convergence of tidal currents from around the north and south of Vancouver Island.

Favorite spots on the passage en route include white-sand Buccaneer Bay and protected Secret Cove for the night. We especially enjoy Hardy Island where there is one of the many marine parks. When the kids were young they enjoyed jumping off boulders in the anchorage then we walked across the island on a pretty leafy path. Along the way we picked black-berries and apples at an old farmstead then enjoyed a red sunset where a rough pool had been made on the beach. Although now much of the island is private it is still a serene place.

The tranquil Harmony Islands have always given happy times with Freil waterfall tumbling down the steep rock face perfectly located for a bracing shower. The steep-sided fjord of Princess Louisa Inlet is a stunning diversion with its sheer granite cliffs rising over 6000 feet, deep turquoise water, and Chatterbox Falls cascading down the mountainside at its head. Just south of Desolation lies Savary Island known as B.C.'s south sea island because of its sandy beaches, and the mossy Copeland Islands that are tiny but lovely and offer a safe anchorage for a few vessels. They were named after Joe Copeland, an American who fought in the Civil War before becoming a homesteader.

"Wow!" is the only way to describe Desolation Sound itself.

The scenery is not only stunning, its grandeur is overwhelming. Peaks tower 7000' with seabeds over 2000' deep in channels that are less than a mile wide. One can spend weeks going from one spectacular anchorage to the next in this lush high-island group that is bordered by the snow-capped Coastal Range. Calm and serene, although with the occasional blow for an exciting sail, it is the ultimate cruising getaway, deserted for ten months of the year with only July and August a busy time. Ironically it was too quiet for Captain Vancouver. He found the islands silent and gloomy hence his name 'Desolation'.

A few of the many popular anchorages include the landlocked haven of Squirrel Cove where it is fun to take the dinghy through the reversing rapids into a lagoon, and pretty Prideau Haven. Refuge Cove has fuel, supplies and mail, Teakerne Arm boasts Cassel Cascade and Tenedos Bay has a trail to Unwin Lake, one of the many lakes that are great for a refreshing swim and laundry for those who, like ourselves, find it hard to tear themselves away.

To the west through the turbulent pass of Hole in the Wall lie the Octopus Islands, one of our favorite areas on this coast. Another marine park, this land-locked group is secluded from commercial boats and less frequented than Desolation Sound. Typical of this coast, it is subject to many moods and changes of character. One day it is sunny and crystal clear, perfect for gunkholing, windsurfing and barbecuing the latest catch. The next day damp fog may descend, its dramatic white swirls enveloping the islands and boats. It transforms the anchorage, and was, in the days before we had radar, a navigator's nightmare.

Those wanting a night away from galley duties will enjoy Blind Channel Marina and Resort in West Thurlow, where a German family has for years served dinner and made wonderful homemade bread. Power and water are available on the dock, including a laundry and showers. The boys loved climbing up through the rain forest here to the 800-year old cedar tree that has a 16-foot diameter.

A passage north on Vancouver Island's east side goes through Seymour

Narrows. With tidal ranges up to 15 feet it is always desirable to transit the many passes at slack tide, but here there is no choice. A third of the waters of Georgia strait squeezes through this narrow gap creating formidable rips and whirlpools, and very strong currents. *Charlie's Charts Cruising Guide* recommends that only boats able to maintain speeds in excess of 17 knots should attempt it at other than near slack; even cruise ships time their passages accordingly.

Now the climate zone changes. The water is colder, making the air temperature cooler. The slopes are steeper and the trees smaller, coming right to the water's edge. Anchorages are fewer and it is more difficult to land ashore. When one does penetrate the forest, it is darker, danker and dripping with decay. Lichens and mosses thrive in excess. Where there is light, foliage explodes in a kaleidoscope of greens; plants have primitive flowers and berries galore. Indian clamshell middens and petroglyphs are common, as are deserted anchorages. Although peacefully relaxing by day, at night the silence can be deafening. A loon's call sounds so eerie it sends shivers down one's spine and the aloneness is almost overwhelming.

As one of our guests aptly expressed, "I feel I'm on the edge of the world."

We could also appreciate Robert Service's lines: 'I've stood in some mighty mouthed hollow, That's plumb full of hush to the brim.' from his *Spell of the Yukon.*

Johnstone Strait is infamous for its strong currents, choppy seas and cool winds that in summer months roar down the channel until after dark. After stocking up at centers such as Port McNeill and Port Hardy, one can either continue north past Cape Caution to Prince Rupert and Alaska, go west around Cape Scott and down the rugged and wreck-strewn west coast of Vancouver Island, or divert to the Queen Charlotte Islands.

Bull Harbour, named after the bull sea lions found in the 19th century, provides a sheltered anchorage to assess the conditions of Queen Charlotte Sound and the Hecate Strait, renowned for their strong winds and high seas. One might also stop for a dive at God's Pocket, known for its brilliant marine life, where colorful sea anemones, large starfish and giant octopus abound. Cruising friends, after several years in the South Pacific, claim this is better than any of their tropical diving.

While cruising the coast it is hard not to become involved in native culture with groups of colorful new totems and ancient ones that have almost rotted away. It is fascinating to find and analyze middens and petroglyphs on walks ashore, and tourist shops display the unique designs of different native tribes' arts and crafts. The Coast Salish live between Victoria and Campbell River, then one enters Kwakiutl territory; the Tsimshian are mostly south of the Alaskan border with the Tlingit to the north. The seagoing Haida live in the Queen Charlotte Islands or Haida Gwaii as they call their homeland.

At Canada's northwesterly point above the 52nd parallel, the Queen Charlotte Islands cling to the edge of the continental shelf, just before the ocean plunges to incredible depths. Culturally rich, ecologically unique, teeming with wildlife and having dramatic scenic diversity it offers fascinating cruising.

The islands lie 60 miles out to sea from the Canadian mainland, 30 miles from the southern tip of the Alaskan panhandle and 100 miles north of Vancouver Island. The passage across the shallow Hecate Strait and Queen Charlotte Sound can be rough, but the weather was benign for our visit five years ago and we even had to motor-sail part of the 130-mile trip from Port Hardy.

It was a memorable night with a deep-red sunset, brilliant phosphorescence glowing in our wake and a bright 'Great Bear' constellation sparkling overhead.

"Look, those are sooty shearwaters," Andy had pointed out excitedly to Jamie, our youngest son. "Do you remember we last saw them as 'muttonbirds' in Australia?"

Albatrosses and storm petrels also hovered about the boat; two birds rested for awhile on the pulpit, cheekily cocking their heads and staring at us with their beady black eyes. Suddenly dolphins were riding the bow wave and then the fishing line buzzed out with a well-timed salmon for dinner. It was wonderful to be back on the Pacific Ocean.

At dawn we were drifting past the Kerouard Islands by Cape St. James, being entertained by the sea lions at play. Barking noisily as they leapt into the swells, they enjoyed a relaxing drift or energetic play before laboriously clambering back up the steep, slippery rocks, only to flop down again into the surf below.

The wind came up for a great sail to SGaang Gwaii (Anthony Island), a rugged, bird-foot shaped island off the southwest coast. Over 300-feet high and constantly battered by waves from the western Pacific, it is home to many exotic birds such as black-footed albatrosses and tufted puffins, and is visited by migrating whales. It also has the best-preserved Haida village, Nan Sdins (Ninstints) which was declared a World Heritage Cultural Site by UNESCO in 1981.

Nan Sdins was home to the Kunghit Haida. Tragically, this once thriving village was decimated by small pox, brought to the islands by missionaries and traders in the 19th century. Of the estimated 7000 Haida in the islands only 600 still survived by 1862. In 1884 twenty-five carved and twenty mortuary poles still stood here. Many rotted away, so in 1957 others were removed and taken to the mainland to be preserved.

The Haida were one of the most culturally rich and highly developed peoples of early North America. They are particularly known as a seafaring nation, as well as for their lavish potlatch feasts and sophisticated art forms. The few centuries-old weatherworn cedar totems that line the beach, with moss-covered beams and pits of tumbled long houses behind, are a moving sight.

We edged cautiously into the bay to the south of the abandoned village, watching the depth carefully as it shallowed to two fathoms, and avoided the rocks and kelp off the rocky point. This small anchorage is open to south winds and only of use in fair weather (as is the northerly anchorage that is currently favored). We quickly launched the dinghy and went around to the village. At high tide (23' range) small boats can enter the short channel, although care has to be taken to avoid the wide strands of golden kelp. Landing on the small, protected, curved gravel beach in front of the village, it is easy to imagine how it would have looked when lined with decorated cedar canoes. At low tide an ancient canoe-launching ramp was exposed that is still usable, although covered with seaweed and slippery.

The warden welcomed us. He had a painting of the original village in his hand and pointed out where we could tread. "The area has been cleared of new undergrowth," he informed us, "and the poles cleaned of moss and propped up to try to help preserve them. Please keep to the worn paths to view them."

The ground was springy under our feet as we walked slowly in the brilliant sunshine, frequently pausing to absorb the sight of the leaning memorial poles in the lush setting of dark cedars and golden grass. It was a moving glimpse of life gone by, a testimony to an ancient heritage. According to legend, the Haida were created here by 'the raven who captured the sun' after he brought life-giving light to the dark ice-encrusted earth. We felt privileged to be able to stand and absorb this poignant scene before all signs of the village disappear into the earth, as inevitably happens in this climate.

SGaang Gwaii is part of the South Moresby Island Gwaii Haanas National Park Reserve that stretches over 60 miles from North to South. It has 138 islands and 800 miles of shoreline that provide spectacular anchorages. Scenery varies from lush green growth to bare rocks, misty inlets to dramatic mountain vistas. There are old-growth rainforests of huge western hemlock, red cedar and Sitka spruce that were alive during the time of the Crusades, and an amazing 500 abandoned Haida sites.

The area has become known as the 'Canadian Galapagos' due to its diverse ecosystem. This developed because, unlike most of Canada, portions of the islands escaped glaciation. Many unique species of plant and animal life have been found, while other species are only duplicated in Japan. We were particularly fascinated by the black bears that are far larger than those on the mainland and we frequently saw them down at the water's edge with their young.

The annual plankton bloom triggers a fish feeding frenzy, which in turn attracts migrating whales and birds. There are many varieties of birds, including one quarter of a million nesting seabirds, peregrine falcons, hawks, auklets and the highest concentration of bald eagles in North America. A variety of whales may be sighted including blue, sperm, minke, sei, gray, finback, humpback and orca, and there are huge numbers of sea lions and seals. Burnaby Narrows has an incredibly rich display of intertidal life with nudibranchs, shellfish, crustacia, anemones and starfish of innumerable colors and shapes, all fascinating to explore at low tide.

Haida watchmen safeguard both the natural and cultural treasures during the summer months. We found them great personalities, well versed in the art of story telling. In Skedans, Charles had taught his serene teenage granddaughter Mandy to show tourists around. With old pictures she brought alive the rotting logs that had once stood proudly as frontal poles of long houses—family symbols of heritage, lineage, status and prestige. Barely discernible bumps and hollows were shown to be carvings of raven,

Andy and Jamie enjoying a hot soak on Hotspring Island

eagle, wolf and killer whale. Even the beaver was present, which was interesting, as beaver was not found on the islands.

"It would have been sighted on one of the expeditions to the mainland, so was even more prestigious," she explained. By the end of the morning she had brought alive the clearing with its few scattered logs to recreate the village and daily activities of a community 700 strong of both the Eagle and Raven clans.

Penetrating the dense forest we came across several pieces of old machinery that were enveloped in brilliant green moss. Out of the gloom we could make out the rotted mounds of buildings. Close-by were gravestones from the turn of the century; several had been pushed over by the large roots of massive trees. Some people had had very short lives in the logging and prospecting camps. It was dark, dank and eerie. We looked at each other and shivered.

"Let's get back to the beach and the sun," I suggested and we quickly retraced our steps.

Clam and abalone shells lined the trail up through ancient spruce and cedar to the small cabin where Mabel lived on Hotspring Island. We scrambled over the rocks to the hot mineral pools that are fed by bubbling sulphurous springs. It was wonderfully relaxing, soaking up to our necks in the steaming water while looking out over spectacular Juan Perez Sound. In the distance a group of brightly-dressed kayakers energetically paddled to their next campsite in a small cove. The day was calm, but a few days later there was a sudden change in weather, not uncommon for these waters. It was amazing how rapidly the winds increased and the seas came crashing in on the shores.

It was due to these fierce winds that the Haida had to develop large seagoing canoes and became the most feared of the Indian tribes, Wesley told us at Windy Bay, where a small replica of Chief Clu's longhouse has been reconstructed. He also told us proudly how the Haida had banded together in 1985 to prevent logging in the nearby old forest. They held out long enough to attract international attention and secure protection for the park and Haida Heritage Site. We climbed up to inspect some of the oldest trees. They were huge, the moss covered trunks making a mockery of Andy's two-meter arm span.

Our three-week vacation had flown by and it was time to hand *Bagheera* over to our friends. We would love to return there one day, although now a trip to Gwaii Haanas National Park Reserve must be planned in advance as there are restrictions on numbers and permits must be obtained (Call Supernatural BC at Tel: 1 (800) 435-5622). The unpredictable weather demands a flexible schedule to come this far north (over 500 miles from

Chief Clu's longhouse

Vancouver), especially by sailboat. Winds can be strong, but sometimes there are several weeks of calm and a reliable engine is essential if running on tight deadlines. The July days are warm ashore but the cool water temperature makes the wind chilly. Although the ocean was unusually warm on our visit, and the fishermen were frustratingly finding mackerel and sunfish instead of salmon, we still needed to wear a fleece and a jacket when underway.

On this trip we had five families sharing our boat for the two-months that *Bagheera* was away from Vancouver. With the vistas, the wildlife, fascinating intertidal discoveries, Haida sites, local personalities, the adventure of cruising in such a remote area and stimulating passages, it turned out to be a remarkable holiday for adults and children alike, one that we all still discuss with animated enthusiasm.

We hoped that we would also have time to take *Bagheera* to Alaska, especially after friends spent the summer there and returned with glowing reports.

"It really is the last frontier," they told us. "Most people just go up the Inside Passage but that hardly touches the surface of the Alaskan coast-line—it's unbelievably vast. The mountains and fjords are amazing, there is so much wildlife and the glaciers and bergs are so awesome they're humbling. It just gets grander and grander the further you go north."

It is not uncommon to cover over 2,500 miles to Glacier Bay from Vancouver or Seattle and with no three-month holiday window in sight we had to rely on the hospitality of others. Besides warm clothing, toques and

gloves we made sure we packed our foul weather gear. Lying in a migratory low-pressure system, the Alaskan panhandle lacks a settled, sunny summer season and can be very wet.

Just ninety miles north of Canada's Prince Rupert lies Ketchikan, Alaska's southernmost Port of Entry. Named 'Alaska's first City', as it was the first stop for mail, this town's colorful history make it worthwhile a visit and there are several facilities for boats along the Tongass Narrows. The world's largest collection of totem poles is especially impressive and there is excellent information on the traditions of the native Tlingit.

The attractive old houses on Creek Street, built on piles and connected by boardwalks, now have shops selling local arts and crafts. Some even have their original furnishings such as the one owned by Dolly, the notorious 'madam' for the visiting fishermen, miners and loggers—who, I read in the hardware store, had the surname of Copeland!

It was fascinating to watch the huge number of salmon run up the Creek, although I felt for those females.

"They look so worn and skinny," I commented. "It's terrible that they have to struggle so hard to find a spot to dig into the gravel to spawn." Even more distressing was the number of females who had died, because they had already laid their eggs.

"Just feel lucky you aren't a salmon!" Andy retorted.

Overhead there were bald eagles in abundance. These birds are distinctive with their snow-white heads and tails, and large wingspan of six to eight feet. They can spot live fish over a mile away and we watched fascinated as they sailed high in the sky then suddenly dropped on their prey.

They much prefer to pick up fish that are dead however, hence their numbers here.

Heading north the fjord-like inlets become steeper, and the snow line creeps lower down the steep sides of the glaciated mountains. Piloting can be tense through the twisting, narrow passages off the main channels. The steep rock-sided anchorages are dramatic and frequently deep. With as much as a 25-foot tidal range, 300 foot of chain is often needed to anchor. Currents can be strong and route planning with tidetables mandatory. As in the Pacific Northwest, there are many logs in the water and a careful watch is required. Those floating are not too difficult to spot, but 'deadheads' (saturated logs that hang vertically just beneath the surface) are a hazard. Fortunately several were tagged with flags as a warning.

The weather was changeable. Winds were either with us or against, gusting up or down the channels and occasionally funneling ferociously through rocky ravines; but mostly there were long calms. Our friends had told us they had sails up for only ten days in four months with a mere five good sails. On many occasions the rain came down relentlessly but at others the sun peeked through, enhancing the bright green foliage on the hills, glistening on the glaciers, creating spectacular rainbows overhead and changing the ocean from its habitual gray to a brilliant blue. Every day we were absorbed in the wonderful wildlife and were glad we had come laden with reference books. There is also great fishing, excellent prawning and endless spectacular vistas.

Although for the most part piloting is straightforward, as with the entire coast visibility is often reduced by cloud and rain, and with deserted anchorages being the norm can come a feeling of isolation. If one misses the cruising community, listening to the Great Northern Boaters' Ham radio net gives a good idea of who is out there, besides providing local knowledge. (0745 PDT on 3870kHz, 0800 on 7280 kHz. Alaska is one hour earlier than BC and Washington State.) Although there are few cruisers there are plenty of fishing boats. The major centers are usually excellent for stocking up, but as everything is brought in by barge produce is much better just after the barge has arrived. Make sure to get to the store before the fishing fleet. We found one shop that been vacuumed out!

Ernest Sound and Zimovia Strait provide a scenic trip to Wrangell, which has a fascinating multi-cultural background. For centuries it was an important trading post for the Tlingit Indians. The Russians built a fort here in 1834 to guard against the Hudson Bay trappers, then later the British leased the area. It was named Wrangell when under the American flag, after a Russian baron.

The mile-wide fjord of Tracy Arm is a spectacular stop with its 2000' cliffs, waterfalls and tidewater glaciers, although currents are strong and there are icebergs to dodge. Originally a gold-mining town Juneau the Alaskan capital can only be reached by boat and plane. Nestled between Mount Juneau and Mount Roberts, this largest city in southeastern Alaska has a scenic approach and many facilities for boaters. It is a good place to stock-up for Glacier Bay and to visit the 'walk-in' Mendenhall Glacier with its informative visitors' center.

At the northeasterly end of the Inside Passage, through the Lynn Canal, Chilkoot Inlet and Taiya Inlet, lies the old mining town of Skagway with its false-front buildings and wood-plank sidewalks. With a winter population of 800 it is far removed from the infamous city in the days of Soapy Smith, when 20,000 made the town their base for prospecting the gold that in 1897 was claimed to be 'everywhere for anyone to pick up'. The museum gives insight into life during the Klondike goldrush days, the characters, the hopes of the gold seekers and the incredibly harsh conditions that prospectors had to endure. Now a thriving summer tourist stop, with excursions to the Yukon by train and bus, it even offers Starbucks coffee!

Glacier Bay, situated at the northern end of the Inside Passage straddling 58° 40'N, is the prime attraction for most cruisers who make the long voyage up the coast. Since John Muir discovered the bay in 1879 few visitors can have been disappointed. Lying in the center of vast Glacier Bay National Park and Preserve which covers 3.2 million acres, the bay is a truly magnificent sight with snow-capped peaks rising over 15,000', dramatic inlets and fjords and sixteen tidewater glaciers. When Captain Vancouver sailed through Icy Strait in 1774 the bay barely existed. Less than a century later Muir found the end of the bay had retreated more than 20 miles. Now the glacier that bears his name is almost 60 miles from Icy Strait. This rapid retreat has revealed plants and animals that are fascinating to naturalists.

The serenity of the bay is breathtaking and as only 25 vessels are allowed in at one time it is rare to see another boat. Even cruise ships are absorbed into the wilderness. To visit the park by boat a free permit has to be obtained less than 60 days in advance from the National Park Service (Fax: 907-697-2230—or go to their website **www.nps.gov/glba**). The rangers seem to be accommodating about changing dates if there is a plausible reason for the delay. On crossing the boundary to the bay you must announce your arrival on VHF Channel 12 then go to the Bartlett Cove ranger station for the informative, mandatory orientation.

Entry is limited to minimize disturbance to the humpback whales, an endangered species, which gather in summer to feed. Almost a quarter of the world's 8-10,000 humpback whales feed in Alaskan waters every summer, but they are just one of many wildlife treasures. There are birds in abundance with several types of gulls, black-legged kittiwakes and Arctic terns. In particular the tufted puffins with their bizarre beaks and orange feet are delightfully entertaining, as are the bears that can be seen foraging at the water's edge.

We were overwhelmed by the vastness and translucent blue of the glaciers. Unlike the lush entrance to the park these monsters grind through stark rock that is almost devoid of trees, and in places over 200 million years old. A special thrill is watching huge chunks of ice break off the glacier face, known as calving. With enormous splashes they join the many other icebergs in the metallic green ocean and we were mesmerized as they passed the boat. Each is unique, some extraordinarily shaped; close-to we could hear them snap, pop then hiss as they flipped over and released centuries-old air bubbles. Many were resting platforms for birds and sea lions, who stared at us unperturbed as they peacefully floated by.

But icebergs can also be of danger to yachts. With most of their mass under water even those that look small on the surface can do substantial harm to a boat on impact. Recently we got a phone call from some English cruisers who had been given our number by mutual friends.

"We're going to be in Vancouver for a while," they told us. "Our boat was badly damaged by an iceberg attack."

Later we heard the details of their frightening situation. They had been anchored in a remote Alaskan bay for the night and were aroused by a 'berg bumping into their bow. They discovered that it had ridden up over their anchor chain and jammed there. But it still carried momentum and to their amazement it then 'climbed' up the chain and toppled onto the deck, where it inflicted considerable damage to the hull and rig. At the time they had been horrified by the possibility that it might engulf the whole boat.

"The dinghy was on deck and obviously swimming wasn't an option," they recounted. They finally managed to break away and limped back to Vancouver for major repairs.

Most who cruise from the south to Alaska get no further than Glacier Bay, although they may go back by a different route, many visiting the attractive old Russian capital of Sitka. The cruisers we've met who have sailed further west, on Alaska's vast ocean coasts, are the few who have undertaken the challenging journey from the Orient via the Aleutian Chain. Wanting to see more of 'offshore' Alaska ourselves we planned to take the Alaskan Ferry, but amazingly a cruise ship was cheaper!

Although not our usual style of boating it was an extremely comfortable way to sightsee from Seward, just south of Anchorage, especially at the end of September when the ocean looked inhospitably gray and cold for a small sailing vessel such as *Bagheera*. As we cruised at triple *Bagheera's* speed we were awed by the rugged terrain, the vastness of the icecap and lack of communities. It was a magnificent sight, especially the massive mountains on the coast that were dusted with new snow and the fall colors of willows and aspen a golden glory interspersed with just a few small, dark conifers.

"Let's set the alarm early for tomorrow morning," I suggested to Andy. He gazed in amazement, this was not my usual call. "I just heard the weather forecast and it promises to be a beautiful day," I continued. "Wouldn't it be great to see the sun rise over the mountains and glaciers?"

We were visiting College Fjord in Prince William Sound, at the north end of the Gulf of Alaska. With a rainfall of over 150″ annually and a surfeit in the Fall, a fine day was a treasure. We were not disappointed. Dawn in this long inlet with continuous glaciers up its western shore, was a spectacular sight. We stared mesmerized as one by one the mountains were touched with an iridescent glow from the new sun, with peaks highlighted from its brilliant rays. Soon light was plunging down the vast masses of flowing ice, accenting their curved paths through the steep dark terrain. Finally the new snow gleamed a sparkling white while the fissured glacier faces became vast, glistening, azure jewels.

Prince William Sound not only provides a respite from the ocean swells, it also rivals the Inside Passage for its spectacular vistas of lofty snow-clad mountains, steep-sided fjords and abundant wildlife. Flanked by the Kenai Mountains to the west, and the Chugach Mountains to the east and north, the Sound covers 15,000sq miles and has numerous inlets and islands, as well as Alaska's greatest concentration of tidewater glaciers, 20 of which are active.

As we cruised up College Fjord we gazed at sixteen of them, some vast, some smaller, pouring down the rocky mountains and surrounded by the debris and scree that was picked up or ground away centuries before. We imagined the delight of the early explorers when they came across this magnificent area. It was Captain Cook who named Prince William Sound in 1778 and the Spanish explorers who followed left behind such names as Cordova and Valdez. In 1791 Russia's Baranof visited and married the daughter of a local native chief. College Fjord was christened by the American railway magnate Edward H. Harriman in 1899 and the glaciers given names of the various universities and colleges that his accompanying scientists attended, including spectacular Harvard Fjord at its head.

Although for Andy and myself the glaciers of College fjord made the greatest impression, it is Columbia Fjord that has the center stage in

Prince William Sound. Named again by Harriman, after New York's Columbia University, it is one of the most spectacular glaciers on the coast and the second largest tidewater glacier in North America. All the superlatives come to play here. It covers an amazing 440 square miles, has a length of over 40 miles with a face 3 miles wide and 260 feet high. It lies at the head of Columbia Bay, a fjord that has depths over 2000 feet. Due to the floating ice it was not possible to get very close but even at a distance the translucent blue face is so brilliant it seems to be lit from within. As we watched, riveted, not one but several huge chunks of ice dropped or 'calved', and we could hear thunderous explosions as they broke off and fell deep into the ocean causing huge geyser-like jets of water.

Another loud sound was the croaking from hundreds of seals that sunned themselves on the icepack alongside. Each summer thousands of harbor seals and Dall porpoises frequent the area, along with humpback and killer whales. The nutrient rich water provides for abundant sea life including our favorite red snapper, salmon, halibut, clams, shrimp and crab.

We were particularly pleased to see sea otters. These animals with cheeky black eyes peering out of their whiskery faces are a delight to watch as they lie on their backs, surveying the world while they nibble clams or sea urchin, human-like, from their paws. We saw several either in groups or in pairs. What fun they have playing, frequently hugging each other as they roll, somersault or dive. Although once found between the Aleutian chain and California sea otters were decimated by fur traders until, of the

A sea otter—such a delight to watch

34

original 150,000, only 2000 were left. They have been protected since 1911 but are still only found in limited areas.

On March 24, 1989 Prince William Sound became known to the world when the Exxon *Valdez* ran onto Bligh Reef. Currents quickly spread 11 million gallons of crude oil, causing the death of thousands of birds and mammals, particularly sea otters. Sea otters keep warm by having an insulating fur coat, rather than blubber. When covered with crude oil, warm air could not be trapped next to the skin, which caused many otters to die of hypothermia. Fortunately most of the shoreline of Prince William Sound was untouched and although the pink salmon stocks may be affected for years to come, other wildlife is in abundance.

As usual Andy had binoculars at hand. There are nearly ninety seabird colonies here with half a million birds taking up residence. This includes 5,000 bald eagles and we could see many of their huge nests high in the trees ashore. The forests are also home to wolves, red fox, black and brown bears, river otters, Sitka blacktail deer and mink. Mountain goats and Dall sheep, the rams with heavy curled horns, are seen on the windswept ridges and in alpine meadows.

Although Captain Cook was met by Inuit when he arrived, there have never been many people in the area. Today there are three main communities—Cordova, Whittier and Valdez, all of which have small boat harbors. Although there are several coves in which to anchor, these docks are convenient for stocking up.

Cordova is a pretty fishing village on the east coast. Its winter population of 3000 is inflated in summer with fishermen, cannery workers and tourists who have come to visit this beautiful area. The town's heyday was when Heney, the builder of the White Pass and Yukon Railroad between Whitehorse and Skagway, arrived in 1906 to build a railway to the Kennecott copper mines. On its completion Cordova became a boom town from the copper ore that passed through its docks but in 1938, strikes and declining prices forced the mine to close. Whittier lies on the west side of the bay and was originally developed as a secret port for the military in World War II. Today it has a population of under 300.

Lying only 25 miles east of the Columbia Glacier, Valdez (population under 4000) is in the heart of Prince William Sound. It is the most northerly ice-free port in the western hemisphere and was named by a Spanish explorer in 1790 after a Spanish naval officer. The town boomed at the end of the nineteenth century when thousands of gold seekers arrived in response to an advertised alternate route to the Klondike. Tragically, it was a suicidal path and hundreds perished. In 1964, the Good Friday earthquake annihilated Valdez. A new town was built four miles away on firmer ground and in 1974 it was chosen to be the terminus for the 800-mile Trans-Alaska Pipeline.

Oil has made the city rich, although fishing is still important. Tourism also helps the economy; the surrounding area is attractive and referred to as Alaska's Switzerland. The people are known to be very hospitable; we certainly found them most friendly on our visit and the facilities for boaters more than adequate. On the docks fisherman and pleasure boaters alike were welcoming and helpful with our questions. Most were power boaters and there were few sailboats to be seen.

We had such a short time in Prince William Sound, but for us it was the crowning glory of Alaska with its pristine, stunning scenery, fascinating history, great opportunities to 'visit' with wildlife and very friendly people.

United States West Coast

3. Washington, Oregon and Northern California

Due to September commitments in Vancouver, we had decided to sail *Bagheera* to San Francisco in August to avoid the notorious high seas and ugly storms that are common later in the year.

"How many miles is the trip?" Duncan asked as we approached Cape Flattery.

"About 700 from here," Andy replied. "It should take four or five days with the present weather forecast, and be a great ride with the wind behind us and not too strong."

Our planned route would take us between 15-30 miles from the coast, which we hoped would be out of the coastal fog and give us lighter, steadier winds than further offshore. It worked well, the northwest winds gave an excellent sail and the Californian current, which is strongest close to the coast, helped us by half a knot. If the weather had deteriorated we would have gone further offshore to gain sea room from this inhospitable lee shore that is known as the graveyard of the Pacific. For those on a flexible timetable, and preferably with a shallow draft, it is also possible to harbor-hop down the coast, but entrances can be tricky to navigate, with bars that become rough, if not impassable, in strong winds.

"I had such a great sleep," said Richard coming on deck for his watch. "What a comfortable cabin." He had the starboard aft cabin that we generally use for guests. With a cozy duvet and thick pillows it is easy to get comfortable whatever the angle. Our cabins have individual hanging lockers, a wide shelf above the berth and lift-up desk so guests can unpack, be organized and feel right at home.

"It's been a quiet watch," I informed him on the hand-over. "Just one ship out to sea and a flat calm. Hopefully the wind will soon pipe up."

"Sounds good. I'm on until 10:30am, right?" he confirmed.

"Yes, three-hour watches seem to work best for us. It's not too long to stay alert but gives enough time off for sleep. We start on the half-hour as it gives time to plot our position on the chart and write in the log on the hour, and it seems to make the watch go faster."

Although we have GPS (Global Positioning System) which gives us our approximate position in latitude and longitude, we write in the log every hour during a passage so we have a recent record of our course and position in case of electronic failure. Information includes: compass course, log (distance in nautical miles), wind direction and strength, barograph reading (for weather), latitude and longitude, sail configuration, speed and water temperature. There is also a column for comments.

Over the next three hours Richard noted 'still flat calm, passed way-point 2 (GPS), shearwaters to starboard, wind up, unfurled genny, off we go, just cruising!'

It was a routine trip, relaxing with four on board, and we soon caught up on missed sleep and gained our sea legs. Except for Andy, who seldom suffers, we had all taken preventative medication for seasickness. I find the British Stugeron (Cinnarizine), now available in Mexico, works well without causing drowsiness. On long passages I also suggest Scopolamine earpatches, although side effects are common and it is important to check with the crew to make sure they are not using other medication concurrently. Since diet is a significant factor in seasickness we keep meals simple, and prepare several in advance to keep time below to a minimum. There is always a good supply of crystallized ginger to finish a meal; not only is it delicious it also cleanses the palate and settles the stomach.

"The wind has shifted. We're now dead downwind and the chute keeps collapsing. Shall I go up to the bow and put on the pole?" suggested Duncan on his watch that afternoon.

Avid racers, we like to have the boat moving well and expect to cover at least 150 miles in a 24-hour period. There is also a safety component to this philosophy. The less time on the ocean, the less one is likely to get caught in bad weather.

Much of the time we could fly our new cruising spinnaker that again had our black cat 'Bagheera' logo with red slit eyes stitched to the center. This spinnaker is far smaller than the old racing chute that we used during our circumnavigation, and much easier to manage as it is launched from a 'sock'.

As Duncan went forward he clipped the tether of his life-harness securely to the jack-line that runs along the deck from bow to stern. This is a safety rule on our boat, reinforced by an experience in the French Tuamotus. One night in the calmest of seas, we were rolled 90° by a freak wave, so never risk going to the bow unattached.

The spinnaker pole is kept on the mast. "Can you take up more on the topping lift?" Duncan called back after he had lowered the inboard end. "That's great," he continued, when I had taken in the line from the cockpit to make the pole horizontal.

Suddenly there were dolphins leaping beside him. They soared and dove in the bow wave, criss-crossing before *Bagheera* in the green depths of the translucent ocean. For half an hour we watched them jumping and diving, tantalizing us as they disappeared then jubilantly returning for a quick spin just as we had given up hope.

"They have the best of lives," Andy commented to Richard. "It's what I want to be next time around!"

Within minutes of the dolphins disappearing Duncan called out, "Whale to starboard." It was a lone fin, some distance away.

Twenty thousand whales pass up this coast in spring and fall during the annual migration of the gray whales between Mexico and Alaska. After the magnificent films in the Imax theatre Richard was particularly hoping to see some. He reached for the binoculars.

"Definitely a whale," he confirmed satisfied. "This is marvelous, a great wind, great sailing, birds, dolphins, whales, it's wonderful being on the ocean!"

The ideal conditions continued, with winds to 15 knots and moderate seas. Comments in the log included 'First albatross sighted (*black footed*), one freighter six miles off, light on starboard bow but no radar blip, 6 dolphins off the bow, caught a fish—lost it, 2 porpoises along for the ride, more porpoises alongside. All copacetic, including the bird (*a boobie rested for several hours on the bow pulpit*), beautiful sunset, full moon, very clear night, spectacular night sky, Orion and Cassiopeia (*star constellations*) prominent, several fishing boats, full moon to starboard—red sun to port (*dawn*), don't forget radio schedule, no wind, motoring.'

Andy, Duncan and I had quickly slipped into the familiar pattern. Richard also soon adapted to the duties on watch and routines on board.

"I think I got everything right today," he commented with a grin. "I remembered to turn off the gas at the stove and bulkhead, use the clips on the drawers in the galley, haven't got any twists in my safety harness, and oh yes," he said added with a twinkle, " I sat down when using the head at all times!"

He joined us up in the cockpit. Duncan had been reading *Charlie's Charts of the U.S. Pacific Coast* as well as some travel guides.

"I know you said it's a rugged coast," he commented, "but it seems every harbor can be difficult. Listen to this. Entry requires a great deal of caution and deliberation, not a recommended stopover, pass by unless one has local knowledge," he read out as he flipped the pages. "The Columbia River has 2000 wrecks at the bar and if you don't get stuck there you can still easily go aground in the mud that came down the river after the Mount St. Helens eruption in 1980. I can see why you didn't plan to stop!"

"Especially with our seven-foot draft," added Andy.

"Wow," Duncan continued, "On a clear day from the mouth of the Columbia you can actually see Mount St. Helen's, which is 75 miles away."

"I do hope you are able to come to visit again," I turned to Richard, "so you can spend more time sightseeing. The drive down this coast is stunning, unbelievably wild with huge rock formations, and the interior is beautiful with the mountains, lush valleys and rural communities."

"Just say the word," he replied. "I'm bowled over! Seriously, I'd love to bring the family out to cruise the Gulf Islands first, then come south by car. It's not just the scenery, the freedom and space here is so different from home. The kids would love it. "

The grandeur and vastness of the Pacific Northwest impresses all our visitors, particularly those from Europe. Running from northern Washington to southern Oregon the towering volcanic peaks of the Cascade Mountain Range divide Washington State in two. In its rain shadow, the land to the east is semi-arid, a sea of golden grasses in summer. To the west vegetation is green and fertile year-round with the Olympic Peninsula having enough precipitation to support a temperate rainforest. Those living in the two largest cities, Seattle and Portland, have majestic mountain views with Mount Rainier rising 14,410 feet and Mount Hood to 11,000 feet. The mountains also offer convenient winter resorts, a variety of summer outdoor activities and endless opportunities to commune with nature.

It took Europeans three hundred years after Columbus' discovery of America to find the mighty Columbia River that is tucked away in the far northwest. Running over 1200 miles from the Canadian Rockies to the Pacific Ocean at the Washington-Oregon border, it is second only to the Mississippi in the U.S., in the amount of water it discharges. For centuries its raging gorge and deadly falls, in one of the few passes in the 1000-km long mountain chain, had been a meeting place for native Indians during the Fall and Spring migrations of salmon. Here tribes from the plains, river and coast met to fish, trade, swap stories and perform ceremonies.

Although there had been many exploration voyages along the coast, this area was first settled by Europeans from the east, with the first white man to cross the continent in 1793 being the Welshman David Thompson, a fur trader. Trappers from both the Hudson's Bay Company and North West Company expanded west, setting up trading forts along the way. One of these forts, Fort Vancouver, became a self-sufficient and expanding agricultural community with its steward McLoughlin encouraging newcomers to move down to the Willamette River valley, a tributary of the Columbia. In 1843 there was a huge boost to the community when 900 people arrived from Independence, Missouri, but this was just the start of a great westward migration.

In the next 17 years an estimated 53,000 settlers trekked the 2000-mile Oregon Trail to The Dalles. From here the pioneers had to either raft themselves and their belongings through the raging rapids of the Columbia River Gorge or struggle over steep Mt Hood and descend by the precipitous Barlow Trail. With its rich soil and mild climate the protected valley became a booming agricultural area with the reputation that 'crops never fail west of the Cascades'. While dairy farms, nurseries, orchards and vineyards thrived in the fertile plain, the dense forests in the lower valley also made it 'the timber capital of the world'. The pioneer spirit lives on, giving Oregon a uniquely different flavor.

We have driven down the Oregon coast on US 101 many times, and the stark contrast of green, cloud-clad mountains meeting the pounding surf never palls. Rocky headlands soar hundreds of feet from the ocean with huge waves crashing below. Beaches are rock-strewn. Large pillars of stone and small islands, that are fashioned into remarkable angles and arches by the swirling surge, are dotted out to sea, disappearing into the blue haze or fog bank that frequently lurks off the shore. As much of this coast is parkland, beaches are readily accessible. Walks are an invigorating battle against wind and spray, with a dynamic intertidal zone at one's feet that is rewarding to explore. Everything here, whether mussels, goose barnacles, clams, oysters or sand dollars, is huge.

Newport, in Yaquina Bay, with its many seafood restaurants, calls itself the 'Dungeness Crab Capital of the World'. It is the first place south of the Columbia River that is easily entered by boat. Besides gorging on crab one can visit the Oregon Coast Aquarium, known as the home of Keiko, the orca in the film 'Free Willy' who is now in Iceland being prepared to return to the wild. The Mark O. Hatfield Marine Science Center and the Lincoln County Historical Museum, which has a large collection of Siletz native artifacts, are also interesting stops. The lighthouse, built in 1871, includes a museum that has been refurbished to the original period. It is one of many along this coast that provide a good reason to get some exercise by visiting.

Ninety miles south, after passing sand dunes 500 feet high, we could see Coos Bay, the most important harbor between the Columbia River and San Francisco. This major port developed around lumber: From shipbuilding to serving the needs of the exploding population in California during Gold Rush times, and meeting the demand for local spruce trees in aircraft building in World War I, it became the largest timber port in the world. Since the 1980's business has declined, as has the fishing industry that gave rise to a large local fleet. Although a good harbor of refuge, with bar reports given hourly, even on a favorable flood the entry passage can be hair-raising, with the roar of huge swells thundering against the jetties.

After three and a half days *Bagheera* entered Californian waters, passing by the massive redwood groves. These are the world's largest trees and before goldrush times the coast redwood forests stretched 450 miles long and 30 miles deep. Only small areas still exist, but walking down the 'Avenue of the Giants' and gazing up at the canopy of the 300 foot boughs arched cathedral-like overhead is not only a breath-taking experience, it is also an awe-inspiring insight into the timelessness of nature. In the 1930's a felled redwood tree proved to be an incredible 2,200 years old.

By this time Richard was getting quite blasé about ocean sailing in a 40-foot boat, despite the reputation of this coast. Up to this point the maximum wind strength had been 20 knots, with frequent spells of less than 10. *Bagheera* was just south of Cape Mendocino when the barometer started to drop rapidly and the wind began to increase. From 9 knots at noon it had risen to 25 knots by 3.00pm. and by 6:00pm was blowing a full gale, gusting 40. We had reefed right down, and were comfortable running before the wind, but the waves were definitely building, the white caps turning to a sea of spume with spray flung violently against the hull. The sky darkened, becoming a mass of turbulent clouds, and we decided to double-up on watches for the duration of the storm, Andy with Duncan, Richard with me.

Unperturbed, *Bagheera* surged along delighted with wind and waves from behind, the autopilot fully in control. Richard and I were in the cockpit, lifeharnesses firmly clipped on when suddenly Richard gasped, "Look, the next wave is huge. Will we go over it? Will we get pooped?"

Bagheera *sleighriding in 40 knots*

I turned quickly. The massive green wall of water was about to break, but it wasn't threatening. We had done nearly 60,000 ocean miles in *Bagheera*, weathering much higher seas, but only once have been pooped and that was in the infamous Agulhas Current off South Africa.

"Don't worry," I reassured Richard, "*Bagheera* is very buoyant in the stern and will have no difficulty riding over these waves."

He kept glancing astern, not fully believing me. "Maybe you should explain again how to work the Life Sling," he suggested, "Just in case there's a problem." Safety had taken on a new meaning to him, as had ocean voyaging.

During the day we heard two 'mayday' distress calls on the radio that were immediately answered by the Coast Guard. They were too far away for us to offer assistance and we didn't hear the subsequent discussion. On arrival in San Francisco we picked up a message to phone our insurance agent.

"How was the trip?" she inquired immediately.

"Pretty routine, with a short blow on one day, but perfectly manageable." I replied.

"Really!" was the surprised response. "We had a new customer who three days ago abandoned ship because the conditions were untenable. They must have been right behind you."

Later we heard their story. Two novice sailors panicked as their boat became out of control as the winds increased. They put out the mayday call claiming 60-knot winds and 40′ waves. The Coast Guard informed them the wind was actually a steady 31 knots with wave height about 12', quite typical and to be expected along this coast. The couple still wanted to be taken off. Three months later we read in a yachting magazine that the boat had been recovered sailing peacefully off the coast of Hawaii.

We always urge new ocean cruisers to become proficient, self-sufficient sailors not only in their local waters but also to seek ocean experience. In the Pacific Northwest an ideal trip is to circumnavigate Vancouver Island. The wild west coast, made famous by Jacques Cousteau as one of his favorite diving sites for wrecks, puts piloting and boat-handling in rough conditions to the test, and, most importantly, the crews' tolerance and ability to cope. Alternatively one can charter a boat in one of the many destinations around the world that will give ocean experience, a great excuse to flee winter blues for some tropical sun. Chartering several types of boats has an added advantage of hands-on exposure to different designs and equipment. It is sensible on a first long trip to take experienced crew along; a new cruiser can also go along to get more experience. Open the many cruising magazines to find both positions and candidates. As with our trip, it is always relaxing to have four on board, with plenty of time for sleep and additional muscle power for maneuvers on deck.

For six hours gale force winds persisted, but finally the storm abated in the night although the seas were still turbulent for several more hours. Our crew fared well despite a comment in the log that reads, 'Don't mix fig newtons, ginger and mushroom soup. It doesn't taste great!'

By morning the sun was out and we were cruising comfortably under full main and genoa. Cousin Richard and I were again in the cockpit, this time trying to get our cell-phones to work. Richard was longing to tell his wife and the office in England about our previous day. I wanted to contact our youngest son, Jamie, who was in Montreal racing a Laser >> in the Canadian Youth Championships. Despite being only five miles off the coast neither of us could connect and were extremely frustrated. Richard had paid for an international service from England; Andy had just purchased a new cell phone in Vancouver and was assured it would work all over the United States.

As I scanned the cloudless horizon the irony of the situation suddenly dawned. We were missing a spectacular sail.

At the same time Richard burst out laughing, "I'm forgetting I'm away from the office, and phone calls can wait. I came for the cruising and this is a perfect day!"

As it had done for Sir Frances Drake in 1579, Drake's Bay gave *Bagheera* good protection from the northwesterly winds and we anchored at the north end of the bay rather than arriving at San Francisco in the middle of the night.

"What a great trip, but how nice to relax!" grinned Duncan as we lounged in the cockpit, drinks in hand. A calm anchorage after an ocean passage is always an agreeable change of pace. What luxury it is to be able to put a glass down without it flying off the table and cook in a galley without a balancing act. There is also a charge of energy that comes from the exhilaration of completing a passage successfully. We analyzed the trip over dinner, animatedly discussing the high points, low points and a few necessary repairs, and finally climbed into our berths, now mellow and ready to sleep the entire night through.

There was a rolling swell, dense fog and no wind for our 25-mile passage to San Francisco next morning. It was an eerie feeling entering by radar, seeing nothing but gray yet knowing the big city was just ahead. Channel markers suddenly emerged out of the gloom. They were crowded with sea lions; most eyed us lazily, although a few lifted their heads and barked furiously as we passed. They were the only sign of life in the ghostly silence.

As the fog began lifting we could feel the heat from the sun and were soon stripping down to t-shirts and shorts. Suddenly there was an arc of metal ahead, floating on the 'cotton batten' below. Soon another span appeared then suddenly the fog evaporated, and we gazed up at a deep blue sky as *Bagheera* passed under the Golden Gate Bridge, one of the longest single-span bridges ever built. To starboard lay downtown San Francisco, ahead the infamous prison island of Alcatraz, and to port was Sausalito.

"Where do you want to go?" Andy asked me.

"Everyone loves Sausalito," I replied. "It was originally an artists' colony and is apparently really attractive, has convenient stores and it's quieter than downtown. Let's go there first."

Clinging precariously to the steep cliffs the spectacular homes and exotic gardens were an impressive sight as we headed in. A Canadian boat was tied to one of several mooring buoys and as we approached I called out, "Hi, we've just arrived from Vancouver and wondered who these buoys belong to?"

But before the owner answered our question he exclaimed, "You have four on board and I need crew. Why doesn't one of you join me? My crew didn't like the trip down and left for good last night."

"I'm sorry," we replied. "Duncan and Richard are leaving soon, then it will just be the two of us on board."

Sadly this is not an unusual story. When we lived in the Caribbean it was quite a common sight to see crew leap ashore, bag in hand, after a TransAtlantic crossing, even before mooring lines were tied to the dock. So many boat owners who dream of blue-water cruising forget that a compatible crew is a major factor in the success quotient.

"The buoys belong to the Sausalito Yacht Club," he finally told us. "Just tie up and go in to register. They are free of charge."

It was the beginning of the wonderful American hospitality that we received all down the Californian coast. We tied up and immediately went ashore to report our arrival to the U.S. Customs by phone.

Next morning we took the ferry across to San Francisco to officially clear into the States, then went into sightseeing mode as Richard and Duncan had just two days left on board. Highlights were visiting Alcatraz where we followed an eye-opening audio tour on tape, wine tasting in the delightful Napa Valley, consuming seafood in Fisherman's Wharf and exploring cosmopolitan downtown along streets that soared and plunged on the steep terrain.

Home to the Miwok and Ohlone Indians for centuries, San Francisco was settled by Europeans less than 250 years ago and was ceded to the U.S.A. in 1846 after the Mexican-American war. Just two years later gold was discovered in the Sierra Nevada and San Francisco exploded, its future assured. The city had a facelift after a huge earthquake devastated most of the buildings in 1906. During World War II the Bay became a center for military operations in the Pacific, and more recently it has been in the limelight for colorful subcultures. Physically spectacular and with an interesting history, cosmopolitan and a trendsetter, San Francisco is always fun to visit.

It was sad to see the lads leave. For Richard it had been a wonderful sailing adventure, with many a story to tell at the bar in his yacht club back home. Duncan had also enjoyed a great trip, and had proved himself a reliable crewmember. His ingrained experience from sailing around the world and recent local cruising on *Bagheera* with friends had been shown in his handling of the boat. After a few more offshore passages with us he should be ready to take *Bagheera* further afield himself.

47

4. Southern California and Preparations for Cruising Mexico

The typical afternoon breeze in San Francisco Bay promotes a great deal of sailboat racing and exhilarating cruising. Covering over 400 square miles, this picturesque body of water is surrounded by attractive communities, and the Delta Region formed by the San Joaquin and Sacramento Rivers, with their tributaries and canals, is a popular cruising destination, particularly for those with a shallow draft.

Bagheera was buffeted by strong currents as we sailed past the prison island of Alcatraz on our way to Alameda, and I shivered, imagining the wind whistling in the rigging was the whispers of old ghosts. Again the yacht clubs were most welcoming. Encinal Yacht Club was especially hospitable and we stayed at their dock for several days getting to know more cruisers arriving from the Pacific Northwest, who were all delighted that their passages had gone smoothly. One afternoon a couple drifted by in their inflatable dinghy, under 'sunflower' umbrellas with drinks in hand. It epitomized the relaxed feeling in the fleet.

There was also time for some serious boat business. While I read cruising and travel guides to plan the timing for our route during the next year, Andy installed a watermaker. It was a luxury that had long been on my 'wish list'. The main reason was to be able to wash my long, thick hair on a regular basis. Andy was reluctant, not having quite the same problem!

"Watermakers are expensive," he argued. "We managed perfectly well for 18 months in the Indian Ocean catching rain," he reminded me. "We are also only away for a year on this trip and much of it will be in the States."

I persisted! "The boat will be so much cleaner with lots of fresh water, the pans and cutlery won't rust, with a cockpit shower we won't get salt below, and guests will be so much more comfortable. Besides which, we will never have to worry about water quality, or have to chlorinate it and the tea will always taste good. I can even come diving when I've just washed my hair!"

Andy had finally been persuaded by my enthusiasm and started to research available DC models, as *Bagheera* has no room for a generator. It was while working the Annapolis Boat Show the previous year that we first saw the Spectra Watermaker. With its amazing output of 9 gallons of water produced by just 8 amps of 12-volt power it seemed the ideal model for *Bagheera*. It was most convenient that we could now anchor off the Spectra office, further up the bay in Sausalito, for Andy to complete the installation. It took three days to shoehorn the unit onto the bulkhead behind the companionway, inside our tiny aft head that we long ago converted to storage.

The watermaker was an instant success, although initially it was quite a shock hearing Andy say, "Aren't you going to use more water?" after all those years of the one-cup ration for an entire body wash-down. Even before family and friends visited we delighted in the great benefit of having 'endless' fresh water on board and hot showers in the cockpit sometimes even twice a day!

Having hunted around for a week, we found a berth in a marina in Sausalito to leave the boat safely while returning home. There was a small hitch when we tried to fit into the allotted spot and found it was too narrow for our 12'9" beam, much to the surprise of the dockman. Fortunately there was one remaining berth vacant at the end of the dock that was satisfactory. It took a day to pack up the boat, leave fridge and systems in order, and deflate and tie the dinghy on deck.

There were two small problems left. A neighboring cruiser solved one by kindly agreeing to take 'Fred', our ivy boat plant. Our budgerigar (parakeet) was the other issue but Craig, a friend of Duncan's who was completing a course close-by, enthusiastically offered his services and suggested he come right away to pick up the cage. It seemed such an ideal arrangement—until his parting comment of, "I'm sure 'Cornflake' and our new kitten will become the best of friends!"

The month back in Vancouver flew by, but it was reassuring to see that the house, our affairs and our children's lives were in order and make realistic plans for friends to join us, now that we had a more definite itinerary.

"Remember this is only an approximate schedule," I warned them. "We might have a breakdown or get caught in a storm and be behind, or have good winds and be way ahead."

'Don't worry," they all replied. "We're happy to take another plane or a bus to find you."

October 5th saw us on a return flight to San Francisco. While Andy went to *Bagheera* in Sausalito, I made a quick trip back east to work the Annapolis Boat Show then returned to Santa Cruz where Andy had taken the boat.

A mammoth shopping trip was necessary and, as our practice is to eat out after a large stowing job, Andy suggested a seafood restaurant along the dock. The seared tuna steaks with scallops and shrimp Mexican style were quite delicious and we praised the owner when he came over to chat.

"You are going to sail to Panama and then up to Nova Scotia?" he said incredulously after we had told him our plans. "That deserves margaritas on the house to wish you a safe voyage." It was a great welcome back to the cruising life.

Our next legs took us 400 miles down the southern Californian coast. What a difference from sailing the shores of Washington and Oregon, with their typical strong winds and few storm-havens for deep-keeled vessels. From San Francisco to San Diego there are numerous harbors and calms are common, especially to the south. Passages can also be made at any time of the year based on a good forecast although one always has to be cautious in rounding Point Conception, referred to in the Pilot as the 'Cape Horn of the Pacific'.

Next morning calms prevailed and it was a motor to Monterey, famous for its Latino heritage and historic quarter. 'Cold, foggy and swelly!' wrote Andy in the log. We searched around for a place to anchor but while filling with fuel the dockman offered us a slip for the day.

It was an invigorating morning walk into town through the attractive oceanfront park, and we were royally entertained by the many pelicans in the harbor. One minute these distinctive birds with their long beaks were in graceful flight, then the next they were swooping down on their unsuspecting prey with huge ungainly splashes. We miss these characters when home in B.C. Apparently they used to come north in summer, before the pilchards disappeared on our coast.

Wood-planked Fisherman's Wharf was bustling with sports fishing, whale watching and sightseeing boats, and Andy was soon drooling over the fresh seafood for sale at the many stalls. Catches of anchovies, cod,

Monterey harbor

halibut, squid, shark, swordfish, tuna, salmon and more, vary throughout the year. The wharf was built in 1846 for trading vessels to drop off the goods they had brought around Cape Horn. It was home to whaling and sardine vessels until the Municipal Wharf was built, where the modern fishing fleet now berths.

We loved wandering around the old quarter. The picturesque 19th century buildings of Spanish-Mexican Monterey are still in good repair and many have fine displays of memorabilia. We learnt that Larkin House, built in 1834, is a mix of the New England and adobe architecture, which together heralded the Monterey colonial style. In Stevenson House Robert Louis Stevenson is said to have written his classic book 'Treasure Island'. Close-by, the Spanish Customs House is the oldest government building on the west coast and all goods headed for Mexico and California had to be unloaded here. Some ancient parts of the building date back to 1827. In 1846 the American flag was officially raised on it for the first time.

It is good to be reminded of California's history as it is all too easy to identify this State with its extremes, such as the glitz of Hollywood, stark deserts, bronzed surfers and natural disasters.

Encompassing 158,000 square miles the history of the huge State has been influenced largely by its geography. The collisions of tectonic plates over some 250 million years have caused the State of California to have a dramatic basin and range topography. There are four distinct regions—

the temperate coastal, the desert, the fertile Central Valley that was once an inland sea and the Sierra Nevada Mountains, a formidable barrier that kept the State isolated from the rest of the country. Snow-capped Mount Whitney in the Sequoia National Park is the highest point in contiguous United States at 14,495 feet and Badwater in arid Death Valley, is its lowest at 282 feet below sea level.

The climate is one of extremes in both temperature and precipitation, and it is not unusual for California to be battered by floods, drought and fires. Most devastating are the earthquakes. The Pacific plate and North American plates slide over each other along the San Andreas Fault, which stretches northwest from the Gulf of California to Point Arena, north of San Francisco Bay. For the most part this movement goes unnoticed, but occasionally an explosive earthquake results causing devastation, particularly in the population mega-centers of both San Francisco and Los Angeles.

The climate is further influenced by offshore currents. The cool California Current that sweeps down from North, is responsible for San Francisco's long, cool summers and persistent fog, while the shallower more fragmented warm current that flows north in the Californian Bight gives the southern region its balmy winters.

The name 'California' came from a romance novel published in 1510 in which a Queen Califia ruled over an idyllic tropical island, rich with pearls and gold, where men were only allowed to visit once a year to perpetuate the species! In 1535 Cortez's men thought they had found this paradise after discovering pearls.

Four flags have flown over the State if California—Russian, Spanish, Mexican and American. Except for a few visits from other nationalities, such as the one by Sir Francis Drake, it was left to the Spanish to settle the coast in 1769 with the establishment of 21 missions to convert the large native Indian population. Even by 1820 the settler population only numbered 3,000 and they were mostly ranchers.

Gold fever was the magic ingredient that caused California to boom. In 1849, shortly after James Marshall discovered nuggets in the foothills of the Sierra Nevada, the United States claimed the territory from Mexico. News spread fast and over 100,000 easterners trekked to the west to seek their fortunes, both overland and by sea, via Central and South America. Later in the year 48 men drew up a draft State Constitution. A quarter of the group were young men who had just arrived with the gold rush and in 1850 when California was admitted as the 31st State in the Union these politicians were some of the youngest in the country.

The following 70 years saw demographic, economic and technological booms that were unparalleled in the county's history. The extravagant spending of the newcomers helped create California's cities and the completion of the Transcontinental Railway in 1869 made it easy for increasing numbers of adventurers to join them. At the same time an agricultural boom was being led by the wheat growers and in 1880 they were finally able to cool railcars sufficiently to ship oranges back to the eastern states and subsequently to England. Between 1880 and 1914, at the beginning of the World War I, the miles of railroad in California increased from 2000 to 8000.

Although the southern half of the State developed more slowly the potential of its benign climate was soon realized. The railway was extended to Los Angeles in 1876 and after a heavy advertising campaign there was soon another rush out west for sun and fun in this exotic 'Mediterranean' setting with its Spanish heritage.

Many of the visitors stayed, totally changing their lifestyles, and it is still considered a place where you can lose the baggage of your past and recreate yourself both mentally and physically. With a population of almost 33 million, (the same as that of Canada) California now has America's most cosmopolitan population with its largest groups being Caucasian, Hispanic and Asian. With this cultural mix and heritage Californians are known for their uniqueness of personality and trends pour out of the State whether in fashion, architecture, food, wine, language, sports or politics.

Despite financial and political setbacks and devastating earthquakes, with the Bay area badly struck in 1989 and Los Angeles in 1994, California continues to boom. While many make their fortunes in the film world, others have joined the world of technology. Of particular significance are the Hi-tech giants of Silicon Valley, just south of San Francisco, whose founders were the techno whiz kids associated with Apple and Intel and their mentor David Packard, founder of Hewlett Packard. There has been an explosion of associated internet companies and now the State's main products include electronic games and computer chips, as well as wine, fruit and rice.

Visitors typically seek out California for its entertainment, whether Disneyland, Universal Studies or the hundreds of strip malls but increasingly nature buffs are realizing that there is tremendous potential inland. Whether it's the fascination of the desert, the strange rock formations and hot springs of the mountains, or the abundant wildlife and unique flora, there is a wealth of opportunities in California away from its commercial coast. These wonders of nature were first extolled by John Muir, a Scot who arrived in California in 1868. He had gone blind as a boy and when his sight miraculously returned he decided to dedicate his life to nature. In particular he explored the Yosemite Valley and initiated lobbying tactics with the government to stop the planned mining and logging, setting a trend for the future. In 1892 he became the first president of the Sierra Club that promotes wilderness experiences and conservation as actively today.

We, too, were enjoying communing with nature as hundreds of sea lions played exuberantly on the harbor wall as we headed out of Monterey harbor.

As I studied the chart Andy commented, "Look how deep it is out here. I've just read about it in Popular Science. It's known as the Monterey Gorge and is like an underwater Grand Canyon. They're doing a lot of deep-sea research here, and have found some bizarre deep-sea communities in waters of 3,000 meters deep. The area is now the largest marine park in the U.S. and second only in size to the Great Barrier Reef."

Sailing south, the mountains faded into the eastern horizon, temperatures were on the rise and we hoped that the warming of the land would induce the typical westerly seabreeze. With a two-day deadline to reach Newport Beach for a Cruisers' weekend, we needed more wind but there was not a breath. A bonus of the flat seas, however, was sighting a pod of humpback whales and we were delighted when they swam towards us then leapt for joy off the starboard bow.

"At least it should be calm around Point Conception," I said optimistically.

Point Conception is an area of extremes; there can either be no wind or too much at this headland and temperatures vary between the cool of the north and the heat of the south. Weather is likely to be calm in the early morning, but as the day progresses the wind frequently builds, accelerating around the abrupt change of the coast and through the Santa Barbara Channel formed by the Channel Islands. Both the strong winds and rough seas contribute in making the passage an extremely uncomfortable ride, and except in calms this point should be given a wide berth.

It was not long before the wind filled in; by evening it was gusting 30 knots, was extremely cold and the barometer had dropped sharply. We passed Point Conception at midnight with the wind gusting west-north-west to 42 knots. The seas were extremely confused, coming from several directions at once, tossing the boat around so unpredictably it was hard to sleep below. Off watch we wedged ourselves in the starboard aft cabin, with pillows on one side and a sailbag stuffed with dirty laundry (firmly zipped closed) on the other!

Our comments in the log bring back memories of an exceedingly unpleasant trip.

'Black night, very noisy surf from the huge confused swells, shivering, ugh, wind howling again, three ships within 4 miles, one ship passed half a mile away we both altered course in the same direction as their lights were confusing'.

"Thank goodness for radar," I said to Andy as we changed watch.

Radar is one of those toys you can manage without until you have one, then, when you become aware of its many uses, it is indispensable! At night, in fog and rain, it gives us confidence and allows us to monitor the movements of other traffic. For landfalls on unlit coasts and transiting passages between islands or entering harbor in poor visibility, we use our radar constantly. Radar bearings and distances are true and do not rely on the accuracy of charted positions like GPS. We can even gauge the severity of tropical line-squalls coming up to us and, in areas such as Indonesia and the Malacca Strait, used radar to warn us of the approach of unlit and possibly hostile craft.

Our current radar is a Raytheon SL72 24-mile LCD unit with a 7" screen and as it has a waterproof display we have it conveniently mounted under the dodger, where it can be seen from anywhere in the cockpit.

South of Point Conception and all the way to San Diego there are innumerable harbors and marinas to explore, as well as the far less inhabited Channel Islands, although these can become crowded during the summer months. I had wanted to stop in the Northern Channel Islands but there wasn't a convenient tenable anchorage in the prevailing weather. We also had hoped to visit a friend in Santa Barbara but it was now way off our course with the current wind direction, so we continued. Then, suddenly, the wind dropped, the sky cleared, the sun shone and we soon had to motor!

It had been a last-minute decision to go to the cruising seminar weekend in Newport Beach that was organized by Walt Gleckler and the Orange Coast College, but it was a thoroughly enjoyable time. Both of us sat on interesting panels, sold many of our books and met some great cruisers, particularly other old-timers and authors. For over 20 years Walt and his wife Anna organized the Sailing Adventures Series and led more than a score of flotillas internationally. We were so sad to hear recently that Walt had passed away and would like to commend both him and Anna for their huge contribution in enabling cruisers to 'live their dream'.

We had great rambles along the water's edge, and were entertained by a creative array of ghosts, witches and pumpkins as it was close to Halloween. Friends from our Dragon sailboat racing days filled us in on the charms of Catalina Island, their main cruising destination and we subsequently enjoyed some small anchorages as well as a visit to the town of

Avalon. It was peaceful there in the fall but seeing the hundreds of mooring buoys and ferries, we could imagine the summer crowds.

For us Avalon was a great stop with laundry completed, mail sent, a grocery shop then a fine, inexpensive lobster dinner. We had intended to spend the night but the mooring charge seemed high so at 8:00pm, when our guest allowance on the mooring buoy had expired, we prepared to set sail.

"But no-one leaves at this time," the Harbor Master argued, amazed. He had come alongside to collect the night's fee just as we were casting off.

"Crazy Canadians!" was his final comment as we started to head out.

There are many yacht clubs in San Diego and with membership of a yacht club back home you can stay three nights at many free of charge. Finding clubs with a vacancy was somewhat of a challenge especially at the end of October, before the start of the Baja Ha-Ha, a sailboat rally down to Cabo, which involved 90 boats. Luckily, West Marine, where we were giving a talk the next day, arranged for us to go into Silver Gate Yacht Club. Almost immediately Jane, Andy's crew from Mustang, an 83' yacht he had captained three years before, was down to welcome us and offer a car for the weekend—what a bonus!

San Diego is ten miles from the Mexican border and is the last U.S. port with amenities—of which there are many for cruisers. Despite resolutions we, like most, went into a buying frenzy particularly at Costco and West Marine. Downwind Marine was also most accommodating. They have an invaluable booklet of Mexican cruising information, which includes a cruising checklist, radio nets and boaters' Spanish terms, and offer mail collection and forwarding. (See their website **www.downwindmarine.com**).). In addition they arrange free transportation, sponsor seminars and have a kick-off party in October/November.

After Ensenada, 55 miles south of the border, there are few facilities down the 700-mile Baja coast until Cabo San Lucas, or better still La Paz. As there are now few banks along this stretch, and those in Turtle Bay and San Carlos in Magdalena Bay do not have ATMs, we had purchased some pesos in advance. We also took on extra fuel, as it can be only be acquired in jerry cans along the Baja coast, except for the dock in Turtle Bay.

Other items purchased were heavy duty plastic containers to decant dry goods, hoping to avoid the inevitable weevils, ziplock bags, cockroach hotels, cleaning materials, insect repellent, film and sun block. It is worth bulk buying staples and favorite luxury items, and there are several lists in circulation that will inform you of 'necessities' not available in Mexico like chocolate chips! Rest assured Mexican food is wonderful and going to local markets is always a highlight in our travels. I also needed a new camera and was pleased to find a waterproof Pentax, with good features and a zoom lens. It was small enough to carry when sightseeing but would also survive the surf when coming ashore in the dinghy.

There were official formalities to complete. A Mexican tourist card had to be stamped by the Consulate. Cruisers must purchase (somewhat resentfully I have to admit), a fishing license for Mexico that then cost $179 which covers two people on board, the boat and the dinghy. It is necessary if you have fishing gear on board, even if you do not intend to fish in Mexican waters. Those planning to use a Ham radio purchased their local Mexican license in Tijuana. We also typed our crew lists in Spanish (from samples provided in *Charlie's Charts of the West Coast of Mexico*) and made more copies of the ship's documents and our passports, so that they would be easier to replace in case of loss.

All chores were completed in time for our planned departure date five days later—except for the matter of communicating with email. Before leaving Vancouver I had made inquiries about sending email via the HF radio.

"Simple," I was told at the Ham shop, "but wait for the new demodulator (the 'dem' part of a modem I was told) that will be out later this month."

I had left by then so thought I would purchase the unit in San Diego. Mitch, on the neighboring boat at Silver Gate, was most helpful. He used SAILMAIL successfully, a service on the Single Side band network, with the advantage, unlike Ham radio, that it can be used for business. He was somewhat skeptical about my getting a system to work in a day—it had taken him six months and he was an engineer!

How right he proved to be. First, the program downloaded from the Internet wouldn't load onto our laptop. After unbelievable efforts to laplink, my learning curve was fast going up; it transpired that our old laptop simply couldn't cope. Then we found our previously reliable Icom radio wouldn't transmit any longer and was deemed too old to repair. In short, after six more days and much frustration we left San Diego considerably poorer with a new Ham radio, new computer and various black boxes but still without the ability to communicate via the Internet!

On the positive side, we had met some phenomenal local people who had been unbelievably kind in trying to get the situation sorted out. There was also a new group of cruisers, with whom we had enjoyed great evenings, and we consolidated long-lasting friendships with those that we had met previously along the way.

On our last night in San Diego *Bagheera* was rafted alongside Rare Metal, fellow Vancouverites. They wanted to leave the dock early to assure their next free mooring spot; this suited us well. There were lots of laughs and we hugged goodbye at 6:30am knowing we would not be seeing each other again on our travels this time around.

The muted pinks and grays of daybreak gave a soft backdrop to masts and palm trees as we motored out of the harbor, passing more buoys draped with sea lions, who this time observed the hush of dawn. We watched the sun come up over the horizon, and quickly grow into a huge red ball. After a few deep breaths the frustrations of the previous weeks slipped right away. It was good to be at sea again and the next legs would take us to a myriad of different cultures and the Tropics!

Mexico

5. The Baja Peninsula, Sea of Cortez, (Golfo de California) & Mainland coast to Puerto Vallarta

Stark but stunning, the long peninsula of the Baja is the first taste of foreign cruising for several hundred boaters every Fall. We have always loved our visits to Mexico. Although part of the North American continent, it is Latin American in lifestyle, language and heritage, and the enchanting blend of colonial Spanish with ancient Indian civilizations has given rise to distinctive regional cultures that have their own architecture, cuisine, music, dance, arts and crafts.

For most sailors this contrast of cultures is also fascinating, a fundamental part of the adventure of offshore cruising. For those without travel experience, however, the differences can be intimidating and we found that several cruisers in San Diego were apprehensive about sailing south. Their anxiety was heightened by the shortage of boating amenities in Mexico such as no Coast Guard for rescue, fewer weather forecasts and marinas, poor charts, questionable water quality, a different language and a lack of well-stocked marine stores and familiar products in food stores.

When these cruisers 'took the plunge' and headed south, however, they were amazed and relieved to find few of their fears realized. They had ignored the fact that Baja California with its desirable weather, endless white-sand beaches, abundant sea life and proximity to the United States has long been a busy tourist destination. With increasing numbers of boats heading south from California each winter (over 1000 this year), officialdom has been streamlined and facilities improved. Within the large cruising community there are endless resources and if there is a problem with the boat there is usually someone close-by who can sort it out. The many radio nets that operate throughout the day are a further source of advice; several also have weather buffs, who broadcast the latest forecast received via their hi-tech on-board electronics.

Our 710-mile voyage from San Diego to Cabo San Lucas was, as usual, a relaxed trip. It is possible to day-sail the length of Baja Pacific coast, with the exception of the last 150-mile leg from Magdalena Bay. The prevailing winds from Fall to Spring are north-westerlies which, with the favorable current, give a comfortable ride when heading south. In contrast, the bumpy passage for boats northbound has been named the 'Baja Bash'. Fortunately, it is now possible to sail north in the Sea of Cortez and have your vessel trucked back to the States from Bahia San Carlos.

Cruisers tend not to head down to the Baja until November, returning by May, to avoid the hurricane season that lasts from June to October. Winds are generally benign although Chubascos, fierce local winds of short duration, can occur in the Fall in the southern Baja.

Just sixty-five miles south of San Diego lies Ensenada, Mexico's first

The Baja—stark but stunning

Port of Entry, an easy day's run for most boats. Boats must clear in with the Port Captain's office (Capitania de Puerto), Immigration (Migracion) and the Customs Office (Aduana), or have an agent complete the paperwork for a fee. It is also advisable to complete the paperwork for the temporary importation of your boat into Mexico, which lasts for ten years. Without this it can be hard to arrange for the boat to be hauled out or have yard work completed.

Crews are welcomed with Mexican charm, although, as with officials the world over, being respectful in one's manner and dress never hurts. Many Mexicans speak English but knowing some Spanish is useful, as well as courteous, and will get a positive response from the locals. Learning to say words for 'thank you, please, good day, how much, where is, goodbye' as well as numbers from 1-10, is worthwhile in any country.

Ensenada is a fishing and commercial port. We love the mouthwatering fish market with its surrounding food stalls and restaurants. Some classic architecture and displays of pottery immediately give a Mexican flavor but there are also large supermarkets, where you can pick up anything you forget to purchase before leaving the States! The region around Ensenada is the center of Baja's wine industry, but if you are a connoisseur, stocking up before you leave the U.S. might suit your palate better. We stick to the delicious local beer or Margaritas.

Having cruised the coast in 80' *Mustang* two years before, we decided on a direct passage down the coast this time in *Bagheera*. As usual it took a couple of days to get into the routine of three hours on watch, three to sleep. We had become spoilt with Duncan and Richard on board.

"It isn't just the sleep I miss," I moaned to Andy. "It's easy to get back into the three-hour routine we did around the world; it's the company, noise and action that's missing!"

"Remember when you were teaching school every morning to the boys when they were young, while everyone else was visiting or going ashore. Now you will have that freedom," countered Andy.

He was right. Although it had been busy, I had enjoyed the school routine with the kids and their enthusiasm for life. It would take me a while to get used to cruising with just the two of us on board and I was heartened by the fact that all three sons would be visiting for Christmas. I was soon back on form. Passage blues are common, but mine seldom last for long.

It was an enjoyable but chilly sail to within a day of Cabo when the wind died and we resorted to motoring. The full moon and bright sky were pleasant for night watches and for tracking the surprising amount of shipping.

'What an easy run,' I noted in my journal on the third day out. 'Washed chart-table cushions, marinated steak, had a great sleep, caught a tuna while Andy was showering on deck and finished *The Perfect Storm.*' (A friend had thought this would make good reading on passage!)

En route, we passed close to mountainous Isla Cedros, a favorite stop for cruisers with its variety of anchorages, unspoiled village, unusual flora and the endangered Cedros mule deer. Circular and protected Turtle Bay, Bahia San Bartolomé was next; this was where we had filled with fuel at the long dock and stocked up on groceries on our last trip. Then came Magdalena Bay, commonly referred to as 'Mag Bay' by the yachting fraternity. When we had visited in *Mustang* in March, we were delighted to find it was filled with breaching, speckled female gray whales and their calves. Later cruisers told us that on their visit two weeks previously, before the males had left to go north, there were so many whales frolicking at the entrance they could barely make their way in.

A brilliant red sky highlighted the distant angular hills as we approached Cabo Falso at dawn. When Andy came on deck for his watch, frolicking dolphins surrounded *Bagheera*. "Wow! This is marvelous," he exclaimed, "and it's much warmer."

"Yes, it's amazing the difference, and right on cue, as we've just entered the tropics! I remember other cruisers telling us the same thing, but I didn't believe that it could happen this quickly."

"It helps that there's no wind," Andy replied, "but it's mainly because at the Cape the cold current takes a turn out to sea. That also means it won't be helping us along anymore."

It had been a fast passage down the Baja. Five days after leaving San Diego the famous arch in the rocks off Lands End was in sight. Then Cabo San Lucas came into view, its hotels and condos perched on the arid cliffs and extending around the white-sand bay. It was 'civilization' with a vengeance. Sports fishing boats were rushing out from the marina; bright parachutes already glided high in the sky pulled along by speedboats.

A tourist town in the extreme, Cabo can be enjoyed for its colorful handicraft markets, regular shopping facilities and availability of American food. If you are in tourist mode a visit to 'The Giggling Marlin' is a must, where you can hang upside-down with others and be fed tequila. It is just as much fun to be a spectator! We like the back streets where you can still find restaurants and bars that serve delicious inexpensive local food.

Sixty sailboats from the Baja Ha-Ha Rally were anchored out and we motored through them slowly, chatting to several cruisers along the way— our first live link for 124 hours.

"What are your plans?" we asked them.

"We'll probably spend a season in the Sea of Cortez," most replied. "But right now we've had a long trip and our agenda is to have no agenda!"

We'd had our fill of Cabo on previous visits and, having no desire to spend half a day with the authorities clearing into Mexico, decided to keep on going, setting a southeasterly course for Isla Isabela off the mainland shore. En route we reminisced about previous visits to the Sea of Cortez, or Gulf of California, a convenient and popular destination for cruisers and one that shouldn't be missed.

Stretching 700 miles to the north, this generally calm stretch of water is the playground for a great number of boats, both large and small. La Paz, the capital for Baja California Sur, where Herman Cortes established Baja's first European outpost, is now an attractive Mexican town. With its spacious harbor, excellent marine facilities, inexpensive open market, good supermarkets, marinas, and easy access to fuel and water, it is a popular base with a ready made social life, and many cruisers get no further!

Daysails to the north are the scenic islands of Islas Espiritu Santo and Partida. Volcanic in origin with the land sloping down to the west they provide numerous anchorages. At their northern tip the high angular rocks of Los Islotes are covered in frigate birds, boobies and pelicans, and huge numbers of noisy sea lions. Best visited in the morning, before the breeze fills in, these islets provide a wonderful nature experience, as the sea lions are exceptionally tame. As in the Galapagos Islands they love to swim with people, and they dart back and forth with glee when snorkelers descend into the water. While visiting previously, one of these sea lions had taken a particular liking to Jamie, and wouldn't leave him alone, excitedly diving around him and 'snuggling-up'. "A little too friendly for me," said Jamie laughing as he quickly climbed back into the dinghy.

The turquoise water, cloudless blue skies, white sand beaches, bright red soil, angular rocks, arroyos (gullies), vigorous cacti and minute but brilliant flowers, set the scene for cruising north in the Gulf. Sunsets are particularly dramatic with the fiery skies a marvelous back-drop for the jagged peaks of the Sierra de la Giganta chain, while the last of the sun's brilliant rays highlight the varying shades of the rock striations. Dry, but striking, 'The Sea' with its twenty-nine islands and many anchorages is such a popular area to cruise that many stay for several years.

We had previously cruised up to Loreto, visiting Isla San Francisco where gold was once mined and pearls gathered. The island was covered with prickly pear cactus, adorned in bright yellow blooms. Here I learnt that it is essential to remove all the prickles before eating the fruit! Circular Punta San Evaristo with its small village, lively school children, dozy donkeys and salt pans was a delightful stop. Several rocky bluffs to the north we gasped at the stark desert beauty of Puerto Los Gatos with its brilliant red rocks, sweeping bay, large rock oysters and huge cacti. Bahia Agua Verde with its dramatic 35-meter high Roca Solitaria at the approach and the emerald green water is another memorable setting.

We enjoyed meeting some local fishermen here and traded for their catch of grouper and snapper. Later we visited their village, a few dwellings perched on a small rocky island. Older fishermen, great characters with faces weather-beaten from a life in the sun, were cutting up shark, sun-drying the fins for the Asian market. Behind there were mounds of bleached dolphin and whale bones.

The area's abundant sea life is another huge attraction. The boat was frequently surrounded by dolphins, not just a dozen but hundreds, the ocean becoming a cauldron from their high arching leaps, tail-walking and backwards spins as far as the eye could see. It is almost impossible not to sight whales, whether humpback, minke, sei, blue, finback or sperm, depending on the season. There were far fewer, we noticed, with the cooler water temperature in March than in November. Deep-sea fish are also abundant and game fishing is popular, especially out into the Pacific.

Protected Puerto Escondido, 140 miles north of La Paz was once known as the 'Hidden Harbor' as it is virtually land-locked. Twenty miles away El Cerro de la Giganta soars almost 2000 meters, the highest mountain in the range. In 1697 Jesuit Juan Maria Salvatierra established the first permanent European settlement in the Californias at the site of nearby Loreto. It is now a modest town but an excellent place for visitors to fly in to join the boat.

Jamie and I had flown in here to join Andy on the 80' *Mustang* two years before. It was a memorable arrival as the authorities didn't want to let us in. "*Permiso*," was all I could understand of the torrent of words. It finally dawned that they wanted a letter of permission from Andy for me to travel with Jamie, who was fourteen years old. Fortunately Andy was waiting for us, quite visible behind the barrier. After this we always made sure that letters of permission for Jamie to travel from both of us were in his passport.

Suddenly the weather turned unbelievably hot and humid and *Bagheera* slowed down, the already light breeze almost gone. Instantly bikinis, or less, replaced the sweatshirts that had been needed at night!

"Flying fish for breakfast," Andy announced jubilantly, holding up three tender, if bony, morsels that had 'flown' onto the deck during the night. "I really feel in the tropics now," he continued, as he disappeared below. Soon wonderful aromas were emanating up the companionway from the galley.

Sunset brought our first green flash of the trip. We love watching for this natural phenomenon that is generally seen only in the tropics. When the sun goes over the horizon the last color refracted is green. Occasionally this can fleetingly be seen as a brilliant, green light as the sun disappears, which has been termed the 'green flash'. It is particularly fascinating, as it is so elusive. Some people cannot see it at all or blink at the crucial moment, and as it happens at the time of sundowner drinks those who haven't imbibed are particularly skeptical! The critical requirement is an absolutely clear sky and it's amazing how often the horizon clouds over just at the last moment. We have seen the green flash many times but it is so intriguing that we always watch for it again.

Bagheera arrived at the tiny island of Isabela at midnight. It was a very black night.

"Thank goodness for radar," Andy commented, "especially as the island is so far from its charted position."

We continued into the small anchorage very slowly. "The cruising guide says there is a submerged rock in the middle," I reported.

"I noticed that," replied Andy, "but with so little light it's hard to assess exactly where it is. We'll have to go in very slowly."

After swinging the beam of the searchlight around the bay he was finally satisfied with our location and went forward to let down the anchor. As we sat in the cockpit watching how the boat settled, the surf was deafening as it roared through the caves beside us, belying our distance from shore. It was a very rolly, hot night, but we did get to sleep for more than our usual three hours!

As usual Andy woke early and went to make tea.

"Liza," he called down from the cockpit, "you have to come up, it's spectacular."

I am not an early morning person, particularly after seven days at sea!

"Come on up," he urged.

It was truly a stunning sight with the black and red volcanic cliffs of the island astern and hundreds of birds swooping around the boat. There were fork-tailed frigate birds, some with their red pouches inflated to impress the girls, four types of boobies, including the blue-footed that we saw in profusion in the Galapagos, and pelicans galore.

As we hadn't yet cleared into Mexico we couldn't go ashore, so instead went snorkeling.

"I can't believe the angelfish," I exclaimed to Andy. "They are huge and there are so many varieties with such bright colors."

"The parrot and butterfly fish are large too, and some of the schools of fish are almost as dense as in the Maldives," he added.

"I've found the rock," he called out later. "It's nowhere near the boat but I'll make a note of its exact position on the chart."

On leaving this magical landfall and cruising the east side of the island, two dramatic pinnacles came into sight, soaring up from the ocean floor. They were silhouetted against the deep blue sky, a photographer's dream. These guano-covered rocks are home to hundreds more birds, and there was frequent movement as they emerged from the fissured face. Many flew high in the sky with an inspirational air of freedom, while others dove for fish bringing us back to the realities of life. It was also time for our lunch and we were soon eating hot fresh bread, whose aromas had been tantalizing our taste buds for the last half-hour.

As usual we trailed a fishing line astern and just as we had started eating the ocean exploded in our wake. We had hooked a mighty sailfish, and it treated us to a magnificent display of tail walking before contemptuously taking off with our favorite lure. Optimistically I had grabbed the squeezy bottle full of alcohol when the line had buzzed out so rapidly, hoping for a dinner-sized fish.

When crossing the Atlantic we had learnt that a squeeze of alcohol on the gills and down the gullet was the quickest, least messy and by far the most humane way of killing fish. Sometimes the larger fish come 'alive' again but another alcohol shot always does the trick. It certainly beats our previous method of bashing the poor fish over the head with a winch handle, with blood and scales flying everywhere!

To the north of our path lay Mazatlan, known as the 'Pearl of the Pacific'. It is famous for its beaches and sports fishing, with over 7000

Isolotes Las Monas off Isla Isabela

marlin and sailfish tagged and released each year. With its spacious protected harbor, marinas, good shopping, great views from the world's second highest lighthouse, picturesque sunsets and pleasant local colonial towns this is another popular destination for cruisers.

Having visited Mazatlan before, we headed to San Blas, a popular stop on the mainland 120 miles further south. We passed by the town as its harbor is silted up, anchoring instead in the deeper big Bay of Mantanchen a few miles down the coast. In the morning Norm came on the VHF radio, welcoming us to the area and passing on local information. We had planned to clear into Mexico here but he informed us that they had closed Immigration which was now in Tepic, inland. He suggested we come ashore with our documents and speak to Customs.

Rather like Tony and Daphne who we met in Kilifi in Kenya, and many others around the world, American residents Norm and Jan spend a considerable amount of their lives helping visiting yachties.

"You are the first boat for the 1998-9 season," he told us when we visited their home.

"Only just," we joked later, as two more boats arrived in the anchorage that night.

One of the couples was elated as they had just finished their circumnavigation. We helped them celebrate in style until dusk, when the mosquitoes and noseeums came out with a vengeance. Although the abundance of fresh water ashore gave rise to lush vegetation it was a perfect breeding ground for bugs, the reason San Blas hasn't developed into a tourist destination.

Back on board we had to check out our VHF radio. It had worked perfectly in Cabo but wouldn't work now. We had been talking to Norm on the handheld, which barely had enough range. Finally we found corrosion in the coax connections from the antenna at the base of the mast and Andy soldered new terminals in place. There's never a dull moment on a boat, but often a few frustrating ones!

On our morning walk along the long white-sand beach we found delicate spined venus clam shells, then left the dinghy with an accommodating 'palapa' restaurant owner to explore the typical Mexican town with its ornate church in the central square. Shopping was easily completed in the market and open roadside shops.

A jungle ride up the river was the afternoon highlight. After surging through a tunnel of mangroves on the local boat our driver roared across a wide green plain. Not only were there orchids galore to identify, the bromeliads were also in full red bloom. Andy was ecstatic over the variety of birds. There were greater and lesser white egrets, snake birds, cormorants, many varieties of duck, kingfishers, swifts, swallows, night-jars, turkey vultures, yellow crowned night herons, cow birds, cuckoos, grackles, great kiskadees, and several of the crane family. As our guide cut the engine and glided in for a closer look, snakes slithered up the banks and turtles dove at the water's edge. After a stimulating hour the trip ended at the Tovara Springs where a huge acquifer (upward waterspout) comes out of the sheer rock face. In the pool below turtles and fish swam to and fro from the river.

"No problem getting fresh seafood in the restaurant," Andy signaled hopefully, but our boat was about to leave!

After a great fish lunch at McDonalds (not the golden arches variety!) in town the next day, we went to see a display of artwork by the Huichol Indians who had settled in the area before the Spanish arrived. They now use tiny, colorful glass beads for their artwork in place of the original gold and local stones. The beads are intricately patterned into gourds and on masks, or made into jewelry. We bought a gourd with a complex design and were told the symbolism of its particular pattern by the attractive, earnest young woman who had crafted it.

"It is a mixture of the old life on the coast and the new life inland, where the people went after the Spanish came," she explained. "The Huichol," she continued, "are determined to preserve their old beliefs and we are reviving our old customs for the young to learn." The peyote cactus is especially significant in their religious life and is vividly portrayed.

We were learning about history ourselves as we cruised down the coast, particularly about the Spanish influence. San Blas became a base for the Spanish for shipbuilding from the late 16th to the 19th century due to the abundance of trees and a small, protected harbor. High above the town stands a fort, built to protect their trading galleons from British and French pirates.

It was an overnight trip from San Blas to Puerto Vallarta and we enjoyed enormous almond-flavored avocados for dinner. Norm and Jan had given us a generous supply from their garden. It was a quiet night but during Andy's watch there was an extraordinary occurrence when without warning the boat was inundated by bees. By the time I came on deck the only sign was a mass of dead bodies; Andy had been busy! Why they had swarmed us so far from land remains a mystery.

With an adverse current and no wind, the trip was agonizingly slow. Little did we know that we would be motoring most of the next 2,500 miles to the Panama Canal! The current was particularly strong as far as Manzanillo, pushing us back as much as 2 miles an hour.

It was 8:00am by the time we arrived at the harbor in Puerto Vallarta so I went straight to the boatyard to make an appointment to haul out *Bagheera*. Andy was keen to install the transducer for our new depth sounder/fish finder that replaced our previous faulty unit. Although we have a regular depth sounder the fish finder not only reads far greater depths; it also indicates the state of the bottom for anchoring.

Much to Andy's relief I could get a time slot but it was expensive to come out of the water for just a few hours. Fortunately there happened to be a boat show in the marina that weekend so as usual I passed the time on the dock with the Beneteau dealer displaying my route map of our circumnavigation and managed to sell a few books. Interestingly, most sales were to Canadians.

Puerto Vallarta is a destination for cruisers and holidaymakers. The attractive setting is nestled between the palm-covered mountains and the large white-sand bay. First settled in 1851, it is now a mega tourist resort although not long ago it was still a small village of farmers and fishermen. Lured by Mexican Airline flights, tourists started coming in 1954 but it was 'put on the map' when Tennessee William's *The Night of the Iguana* was filmed here in 1964, when the Richard Burton-Elizabeth Taylor romance was blossoming.

Not only is it a good hurricane shelter for yachts, there is long-term marina moorage and excellent facilities at hand. Many yachts never venture farther; for many long-distance sailors this is the last major port of call before heading for the South Pacific. We met several cruisers whose boats had been at the dock for years; some work locally while others treat their boat as their winter residence in the sun, and go north to visit the family in summer.

Life is comfortable and relatively cheap in pleasant surroundings. At the end of our dock was a hotel swimming pool where the yachties gathered late afternoon. Laundry was $5.00 for two loads, done for you and neatly folded (although the local soap powder has a 'different' smell), and there are several inexpensive restaurants around the harbor, all serving excellent ice cold beer and powerful margaritas. After hauling out and working a boat show in the high heat and humidity, who needs to rationalize to visit them?

We were also able to see an old friend from our Caribbean days. We had visited Maria a few years previously when she and her husband had been running the luxury converted ocean-going tug *Itasca* and had also toured the area by car staying at their colorful hilltop home in Sayolita with its spectacular view of the ocean. It was great to reminisce about Caribbean cruising in the '60s and wonderful to be whisked around in a car to do the chores.

Andy worked on our Ham radio, over-hauling the antenna connections and lead wire, which we thought might be corroded, as despite the new radio and tuner we still weren't transmitting well. By Monday he felt he had done everything possible. By this time we had met Barrie aboard *Minerva*, from Victoria, B.C., an expert on radios. He is now a Mexican resident with wife Carole, who does canvas work on her large industrial machine on deck.

Barrie confirmed that both reception and transmission now checked out well with a final talk to New Zealand. It was a huge relief, as the radio is our precious link to the world of communication and weather. I also went on the morning chat net between boats on the VHF radio and asked if anyone was using radio e-mail satisfactorily. One man responded. He came over that morning and spent an hour sorting our connections. Finally he got through on the Ham bands—another relief, although we were still missing one fitting that we couldn't get locally. Neither would accept any payment, an example of the wonderfully supportive yachting community.

All systems in order, it was time to leave this nurturing yachting community and head south, if we were to be in time to meet our children for Christmas in Costa Rica. There was another 1000 miles of Mexican coastline beckoning to be explored, then a crossing of the notorious Gulf of Tehuantepec to be achieved before reaching Central America.

6. Southern Mexico

Puerto Vallarta to Puerto Madero, Across the Gulf of Tehuantepec

The lush Sierra Madre Mountains create a dramatic backdrop to the central Pacific coast. Between Puerto Vallarta and Huatulco are found some of Mexico's favorite tourist destinations, but there are also beautiful quiet bays. Cruising this area is becoming increasingly popular, particularly because a comfortable winter circuit is possible from the Sea of Cortez.

The coast itself is a combination of long sandy beaches and headlands, with many rocks scattered off the shore. Few of these are marked accurately on the charts so we decided to stay well out to sea. It was an overnight passage from Puerto Vallarta to Careyes Bay, and a pitch black night but calm as we motored past Cabo Corrientes. Although there was some adverse current we were pleased to weather the point so easily. As at Cabo Falso and Point Conception local winds can accelerate around this cape causing disturbed seas and strong currents.

A few miles before our landfall a voice came over the VHF radio. We could just see the bow of a boat peeking out from behind the rocks in the tiny anchorage inshore.

"We haven't seen another sailboat for weeks," the American couple told us. "It was so exciting to see a sail we just had to call. Where are you headed?"

"We're planning to be in Costa Rica for Christmas, then continue through the Panama Canal. We've met tons of cruisers leaving the States this year but it will be a while before boats get this far south. What are your plans?"

"We're off to the South Pacific and waiting for the cyclone season to end."

"Great. You'll love it down there."

"You've been already? Where did you like the best."

"Everywhere! French Polynesia, Raratonga, Tonga and Fiji—all the islands are marvelous to cruise."

"We can't wait. Enjoy southern Mexico and Central America."

"Thanks and you have a good trip to the Marquesas. *Bagheera* clear and back to channel 16."

The interchange stimulated many a memory of our 1987 crossing of the South Pacific with our young children. Distances are vast, with several long passages required, but the rewards are outstanding on arrival at the island groups.

We soon arrived at Careyes, a small triple-lobed bay with tiny islands in the center. A Club Med, hotel and brightly-colored condo development line the shore. We decided to call in here because a yacht club friend owned one of the condos. They weren't in residence but it was fun to wander around the spacious units that are attractively piled up the steep cliff and lavishly smothered in tropical flowers. We were treated to another interesting snorkel, in water that was cool enough to be refreshing. Ashore at the hotel they served formidable Margaritas!

There was a light breeze for a sail to Bahia Tenacatita, just eighteen miles to the south. This large, tranquil bay has jagged rocks at the entrance and several were just awash.

"I'm glad we're not making our usual night entry," commented Andy as he marked the rocks on the chart accurately. We were attracted by the many palapas lining the beach in the pleasant outer northwest bay. With their palm-frond shades these restaurants are so simple yet so cool we couldn't resist going ashore for a seafood lunch. It was quite delicious and only $10.00 for two large fish lunches and three bottles of beer.

"Are you from the sailboat at anchor?" asked some tourists as we were contentedly wandering back barefoot, luxuriating in the feel of the soft, warm sand. We stopped to chat and learned they lived just down the road from us at home!

We launched the dinghy through the frothy surf without getting totally drenched. Taking off from the shore through ocean swells is always a little unpredictable. By this time we had perfected the technique for landing the dinghy in the rollers. Andy puts down wheels on the transom of the dinghy before reaching the breaking waves, then we surf in on a big one, leap out in the shallows, both grab the line under the bow and furiously wheel the dinghy up the beach—much to the amazement of the locals! Launching is more difficult. Waiting for a break in the large waves we rapidly push the dinghy out into deep water, climb in at the last moment and frantically start the engine before we are turned broadside to the next big breaker. Wrong timing or the engine not starting generally means a soaking!

A river in the inner bay looked inviting. We took *Bagheera* around and anchored next to an American vessel. It was disappointing that no one was on board; we miss getting together with other cruisers. At low tide the river mouth was shallow but we wheeled the dinghy around on the beach to deeper water. After motoring for a bit up river it became shallow again and we were about to turn back when around the bend ahead came a dinghy filled with gringos! They were, of course, from the other boat and told us they had visited the Palapas by river, and that there was enough depth to use the outboard the whole way.

It turned out to be another great river exploration through the mangroves. Again there were birds in profusion. Groups of pelicans relaxed in the higher branches, and lower down there were nightjars, kingfishers, gray herons, night herons, ospreys, cormorants, our first ibis, and white egrets that startled us by launching into flight right in front of the dinghy, then leading us up the narrow and winding stream. Soon we were ducking under the vine-like branches, and passing close by the dense masses of interwoven mangrove roots that were covered in bright red crabs.

Dusk was falling as we headed out of the bay. Andy was in despair when I came on watch at 10:30pm that night.

"There is no sign of wind and we've been averaging barely three knots over the ground," he moaned. "I've been motoring all the time and if the current continues at this rate against us our fuel supply won't make it to Zihuatenejo. I've been looking in the cruising guide and except for Manzanillo, at all the other anchorages we'll have to inflate the dinghy to get ashore then get a taxi to a Pemex gas station for diesel."

In all of our 60,000 miles of cruising on *Bagheera* we had never moved so slowly, or used so much fuel. We decided it was prudent to stop at Manzanillo, so crossed Bahia de Santiago to anchor in the small bay on its eastern shore. Again it was midnight and entry was a little confusing, until we realized that the flashing red and green lights at its inner end were part of the local disco, nothing to do with aids to navigation!

Opulence greeted us next morning with huge mansions and the arches of the famous Las Hadas Hotel adorning the hills, but the marina had no

Manzanillo

diesel despite its prominent fuel tank. There were three sailboats at the dock stern-to, besides a number of powerboats. The first was British and had attracted our attention as its anchor line was covered with balancing pelicans who were having a great game of 'who can I make fall off when I land'. You could almost see them laughing.

The other two boats were American, both with signs of life on board. They kindly gave us directions for finding fuel at the other end of the harbor, several miles away. At the very far end of the port, past all the naval ships that had seen better days, at the very last wharf, there were pumps for fuelling the local fishing fleet. At least it was easy to get diesel on board and remarkably cheap; fortunate, as we had just enough pesos. We had expected to use a credit card when we thought we could get fuel at the marina.

As we headed on southeast the current eased and was even in our favor occasionally; the wind also came up at least for part of the day. "Sod's Law!" exclaimed Andy when I told him the good news. "We could have made it after all."

Zihuatanejo is a popular destination for cruisers completing a Mexican circuit. Its bay is protected, although for those who would like to be at the dock there is a marina at the near-by tourist development of Ixtapa. Just be sure not to swim there, the lagoon is the home to several crocodiles and they can sometimes be seen looking for a tender morsel!

Initially we were unable to set the anchor in Zihuatanejo, then it suddenly caught, stopping the boat abruptly. Andy and I looked at each other;

this was an ominous sign. Ever since Portugal, where our anchor had jammed under an ancient ship's chain and the anchor windlass had been torn out, we were wary of debris on the bottom, but we decided to stay. This time our concern was unfounded and the anchor came up easily next day.

As we sat down in the cockpit with drinks in hand, right on cue a band started ashore. The accomplished musicians were playing traditional guitar music and singing in harmony. We lay back, lounging in the light of a full moon and savoring the soothing melodies.

"A perfect way to relax after a trip," I commented sleepily. By the time the fervent freedom speeches began (it was Revolution Day, the anniversary of the Mexican revolution of 1910) we had already retired.

Dawn showed us a pretty bay with pleasant beaches and thatched hotels, although we had woken earlier than intended. A cruise ship had arrived and the tenders laden with passengers were passing unnecessarily close to *Bagheera*, their wakes violently rocking the boat. Andy called the ship on the radio. A very British voice answered and it was amusing to hear the two formal British accents in the middle of Mexico discussing the problem, each a match for the other! The ship agreed to reroute their craft.

Although becoming more touristy, Zihuatanejo is a charming Mexican town. It was Saturday and the busy market was excellent with a far greater variety of fruit and vegetables than we had seen previously.

We had coffee on the sea front and were asked to comment in the restaurant's visitors' book for cruisers. Again, we were the first of the season to sign. They told us there were generally 80-100 boats passing through in a year. There were also attractive souvenir stores and stalls along the front. One had some appealing and inexpensive Mexican pottery and pewter. We had decided to buy some items for gifts on our way back to the boat but the store was now closed. It was a reminder that, like taking photos or buying seasick pills, one must always 'strike while the iron is hot'!

Coming out of the bay, past the light at Punta El Faro, high islands were clearly visible.

"Look at the chart Andy, those large islets are just marked as pinpricks."

"Yes," he agreed, "It's amazing how poorly charted the rocks are and I suspect the charting will get worse as we head south." He was right.

The luminous white rocks ahead were home to numerous seabirds and it was the first time on this trip that we had seen the long-tailed tropicbirds. Passing close-by we were amused by the reaction of the immature brown boobies who behaved like cheeky teenagers as they wheeled close to the sails and across the bow. It was a great diversion from the heat, 95°F., and not a breath of wind. Thank goodness for Mexican beer and efficient refrigeration!

After a night of thunderstorms, always worrying after our lightning strike off South Africa, we arrived in Acapulco at dawn, far earlier than expected as there had finally been a strong, favorable current. Acapulco is an impressive natural harbor, and almost entirely surrounded by a white sand beach. We went to the Club de Yates and were pleased that we could get a discount on moorage on presenting our Vancouver yacht club membership card.

A bit of civilization while cruising is great for the body and soul and it was thoroughly enjoyable having waiter service as we lounged in chaiselonges beside the club swimming pool. There were several members enjoying a relaxing Sunday, many with extended families. All were welcoming and we were also joined by more cruisers. They were a group of South African lads who were completing a fast passage from the United States to Bonaire, a Dutch island off Venezuela. We had met them in Puerto Vallarta when they had also been profiting from the boat show, by modeling clothing.

"Have you done the trip to Bonaire from Panama?" they asked, after hearing that Andy had lived in the Caribbean for seven years.

"I've done part of it and I have to say it was a long slog, as the wind frequently blows 30 knots or more in the southern Caribbean. So it's a hard beat in itself but you will also have two to three knots of current against you." We suggested coastal hopping, doing passages at night when the wind eased.

"We are on a delivery," they explained, "so need to go direct."

"Then go on a long starboard leg north to get out of the current and tack back on port to fetch Bonaire," Andy advised. We heard later that they had arrived, but it had indeed been a tough ride.

A swim and siesta rejuvenated our enthusiasm to explore ashore. First stop was the large five-fingered Spanish fort that is well maintained and has an informative museum where we learnt about Acapulco's long and illustrious trading history. Soon after the Spanish explorers discovered the Bay of Acapulco in 1512, trading routes were established with Mexico City and the Caribbean coast, linking Spain with the Orient. From the early 16th to the late 18th century Acapulco was the only port in the New World authorized to receive Spanish trading vessels from the Philippines and Japan to sell their wares. By the 17th century trade was flourishing and the fort was built to ward off English and Dutch pirates.

When a ship arrived four and a half centuries ago so did traders from

Europe, to buy, to sell and to party. Now, international tourists come to play in the high-rise hotels, of which hundreds are visible from the top of the fort, while the traders walk around with their wares, plying the beaches and streets. For the most part we found the Mexican vendors charming and the children attractive, although very young to be working. We chatted to several while relaxing by the cathedral in old Acapulco. The children were fascinated by my guidebook, inquisitive about the places in the pictures and delighted when they came across one they recognized. We were happy to learn from their mothers that education of the young is taken very seriously, and that school came first during the week.

The old tourist area is now full of character and enticing inexpensive restaurants. Here we ran into more Vancouverites, including another author with whom I had been put in touch when writing *Just Cruising*! Finally, we couldn't resist the lure of the seafood (only $6 for two, this time with drinks), and then made the steep climb to watch the clavadistas of La Quebrada make the incredible leap off the cliffs. Four young boys made a graceful dive into the narrow crevasse where ocean swells dramatically rise and fall over jagged rocks, continuing a dangerous tradition that has been practised since 1934. The last diver even did a somersault on the way down the 45 meters from the top of the cliff, where he had first prayed at the shrine.

The passage from Acapulco to Puerto Madero is over 500 miles. There are few anchorages and this stretch also includes the treacherous Gulf of Tehuantepec. We decided to pass by touristy Puerto Escondido, renowned as a hangout for hippies in the 60s, and instead arrived at dawn at the delightful bay at Puerto Angel, dropping the hook on the west side of the bay. It was a picturesque setting with a small sandy beach covered with palapas, local boats at the water's edge and a cemetery filled with blue and pink tombs clustered on the steep hill behind.

Almost immediately and to our surprise, the Mexican military arrived by panga. It was only later that we realized their headquarters was right beside us! The two Mexican workboats were filled with men and two dogs. Seven armed soldiers climbed aboard with one dog, friendly but with authority. While Andy assisted with the Spanish paperwork the commandant indicated that the dog should be taken below. He signaled for me to follow and as I climbed down from the coach roof one of the men jumped up and continued pumping up the dinghy in my place! I was impressed.

Down below lockers were being opened and the black retriever sniffed thoroughly inside each one. Then the guard opened the door of our starboard aft cabin. This is where the dirty laundry is thrown when no guests are on board. The poor dog rushed in with his usual enthusiasm, then backed off so rapidly he leapt off the floor and crashed into the table. It was hard not to laugh as he sat on the sole (floor) with a defiant expression that read, "It's a no go here, I've had enough. When can I leave?"

We learnt that two years previously security had been stepped up because of the Indian uprising in Chiapas, particularly after guerrillas overran the small Navy outpost in Huatulco, just 20 miles away.

The small village of Puerto Angel has good roadside stalls for produce and a supermercado. "We've run out of margarita mix, lets go in," suggested Andy. We were lucky. The shelves were filled with booze, hot sauce, toilet paper and soap.

Ambling back along the beach we were touched by the many shrines that were adorned with vases of freshly-cut flowers. A colorfully dressed woman came up, pointing to the goods that were piled high on her head.

"Would you like to look at my hammocks," she invited with an infectious smile.

She immediately hauled down her wares and unloaded hammocks and bags that were skillfully woven in bright tropical tones. I settled for a two-dollar bag. When we returned an hour later she was quite delighted to see that Andy was carrying it laden with produce. Gleefully she pointed it out to some tourists, and immediately completed more sales!

After an hour of walking in the heat it was time for a beer on the cool deck of a restaurant. In front, the fishermen were hard at work driving their laden pangas up the sandy beach under full throttle then unloading their catch of yellowfin tuna, helped by their wives and children. We struck up conversation with an English couple at the next table and they joined us for a snorkel and an enjoyable palapa dinner. He worked for the British Tourist Board and covered Africa and the Middle East. They wanted a change of scenery for their holiday so had come to Mexico. The big question was whether to travel north or south from here; it was a dilemma as both have great appeal.

Puerto Angel is at the north end of the Gulf of Tehuantepec, feared for its frequent 60-knot winds and high seas. Motoring south we debated giving the last safe port, Huatulco, a miss. The weather had been benign all month and there wasn't a bad weather warning.

After discussion, however, we decided it made good sense to call in and visit the Port Captain for the very latest forecast. Ashore a small inner harbor has been developed as a shopping area for cruise ships but it was pleasant enough to wander around looking for Christmas stocking stuffers while waiting. The 4:00pm forecast was perfect—winds to be NE at 15-20 knots, with seas 5-8 feet. Occasional scattered thunderclouds. The actual at Salina Cruz, midway across the Tehuantepec, was only NE 30km (16 knots). We left with confidence, but were soon to be disillusioned.

As the evening progressed the wind built and continued to increase until it was gusting 46 knots on the nose. Termed a strong gale on the Beaufort Scale, it is characterized by high waves, rolling seas, dense streaks of foam and spray that reduces visibility. We know it well. The seas were extraordinarily uncomfortable and the spray that was blown off the tops of the waves stung our faces. Huge quantities of green water came over the deck, and unfortunately through a port we had failed to close tightly, and onto the laptop computer. But we were again impressed by *Bagheera's* ability to progress to windward even in these extreme conditions.

At 11:00pm our autopilot failed and we had to hand steer on two-hour watches throughout the night until we could get the windvane mobilized at dawn. Earlier we had hoped that the northeasterly winds would be on our beam, but as we hugged the shore to stay in the smoother seas *Bagheera* was heading straight into wind. We reached Salina Cruz next afternoon and thankfully entered the harbor.

When there are big waves and white caps even in the inner harbor, you know this is serious weather. In fact the port had been closed to shipping and there were two ships waiting, anchored outside. There was no safe dock to tie up, and the sea wall was on the lee side of the harbor and unattractive, particularly with the two-meter tidal range. Seeing our dilemma some fishermen beckoned us to come alongside their vessel. We gave them some small bottles of whisky in thanks; they laughed at the meager alcohol content, and went back to their home brewed tequila. We declined the offer to swig from their bottle, saving face by holding up our bottle of wine!

Being a commercial port the authorities were used to agents completing a ship's clearance documentation and demanded that we also hire one. The agent's usual fee was $50.

"But we are just a small private boat," we argued. "We can't afford $50 and only came in here as a harbor of refuge."

"But the paperwork is the same as for a ship, and must be done," the official replied.

"How about $20?" Andy finally suggested. We settled on $25 and in the end the agent was extraordinarily friendly and helpful.

Next morning the fishermen watched over *Bagheera* while we went into the bustling town. When we came back laden with produce and seafood from the well-stocked market they were crowded around a small radar unit.

"Do you know how to work it?" the captain asked Andy. "We don't have a manual."

"I don't know that model, but it looks similar to ours." Andy replied.

We all piled up the steps into their stark but surprisingly well-equipped bridge.

Andy was soon able to work out the radar's basic functions. The fishermen were delighted and more tequila appeared. Yet again we declined. Later, when Andy came out on *Bagheera's* deck with his pint of tea they asked what it was. "Tea," he replied. "Ah, una tequila grande?" they teased back. "No, té," Andy rejoined in Spanish with a grin. There was great laughter all round.

"Party tonight?" they asked us with beaming smiles.

Marine Control was most informative with weather information and told us the wind would be down for us to leave the following morning. We hoped for a great sail to Puerto Madero, but as predicted by the fishermen, the wind died after a few hours. Just before we resorted to motoring, two pink flamingoes flew past our stern. They made a beautiful picture silhouetted against the deep blue sky, flying so serenely over the sparkling ocean.

It was hard to believe that there had been such a raging storm just two days before, and in all likelihood there would be another in two days time. Back to reality, it was a good time to get the laundry done. Soon I'd strung lines and the cockpit was full of clinging wet clothing. It was great having ample water to do it! Meanwhile Andy checked for chafe on the boat and we completed routine chores.

Along the way a sailboat passed by inshore, tacking north. Andy called them on the VHF.

Changing the paper on the baragraph

"We've been cruising in the Caribbean for three years," they informed us. "Now we're making our way back to Canada."

"We just left there in August," returned Andy. "Are there many boats down south?"

"We haven't seen too many since the Canal," they replied. "But the cruising has been great. Be sure not to miss northern Panama."

Puerto Madero, the last port in Mexico, is one hundred and ninety miles past Salina Cruz. The coast consists of low, sandy beaches with the mountains of the Sierra Soconusco and Sierra Madre behind. The winds from the Caribbean funnel through these mountain ranges causing the strong winds in the area. The southerly portion of the Gulf of Tehuantepec is generally less affected than the north, according to the locals.

It was dark when we arrived at 9:00pm, which made the entry through the breakwater interesting; initially all we could see was surf! Red and green can buoys mark the dredged channel but they were unlit and we almost passed one on the wrong side. After that we had the searchlight at hand and moved forward cautiously. The first anchorage, off the palapa beach, was too shallow; so we continued past many pangas that lined the shore and on into the inner lagoon.

It was a peaceful night but there was an early hail the next morning asking us to move for the dredger. Soon another vessel arrived; a large multi-passenger sightseeing boat headed for California to join a whale-watching charter fleet. It had been brought down from Connecticut and through the Canal. The skipper and I went to the new Port Captain's office together. As he cleared into Mexico, I cleared out. (It is necessary to clear out of almost every country in the world except the U.S. to be allowed to enter the next.) The Port Captain was charming and extremely helpful, asking one of his men to drive us to the airport for clearance with Immigration. He also offered to Federal Express our package of Christmas cards to Vancouver!

There was one final matter to attend to—fuel. Although there was a fuel dock for the fishing fleet and diesel was generally available, there was a severe shortage due to Hurricane Mitch, which had devastated Central America a month before. The sightseeing boat had ordered a fuel truck from Tapachula, about 20 miles away. As the day wore on with no fuel in sight the owner suggested he give us the few gallons of diesel we needed from what was left in their tanks. Besides this generous offer, they also gave us their Costa Rican courtesy flag.

"At least they should have a good trip across the Tehuantepec," I commented as we headed out through the breakwater that was much easier to navigate in daylight. "The Port Captain just told us that there would be light winds for the next two days."

"That's interesting," replied Andy. "The forecast I just got from the States gave out a Tehuantepec warning!"

Andy put out the fishing lines. "It would be really nice to catch some fish to make up for that license fee," he remarked. "There must be some around, look at all the fishing boats."

Fishing had been decidedly poor lately with only three bonito that were oily and poor eating, and one yellowfin tuna that was delicious. The rest of the fish had either escaped or been eaten by sharks. Andy had also caught the huge sailfish, that provided some entertainment but had also escaped with our most expensive lure!

The busy Mexican fishing boats ended in an abrupt line; we didn't need to look at the chart to know it was the Guatemalan border. It seemed strange to be leaving Mexico after so many miles of cruising its coast. We had thoroughly enjoyed the extroverted people, the food and the culture, and seeing more of the country than on our previous visits. Now there was the special anticipation of exploring a whole new cruising ground, and adventuring ashore in Central America.

Pacific
Central America

7. El Salvador to Costa Rica

Except for its physical location, and its reputation for volcanic eruptions and political strife, we knew very little about Central America and the feasibility of cruising its shores. I was particularly eager to see Guatemala. Many years ago my interest had been piqued when a school friend had vividly described life on her father's ranch, the exotic birds and animals, and brilliant flowers. Her excitement about landing in the jungle on the new airstrip that had been built beside the temples at Tikál had been so infectious it had stimulated a class project on the Mayan culture. It was at a time when excavations by the Museum of the University of Pennsylvania together with the Guatemalan Instituto de Antropologia y Historia were stimulating an explosion of interest in the Mayan civilization throughout the world.

While Andy installed the watermaker in San Francisco I had researched the countries we planned to visit, to make realistic cruising and sightseeing plans. The boys' school atlas to show the physical boundaries of the countries involved and Lonely Planet's *Central America on a Shoestring* gave some excellent historical background and places of interest to visit. By using the British Admiralty *Sailing Directions* for the *West coasts of Mexico and Central America* and some cruising guides, I was able to plan our route. We also made inquiries about the current political situation and safety for inland travel.

In recent years the term 'Central America' has generally been used to include the seven countries of El Salvador, Guatemala, Nicaragua, Belize, Panama, Honduras and Costa Rica, that lie between Mexico and Columbia. Although the area is small, about a quarter the size of Mexico and with a maximum width of 175 miles, it has a strategic location, dividing the Pacific and Atlantic Oceans and joining the continents of North and South America. The Panama Canal, the operation of which has recently been handed over to the Panamanians by the United States, is of particular importance to world trade.

This land bridge is primarily volcanic in origin, with over 250 volcanoes, several mountain chains and fertile valleys. It has been heavily populated for thousands of years by people who, it is believed, migrated from Asia. Speculation also includes migrations from Africa, particularly Egypt. Historically, the lowlands of Costa Rica and Nicaragua formed the boundary between the indigenous peoples of the south, including the Incas of Peru, and the northern tribes of Mexico. Of these, the Maya were particularly significant as their empire stretched through Belize, Guatemala, El Salvador, some of Honduras, the Yucatan and Chiapas.

On his final voyage in 1502 Christopher Columbus, a Genoese, discovered Central America for Spain, while looking for a western sea route for the Asian spice trade. Centered in Panama, Spanish exploration branched across Central and South America. As gold, pearls and other wealth came up from Peru, and precious metals were found locally, they were taken from Panama City, across the isthmus to Portobelo and shipped to Spain. Colonial rule in Central America lasted until 1821 by which time both Mexico and old Guatemala (which was Central America today without Panama) had declared their independence from Spain. By 1838 almost all of the states of the old Guatemala had become independent. Since then Central American politics have been volatile both within and between individual countries. Recently, however, there has been political stability and the positive articles on both cruising and travelling in the area convinced us that these countries would be fascinating to visit.

Departure from Puerto Madero had been in the late afternoon and, on entering Guatemalan waters, we were treated to a double green flash at sunset as *Bagheera* rose and fell on the ocean swells. The night saw little traffic but at dawn I was startled by a sudden loud bang. Andy had just woken me for my watch and I leapt up on deck.

"What was that noise? It sounded like an explosion."

"Just another volcano going off," replied Andy nonchalantly. "There have been several."

The volcano abeam was now belching huge clouds of smoke; another boom produced a long silver plume from a different peak. It hung suspended, a trailing white pennant against the dawn sky.

During the morning several fishing pangas passed us as they headed out to sea. We were also fishing and despite my calls and waves of warning, a boat passing our stern caught our line. The fisherman was quick to respond, lifted up his outboard and unwound the line from the propeller. He held up the lure, showing me it was still in place, then rushed off with a friendly wave.

'Liza catches an 800lb Panga,' Andy wrote in the log. His comment soon came back to haunt him as shortly into his watch there was another 'catch'. He decided to wind in the fishing line!

There are two ports of entry along this coast, Champerico and Puerto Quetzal. Our cruising guide informed us that Champerico is now a desolate open roadstead with a decrepit wooden pier. In contrast, the new port of Puerto Quetzal, which replaced the old port of San Jose, is thriving and has become Guatemala's principal Pacific port. It has a yacht anchorage and dinghy dock that is conveniently separated from the commercial activities and guarded by the navy. Recent cruisers have commented favorably about leaving their boats here to travel inland, although the fee of $100 for five days seems steep. *Bagheera* motored by in the middle of the night; it seemed to take a long time to pass its bright lights.

For years cruisers have extolled the pleasures of visiting Guatemala from the Caribbean side at the Rio Dulce where there is a choice of marinas, so we decided not to stop along this short Guatemalan Pacific coast. (Had we known the trauma of getting *Bagheera* over the bar into the Rio Dulce, we might have decided otherwise!)

We were motoring again when I came up on watch at dawn, but this time Andy was happy!

"No Papagayos, I'm pleased to say," he commented.

South of the Bay of Tehuantepec, from November to February, the Pacific coasts of Guatemala, El Salvador, Nicaragua, Honduras and Costa Rica are plagued by violent winds called Papagayos. These are instigated to a large degree by the weather in the Northwest Caribbean that spills across the narrow peninsula. Cruisers hope for low pressure in the Gulf of Mexico when few Papagayos develop. Although these winds generally don't exceed 45 knots, it is always helpful to have warning of gale-force winds and with a weatherfax on board we usually have a good idea of what to expect. But here it was a problem getting local weather information. Our location was off the weatherfax picture that we had been receiving from San Francisco and other faxes were too general, covering too large an area.

"How about voice forecasts?" I questioned.

"You won't believe it," Andy replied, "When I tuned in, the U.S. high seas forecasts from the west and east were being broadcast on the same frequency at the same time, making both unintelligible."

Later we were pleased to link into the Ham net called the Central American Breakfast Club on LSB 7.085 kHz at 1300z. Its participants were located between 20 degrees north and south, around Central America. They included some currently cruising, as well as others who live ashore, and they had much useful information to share. Later the SSB Papagayo Net on USB 4024-4030 kHz at 1400z became active, with excellent weather predictions.

As it turned out, travelling in November/December worked well for us, although we subsequently met cruisers who, only a week behind us, experienced strong Papagayos all down the coast.

Fifty-seven miles past Puerto Quetzel lies Acajulta, El Salvador's largest port and a popular beach resort. Although a breakwater gives some protection, this is an open roadstead. A more attractive alternative is the large Bay of Fonseca, bordered by the three countries of El Salvador, Honduras and Nicaragua, and filled with high volcanic islands. (There is also now a Barillas Marina on the coast in Bahía de Jiquilisco.) We had purchased large-scale charts in San Francisco having found that the chart book we were using (which covered the Mexican border to Panama), omitted details of the entire Fonseca area.

Dolphins joined us as we turned into the bay. I was entranced by their leaps at the bow that were in perfect unison. Suddenly Andy intruded, "Wow, look at the sky!"

The starboard side of the boat was a brilliant orange and the last of the gleaming rays reflected a rosy glow onto the sails. This is what cruising is all about and we felt a nurturing peaceful contentment. In contrast, to port a huge moon had made a rapid ascent, and its white light induced a totally different mood. Starkly outlining the volcanic hills in the background the severe black, white and gray created such an aura of harshness, intrigue and mystery that I gave an involuntary shiver. We became mesmerized, repeatedly turning back and forth in unison. These unexpected visits with nature, and our vital responses to them, are glories of the cruising life.

On entering the large, shallow bay the strong current made progress slow so we decided to anchor for the night. I had just finished making the El Salvador courtesy flag from spinnaker cloth. These always take longer than expected and I was quite pleased that with some stars added from self-adhesive repair cloth the same flag would also serve for Honduras.

Andy was awake early, keen to leave.

"The fishermen are already out to sea," he informed me. "It was so nice to see them sailing their dug-out canoes."

Deep into the bay at the base of a volcano is La Union, a Port of Entry, that offers a sheltered, if shallow anchorage. After passing a U.S. Navy patrol vessel, we anchored as instructed off the El Salvadorian Naval Base at the port of Cutuco and waited for clearance. We were hopeful the procedure would go quickly as the police had a smart launch, prominently visible ashore. Every time they headed out from the dock we thought they were coming over to us, then they would turn away. Finally we realized they were doing circles to practise docking their new vessel! Andy was getting itchy feet. He had just realized it was Saturday, not a good day to clear into a country.

"How long are we staying here?" he demanded.

"Two days," I responded.

"It will never work at a weekend!"

"But it's still early!"

"Why don't we leave?" Andy pursued.

"I want to see something of El Salvador, it's the one Central American country that doesn't have a Caribbean coast," I replied, then quickly went on deck to pump up the dinghy!

El Salvador is the smallest, most highly industrialized, and most densely populated country of Central America. With its total area of 124 sq. miles it is about the same size as Wales, while its population of almost six million, is double. Having no precious metals it remained largely isolated from the Spanish conquest, although plantations of cotton, balsam and indigo were productive due to the country's fertile soil. It was the introduction of coffee at the end of the nineteenth century that caused the population and prosperity to grow and by the twentieth century 95% of El Salvador's income came from coffee but only 2% controlled the wealth.

Efforts to redress the country's social and economic ills resulted in repression, political turmoil and violence. In 1979 a military coup overthrew the president and formed a junta. When they failed to improve conditions the opposition parties banded together. The successful socialist revolution in Nicaragua encouraged others to believe armed warfare was the only solution. In 1980 a civilian, Jose Napolean Duarte, was elected to be president for four years. He was heavily supported by the U.S. but when guerrillas gained control of the north and east the military retaliated. A civil war ensued, thousands were killed, the land was destroyed and the economy foundered.

It wasn't until 1992 that civil war ended with a peace agreement between the guerrillas and the government, and the establishment of free elections. Since then efforts to diversify away from a dependence on agriculture have resulted in a large manufacturing industry. Now coffee, sugar, shrimp and textiles are the main exports. Although El Salvador now has one of the strongest economies in Central America, many still live at a subsistence level and the main source of the country's revenue is from El Salvadorans living in the U.S.. The country also has the highest level of environmental damage in the Americas, but other travelers had enjoyed their visits here and I was interested to see this country that has been redefining its present and future.

When the dinghy was inflated we went ashore and were told that officials would be on board within the hour. The Port Captain arrived at midday and was charming, and fluent in English. While he was completing the paperwork he suggested we go into town to visit Immigration; there was a dock where we could tie-up the dinghy. Fate was not with us. The tidal range here is nearly ten feet. It was unfortunately still mid-tide and there were many meters of thick, stinky mud to wade through, and drag the dinghy across, to get to the wall— the only place to tie up the dinghy. We also had to avoid the many colorful fishing boats. The locals were laughingly leaping across the goo, but as Andy's thongs were suctioned deeper and deeper he was less than enamored.

After the dinghy was secure he bent down to wash his hands in the water that had gathered in the bottom of the dinghy. "I never thought I would be glad that the dinghy leaks!" he commented wryly.

The Immigration office was the shabbiest we could recall ever seeing. The officer charged $20 which didn't seem unreasonable until he demanded, seemingly as an afterthought, another $20 to simultaneously clear us out.

"Outrageous," declared my spouse. "It is too much for such a short stay. We will leave now and we want our $20 back!" The official was reluctant but finally our money was returned. We went to the Port Captain's office to collect our papers, and explained the situation.

"No problemo," he said with a smile. "Do everything you want before leaving, take your time, enjoy El Salvador!"

We wandered through the small busy town and visited the raucous Saturday market. Despite the heat, under the thick black plastic tarps that covered the stalls, the people were full of fun. A girl befriended me, linking her arm in mine and bargaining hard for us, although after the floods from Hurricane Mitch the produce was sparse with lettuce, tomatoes and cucumbers our only purchases.

After receiving big kisses on both cheeks, we extracted ourselves from our newfound friend, then collected our jerry cans from the Port Captain's office and took a cab to get fuel. By this time it was extremely hot but to my amazement at the gas station there was a sign that said 'Walls'.

"Surely it can't be Walls ice-cream," I said to Andy. I couldn't believe that here, in Central America, they were selling the favorite English ice cream of my youth. A Walls ice cream has never tasted better!

When we returned to the dinghy it was floating—a relief! Later we realized an oar had been taken. Although theft is understandable where there are so many poor it is always disappointing, but soon the breeze came up and an exhilarating sail to the island of Conchaquita quickly dispelled all negative thoughts. Typical of several lush islands in this large bay, it had a small community scattered along the shore. As we anchored we could see there was a party that night and drifts of music floated over the water. The village was brightly lit, as were the homesteads that wove high up the mountainside, and the lights burned all night. While sailing down the coast, we came to realize that electricity was readily available throughout Central America.

Next morning we relaxed in the delightful ambience of island life. Areas had been neatly cultivated up the green hillside; pigs and cows wandered at will through the village and across the beach. The fishermen called out friendly greetings as they headed out to sea. Ashore we could hear children laughing as they tossed their bags while scampering along the beach on their way to school. Homes were tree-shaded and covered with flowers; several locals gathered round the small store that sold soft drinks and a few staples. It was a good note on which to leave El Salvador.

As we left the Bay by Punta Cosiguina we were already in Nicaraguan waters. Next time we would spend more time in this little visited bay, exploring some of the Honduran islands and anchorages as well as those of Nicaragua.

Nicaragua is the largest of the Central American countries and slightly smaller than the State of New York. It has three distinct geographic regions: the Pacific lowlands, the north-central mountains and the Caribbean (or Mosquito) coast. Like most Central American countries its population (5 million) is predominantly Mestizo, a mix of Amerindian and Spanish, plus 17% white and 9% black. The earliest traces of human habitation, found within the city of Managua, are known as the Footprints of Acahualinca and are 6000 years old.

The country has much to offer with its islands, deserted beaches, volcanoes, colonial cities, lakes and navigable rivers. It also, however, has suffered extreme political strife since its independence from Spain, particularly during the 20th century. Although one of the poorest countries of Central America, the government has recently been pursuing a number of impressive economic reforms and the country is starting to prosper. Tragically, it was the country hardest hit by Hurricane Mitch, particularly its all-important agricultural sector.

Of four possible anchorages along the Nicaraguan Pacific coast only San Juan del Sur in the south appealed to us. Although Puerto Corinto is an almost landlocked harbor we had been warned of high charges. The small port of Puerto Sandido has a small cargo and discharging facility with a poorly marked channel and questionable depths. Another bay further south was reportedly attractive for its good shelter and palapa restaurants.

The cruising guide describes San Juan del Sur as the perfect crescent-shaped beach complete with palm trees and gentle surf. It is also known for its 'Indian face' naturally etched on the mountains behind and its many white-sand beaches. Many wealthy Nicaraguans have vacation homes here and there are good facilities. I was fascinated by its history. Once a terminal for Cornelius Vanderbilt's transport company, it became an important passenger ship port for those who sought a prosperous new life on the U.S. West coast. Ships transported these adventurers from the East U.S. coast to the Caribbean then up the River San Juan to Lake Nicaragua. From here it was a 12-mile ride by coach to board the ships for California.

'I'd really like to bear away," said Andy as I came up on deck. "Those green mountains ahead are Costa Rica and now the wind has come up it's on the nose for San Juan del Sur."

Andy raising the Costa Rican and quarantine flags

"I could tell he was in 'homing pigeon' mode, wanting to get to Playa del Coco where we would be meeting our sons for Christmas. It was the best wind since Baja and *Bagheera* raced excitedly into Costa Rican waters and around the high knife-edged point of Cabo Sante Elena. Now in the Golfo de Papagayo we seemed to be entering a different climate zone; there were puffy white clouds over the hills and the air was cooler. We even had a hint of rain, our first since leaving San Francisco.

Protected by the Peninsula de Santa Elena, on which stands Costa Rica's largest National Park, *Bagheera* continued her sleigh-ride past the rocks of Islas Murcielagos. A yacht was tucked into peaceful Bahia Potrero Grande and we noticed several in Playa Hermosa before we entered the attractive bay of Bahia del Coco and anchored among the fishing boats, a day ahead of schedule.

It was time for reflection and congratulation. It had been a long haul of over 4000 nautical miles down the west coasts of the United States, Mexico and Central America. We had survived the rigorous routine of watch-keeping, explored some fascinating places, gorged on seafood and enjoyed some great people. It would have been wonderful to have taken more time, but in a year one can only achieve so much.

8. Costa Rica

Although surprised to see that the sand was a dirty gray, we awoke to a pretty palm-fringed bay, and ate breakfast in the cockpit with binoculars in hand.

"The pier has almost washed away," Andy commented. "No wonder we couldn't find it last night." It was to have been our landmark for a safe anchorage away from the rocks.

Playas del Coco is Costa Rica's northernmost Port of Entry. The few prominent buildings around the bay belie the size of the town, which is growing quickly from a fishing village into a tourist destination that now stretches several blocks inland. There were a number of powerboats anchored off but only three other sailboats. We learnt that two were local and the third was being looked after for a Hawaiian owner.

Noticing the breakers ashore, we put the wheels on the dinghy and landed in a lull between the waves north of the ruined wooden peer. Immediately a man came down from a restaurant and with a welcoming smile helped us pull the dinghy up to the top of the beach.

"It will be quite safe here," he assured us. "Customs is just up the street on the left," he continued. "Immigration is a bit further on the right."

The road was lined with stalls and it was a colorful walk, past displays of string hammocks and clothing. Other vendors plied the streets with carts and bicycles, all piled high with an unbelievable variety of knick-knacks, and advertised their presence with loud latino music.

We were about to enter the Customs building when two Americans appeared. "You have to visit Immigration first," they informed us.

"How were they in Immigration?" Andy asked. "We didn't get our passports stamped out of Mexico and hope there won't be a problem." After our quick visit to El Salvador this was our last official port.

"She was very charming. Our crew didn't even have passports, let alone a stamp," they replied.

Andy was relieved. We had read that the Costa Rican officials were sticky about exit stamps from the previous country visited but when I had cleared out of Mexico the Immigration Officer had said it wasn't necessary, and I couldn't persuade him to indulge me! But all went smoothly with clearing-in and in no time we had been through Immigration, Customs had promised us a cruising *zarpe* (permit) to Puntarenas, and we had purchased the inexpensive fishing license.

Our official arrival demanded a celebration. There were no palapas so we settled for a restaurant by the beach. Andy ordered a local Imperial beer but I decided on a papaya drink having heard the *refrescos naturales* were excellent. Costa Rica produces huge papayas that are pink inside and quite delicious in flavor, especially with a squeeze of lime. Having sampled a few around the world these rank with some of the best. The refreshing fruit drinks became my preferred choice when ashore with *cas* (a local blackcurrant), *maracuya* (passionfruit), *piña* (pineapple) and *tamarindo* (a tropical tree with fruit in a long pod with seeds) favorite flavors. The lunch was typical Central American fare of rice and beans, with fish or chicken. It was quite palatable but we found interesting food is not one of the country's fortes, although the *casado* that is frequently offered at lunchtime is very economical.

It's easy to spread into empty spaces on a boat and it took me two days to remove all our belonging from the aft cabins and prepare for our children and a friend's arrival. While I was at it, I retrieved the Christmas boxes and some supplies that I had stowed under the aft mattresses at the stern. For three weeks we would be six on board, so not only would the boat shrink, but recovering items from such inaccessible places would also cause a major upheaval. I also completed a massive laundry to get rid of the salt that always permeates below and makes everything damp. Ironically we had a torrential downpour before it was dry, almost the only time along this coast that it rained!

Meanwhile, Andy went into routine maintenance mode and changed the engine oil, cleaned the stainless on deck and varnished the brightwork. After we had both polished the hull from the dinghy and cleaned the waterline while swimming, *Bagheera* was gleaming inside and out, all signs of the long trip removed. It was tiring work with temperatures constantly in the nineties and when all was completed we relaxed on the third afternoon for a well-earned siesta!

With so many guests arriving we were pleased that it was easy to replenish food stocks at the local supermarket, which had a fine supply of products including some American items and good produce. The best produce, however, came into town twice weekly by truck from the capital, San Jose. We found these trucks everywhere and were impressed with the reasonable prices and excellent variety of fruits and vegetables. We were also delighted that we could purchase shrimp from the fishermen and could never resist being lured into the bakeries by the most enticing of aromas. For a larger provisioning shop, Liberia, about a half-hour drive away, had several supermarkets.

After chatting up the lad behind the desk at the hotel, who fortuitously had a Canadian mother, I was able to call home to make sure everyone was on track with travel plans. The local phones in the town square frustrated any attempt at overseas phone calls although we could send faxes from a store in the main street.

The 5 1/2 hour bus ride to San Jose, to meet Colin and Jamie, passed quickly: I was interested to see this country that is so highly recommended by the travel industry. Unlike its neighbors, the Republic of Costa Rica has avoided volatile politics, military coups and despotic dictatorships and is one of the most peaceful nations in the world. Since the 19th century Costa Ricans have prided themselves on having more teachers than soldiers and the armed forces were abolished after the civil war in 1948.

The country also has a reputation for its enlightened approach towards conservation, with 12% of the land in national parks and another 15% protected in some form. Its biodiversity attracts nature lovers from around the world and the lush tropical forests are home to over 200 species of mammals, including sloths, armadillos, tapirs, jaguars and four types of monkey. There are over 850 bird species including the colorful macaws and toucans, 50 varieties of hummingbirds and the elusive quetzal, plus some 200 species of reptiles and an ever-present array of resplendent butterflies.

Costa Rica covers nearly 20,000 square miles. Topographically the country is split in two by a series of volcanic mountain chains that reach 12,000 feet, with the coastal lowlands of the Pacific and Caribbean on either side. In the center lies a high altitude plain that houses over half the population. The swampy Caribbean coast is only 131 miles long but the more rugged Pacific coast, with its peninsulas and islands, offers 630 miles for cruising. Like most tropical countries Costa Rica experiences two seasons. The dry season generally lasts from late December to April (called summer) with the wet season the rest of the year (called winter), although the Caribbean side gets rain all year round. There is a remarkable difference in temperatures with the altitude. San Jose at nearly 4,000 feet has a pleasant climate that is referred to as 'eternal spring'. On the coasts it can be hot and steamy averaging over 86°F. during the day on the Caribbean side with even higher temperatures on the Pacific Side, that can make it uncomfortably warm on board.

The streets around the many bus stations in San Jose were humming. Having been warned this area wasn't safe I took a taxi to a backpacker's pensión, passing the impressive Teatro National, with its statues of Calderón de la Barca (a 17th century Spanish dramatist) and Beethoven at the entrance. I quickly set out to explore the town, wanting to find some unique presents for Christmas that symbolized the culture. What I found was a cosmopolitan city with department stores, shopping centers, shops full of bargain t-shirts and jeans, and local and American fast food chains but few local handicrafts that weren't expensive.

Later in the day huge crowds gathered for the Christmas 'Festival of Lights'. The many bands from around the country and huge flamboyant floats formed a long parade. It was delightful to see so many children taking part and they proudly strode forth, playing their instruments to perfection. All were immaculately dressed, but there was a tartan theme rather than a native one as seen elsewhere in Central America. My guidebook explained this lack of Indian influence.

Although human habitation of Costa Rica dates back to at least 5000 B.C. there were far fewer Indians in Costa Rica than in other regions of pre-Columbian America. When Christopher Columbus sailed along Costa Rica's Caribbean shore in 1502 he saw many of the natives wearing gold so gave it the name of 'rich coast'. However, the hoped for hoards of gold did not materialize and colonization came later than in the surrounding areas. When the Spanish soldiers and missionaries did arrive the indigenous people resisted violently but were quickly suppressed. Those who survived this onslaught soon fled or died of European diseases. As a result, unlike the rest of Central America, Costa Rica's population is mostly of Spanish descent with just 2% of African and 1% of indigenous Indian descent with some Chinese. The few examples of indigenous culture that remain, including the impressive collection of jade at San Jose's Museo de Jade and the Guaybo archaeological site, suggest that the Indian societies were modeled on both the Incas of Peru and the Maya. We found the Costa Ricans, locally called 'Ticos', friendly but reserved. They are always extremely helpful and with compulsory education through Grade 9 (age 14) the literacy rate is over 90%, among the best in Latin America.

It was great to see Colin and Jamie and catch up on their news. Colin was studying Fine Arts at Langara College in Vancouver, while Jamie had chosen to go to Shawnigan Lake School on Vancouver Island for Grade 11 while we were away. Although he liked the school, boarding had been a huge adjustment in lifestyle and he was upset that I hadn't phoned more often. How ironic, I thought, as Andy had complained I had spent far too much time going ashore to phone and I had left frequent messages at the school office! Although I had explained to Jamie how difficult it was to make overseas calls from small villages, especially at a specific time, it's always hard to believe when accustomed to a phone being readily at hand.

Although I had been sending some e-mails from the boat we found we had bad RF (stray radio frequency problems) that made the lights on the panel glow on and off with each transmission, which froze the computer. I had been waiting for some ferrite chokes to attach to either end of the leads (recommended for all electronics). After these were installed it was delightful to be able to communicate daily with family and friends through the laptop, demodulator and Ham/SSB radio, although it did require some patience waiting for a frequency to clear.

Little was open at midnight as Colin, Jamie and I wandered around downtown San Jose looking for a place to eat. Inevitably the boys were starving! Jamie stopped by a 'soda', the inexpensive snack bars that are popular with Ticos looking for a cheap meal.

"Two dollars for two pieces of chicken, a tortilla and a beer," he translated triumphantly from a sign in the window.

"And a beer?" I raised by eyebrows.

"I deserve it after being cloistered away for three months," he replied grinning.

"Okay," I replied. "If you can order three meals you can have the beer, but this is not going to become a habit!"

He had just started Spanish lessons and is not a natural linguist but 'where there's a will there's a way' and in no time we were tucking into succulent legs of chicken and happily swilling them down with ice cold beer. Two days later Duncan and friend Micha arrived in Playas del Coco. We went ashore at their arrival time only to find the bus had come early. Duncan and Micha were already in the most popular bar happily chatting to locals, *cervesas* in hand. The Christmas holiday had begun!

We had initially planned to head north to check out some of the anchorages that *Bagheera* had glided past on our arrival. Bahia Potrero Grande, an isolated beach in the northeast corner of the Golfo de Papagayo, which is a nesting site for olive ridley turtles, looked attractive, but the wind favored heading south. Wanting to give everyone an easy ride on this first day we cruised down the coast to, confusingly, another Bahia Potrero and anchored off Marina Flamingo. It was a pleasant sail with the spinnaker flying.

"Just how I imagined it would be," sighed Micha contentedly, lazing back in the cockpit.

In contrast it was a windy night and *Bagheera* squirmed around on the anchor in the frequent squalls. "With the wind in this direction we are now on a lee shore," commented Andy, as yet again he bounced up to peer through the hatch in our cabin, "A bit worrying; it's so shallow."

We found, as we cruised down the coast, that Costa Rica has few protected anchorages but as calms were far more prevalent than strong winds we could cope with having to anchor on a lee shore. Far more irritating was the constant roll from the Pacific swell that is tiring whether cooking or sleeping. It was also very wet getting ashore in the dinghy through the breakers and in six years of circumnavigating there had never been so many sodden, salty clothes hanging up to dry on the foredeck. The watermaker was a boon but as it takes a huge amount of fresh water to get out a drenching of salt water, (particularly from the fashionable 100% cotton fabric) many items had to be left until we could find water ashore.

Marina Flamingo, one of the few marinas in Costa Rica, is tucked into the southeast corner of Bahia Potrero and formed by rock breakwaters. Next morning we dinghied ashore to inquire about fuel and were glad we'd seen the shallow depths inside and had checked-in first with the marina operator, who warned us about the shoals when entering.

In the expensive tourist facilities ashore I was pleased to find a travel agent to book a flight for Colin from Quepos to San Jose at the end of his trip. I learnt that there are two main internal airlines, Travelair and SANSA and I booked a seat on the more expensive Travelair; the airline that I was assured was very reliable. I was relieved, as travel arrangements can be hard to organize when off the beaten track. It wasn't until I confirmed the flight two days before Colin's departure that I learned this flight didn't exist!

A short walk along a rocky peninsula brought us to a stunning view to the south of Bahia Brasilito. This large bay with its lovely white sands below, spectacular pinnacles of rock out to sea and a shell beach at its southern end definitely demanded a visit and we proposed it for tomorrow's plan.

Meanwhile, when we had managed to stir the slumbering troops, (it was an adjustment getting used to the hours of the young again!) the consensus was to go snorkeling. To the north, the bays and islets looked promising diving destinations so we headed out, pulling the snorkeling gear from the lazarette so everyone could get fitted along the way. To find the best area, I went in the dinghy and towed the others behind.

"How is it?" I asked Duncan as he approached the dinghy after they had been snorkeling in an area for a while.

'Quite murky," he replied, "and not many fish or much coral."

This did not sound encouraging. When listening to the radio in Coco I'd heard the dive boats mention the murky conditions, apparently not unusual for this region that has considerable run-off from rivers. Clear water as well as sun is required for the growth of coral and the only coral we had seen recently was in Playas del Coco and it had been covered with green and brown algae.

"Come over here," called Andy suddenly, gesticulating urgently. The group quickly joined him and hovered heads-down for a long while.

"Liza, you must look at this," he called out swimming over. "There are several huge spotted stingrays and they don't seem worried by us at all."

The beach ashore was perfect for a barbecue. The boys enthusiastically collected wood and soon wonderful aromas were emanating from a travally, one of the fish we had caught en route. Meanwhile a jumping competition was in progress and Colin had found one of the rarest Costa Rican shells. Feeling thoroughly content we lay back to watch one of Costa Rica's famous flaming sunsets, but before the light completely disappeared we searched for land crabs. Micha had been promised crab races and Andy drew large circles in the sand.

"I've a definite winner," said one triumphantly.

"Not nearly as active as mine!" called another.

Finally everyone had a perfect hermit crab with a shell on its back. All were placed in the center and the race to get to the outer circle began. The noise was deafening as each urged on their own. Andy's almost made it only to turn back to the center before touching the outer ring. Duncan's was unbelievably active before deciding to hibernate for the night. The other crabs barely moved!

We carefully cleaned the beach before leaving and put the crabs back in their familiar environments. It had been a great cruising day.

Disappointingly, the shell beach of Playa Conchal at the southern end of Bahia Brasilto had only broken clamshells, but it was a great walk to the resort at the far end. Reading the guest activities' notice board I found a tour to watch the leatherback turtles nesting. It was too expensive for us to consider, but the tour operator suggested we visit the site from Tamarindo, a tourist town down the coast that was close-by.

Andy was skeptical about spending another night in an open roadstead but there were no alternative anchorages. Following the chart and guidebook we made our entry into Tamarindo cautiously, but were being catapulted forward by huge ocean rollers that were coming from astern. As usual *Bagheera* took these waves in her stride, but we became concerned when the depths shallowed and we were tossed over the peaked crests then plunged deep into the troughs. Suddenly the keel banged on the rocky bottom, so quickly and sharply that it was almost as though it hadn't happened. The depth sounder, to which my eyes were glued, never went below 15 feet. We held our breath as we continued in, committed but dreading another jarring grounding. Finally *Bagheera* was past the rocks and tucked into the southeast corner of the bay. We anchored thankfully but found the holding was poor. With sudden squalls blasting down from the northeast it was obviously an unsafe anchorage, so Andy opted to stay with the boat while the rest of us went ashore.

The next challenge was finding a spot to land the dinghy. Although it was relatively windless the surf was huge all round the bay, and the surfers were making the most of it. Finally we made an exciting run for the beach, got drenched as we leapt out, then quickly carried the dinghy to the top of the sands.

It was fun to be back in backpackers' civilization with street vendors, latte bars, a good supermarket and international telephones. Soon everyone was dialing out, anxious to find out the gossip from home!

The locals informed us that the turtles used Playa Grande to the north of the bay in the Tamarindo Wildlife Refuge, but the chances of us visiting did not look promising. The turtles wouldn't be climbing the sand until midnight, not a great time to land or take off from the beach in these conditions. There were also rip tides and huge breakers over a sand bar that had to be crossed. We were all disappointed but after the boys had tried surfing, and been tossed around by the waves, to say nothing of being thrown airborne in the dinghy when trying to leave the beach to return to *Bagheera*, we all agreed it would not have been prudent.

Our trip the next day, however, was a great compensation. While *Bagheera* peacefully ambled down the coast with just the spinnaker flying everyone settled on deck, relaxing on cushions to soak up the sun.

"What's that black blob in the water," Duncan called out from the bow.

I put the autohelm on standby and steered over to investigate. It was a sleeping turtle and soon there were so many that we had to keep turtle watch. They were olive ridleys and were quite unperturbed when we drifted up close to take photos. "There's a ray." Micha called out enthusiastically later. As we waited for it to surface Duncan set his camera on full zoom, but the manta ray was so vast only a fin appeared in the lens! Soon dolphins galore were leaping and frolicking all around the boat, and astern a mahi mahi was on our line and gave a spectacular leap clear of the water before getting away. Just before landfall we caught another fish and this time landed a perfect dinner-sized yellowfin tuna.

Our anchorage for the night was beautiful Carrillo Bay with its curved sandy beach and picturesque avenue of royal palms. Arriving in good light and at low water we could appreciate the extent of the reef that reduces the navigable entrance to less than half a mile. We anchored on the east side, near a small beach and hotel. Initially Colin, Andy and I went ashore and after climbing the steep hill had a lovely country walk. Choir practice was taking place in the small church and the vibrant voices and beautiful harmonizing took us back to cruising in French Polynesia.

We met the others on the deck of the hotel at the top of the hill and watched the most magnificent of sunsets. The sky turned a flaming red, then orange, and then a dying gold with *Bagheera* beautifully silhouetted in the foreground. Frustratingly it was one of the few times I had forgotten my camera and soon Andy was complaining and jumping about like a mad thing. The mosquitoes had come out with a vengeance; fortunately Duncan had taken a photo and the restaurant had a good supply of repellent, so calm was restored!

Although not a safe anchorage, we made a stop at Montezuma that was recommended by friends who had visited with their three sons. We were surprised at the small size of the town but despite anchoring in the big Bay of Ballina six miles to the east, the boys had some good times here, including Jamie's sixteenth birthday celebration.

The day was spent horseback riding up to some stunning waterfalls. After a hot gallop along forest trails it was bliss to bask in the cool water, drooling over the sweet, succulent pieces of pineapple that Roger, our guide, had peeled for us, while the tumbling falls gave our backs a natural massage. Back at the *finca* (farm), Roger's pet howler monkey called out to greet us and leapt affectionately to his shoulders, nuzzling his ear. Roger and his wife had found the monkey abandoned as a baby and were in the process of reintroducing him back to the wild.

"The problem is he's getting quite aggressive," Roger told us, "and he keeps us awake at night."

Later, on an early dinghy ride up the river from Ballina Bay, we heard the howler monkeys calling from tree to tree, and learnt just how deafening they can be.

Jamie turns 16 and fun was had by all!

It was necessary to visit Puntarenas to extend our cruising zarpe. Although there are several islands in the Gulf of Nicoya these are often busy with tourists and as *Bagheera's* entrance into Puntarenas would also have to coincide with high tide, we decided instead to go by bus and ferry. The ferry leaves from Punta Naranjo, a pretty anchorage, and takes 1 1/2 hours to reach Puntarenas, Costa Rica's major port during the 19 th century, although Puerto Limon and Caldera now take most of the shipping. Puntarenas is a long, narrow town situated on the end of a 5-mile long peninsula that is only 650 yards across at its widest point. There are several boat facilities here and a hospitable yacht club. The paperwork was quickly completed and we received a *zarpe* to Golfito, the most southerly port.

Puntarenas has seen better days but we had a most memorable stop at the bustling market. After wandering through the fruit and vegetable section we came to the seafood. Abruptly Andy stopped.

"Look at those huge fish," he exclaimed, peering round a stall.

He pointed to a shark that I certainly wouldn't wanted to have come face to face with in the water. "It must weigh at least 200lbs." he estimated. "And the marlin must be over 300."

"But how disappointing that they are selling turtle eggs," he continued after glancing at the next vendor.

We were able to purchase many Christmas gifts and were pleased to find local handicrafts—uniquely carved items in attractive two-tone wood, ceramics, leather masks, hammocks and woven goods. We lunched to the sounds of a xylophone band, but on arriving back in Ballina Bay there was no sign of Duncan and Micha. They had returned on an earlier ferry and promised to come ashore by dinghy to pick us up. Dusk had already fallen when there was a loud honking from the road behind.

"The outboard wouldn't start" explained Duncan. "I think there's water in the fuel." The dunkings in Taramindo had finally caught up with us.

With no motor to get them back they had rowed ashore to the nearby yacht club and had been driven around by the manager, the daughter of Heart, the designer of Heart inverters. The family had sailed here several years previously and stayed in their piece of paradise.

After roaring down rutted lanes under flashlight, the battered jeep's own lights being non-existent, we arrived back at the club.

'We've just decided to put on a traditional Christmas dinner here," they informed us, "Are you interested?" At $20 a head it sounded very appealing, especially as I had just cooked a leg of lamb on board for Jamie's birthday and nearly expired in the heat while doing so.

Christmas in the tropics is never quite the same as in a cool climate but a few festive decorations and Christmas music go a long way in achieving the right atmosphere. To the ornaments that had been made and collected around the world we had added a fiber-optic Christmas tree, purchased in Puntarenas, that had even Colin impressed.

It was a relaxed Christmas day, stockings were opened at 11:00am, breakfast cooked by Duncan at noon, swimming and canoeing in the afternoon, and a great turkey and lamb feast that evening. To our surprise, it was served to us by a Canadian, who runs a stable in Victoria, B.C. in summer and was now wintering in her local home. She had come along to help and made sure her compatriots lacked for nothing!

Time was running out for Colin who wanted to be home for New Year, so we made an overnight passage to Quepos, situated about half was down the Costa Rican coast. Once a bustling banana exporting port, the town's economy was crippled when Panama Disease killed banana production in the 1950s. Now serving the tourist industry of close-by Manuel Antonio Park, Quepos has interesting shops, a good market and a personable travel agency. I had met a young couple who had spent six months cruising in Costa Rica who had said this was their favorite place, and we too really enjoyed this up-and-coming town with its macadamed roads that were laid just three years before.

While talking on the Ham radio net, the Central American Breakfast Club, I had 'met' George. On our arrival in Quepos he and his wife Keiko treated us to a wonderful tour along the high winding road to Manuel

Christmas dinner: Andy, Liza, Micha, Colin, Jamie and Duncan

Antonio, then out to their finca. Several years before they had trouble in a storm while cruising the coast and had been towed into Quepos. Enchanted by the area they bought a farm, and raise cattle and graze horses for rent. They also have a large orange grove and supply many of the hotels and hostels we had seen on our coastal drive with fresh juice. As always it was fun to travel inland and to hear about their local community, with whom they have become very involved.

The boys wanted to go on a jungle canopy tour but it was booked up so we settled on white-water rafting for Colin's last day. A group of us gathered at one of the many backpackers hostels to be taken by truck to the hills and there was great anticipation as we bounced down muddy paths and finally arrived at the river. The class 3-4 rapids looked impressive and we had soon donned lifejackets and had been divided into boats. Andy, Colin, Jamie and I were to go in a four-man with a guide. Duncan would go in a two-man with a guide who was in training.

It was most exhilarating following the instructions from our guide, a girl from Washington State. On command we paddled in unison forward or backwards, or just to the right or left, as we catapulted down through the surf and around huge rocks. Our craft became stuck in the rocks only once, but stopped so abruptly that Jamie and Andy flew out over the bow. Jamie quickly jumped back into the boat but Andy was whisked away down the rapids. Our guide galvanized into action and had soon grasped his lifejacket collar, holding on with an iron fist until we were back in calm water. Andy took the dunking calmly but the rest of us had been concerned.

"You don't have to worry," Duncan assured us at the next stop. "You will never go very far." In his two-man raft he had spent most of his time upside-down or swimming!

The sun was setting as we glided through the lower stretches and a full rainbow arched over the river, each end fading into the lush green valley. Faint calls of howler monkeys occasionally broke the silence, together with a burst of song from the many birds. The delicious tropical dinner provided gave a perfect relaxing ending to an adrenaline charged day.

It was sad to see Colin depart but there was much work to be done before Rob, Vicky (Andy's daughter) and 14-year old Cynthia's arrival that afternoon. We weren't sure whether they would come by bus or by air so had e-mailed them with instructions to go to the Port Captain's office and call us on the VHF radio. In the end they passed us on the street, although they were coming from the airport and we were walking to the bus station!

Manuel Antonio's beach beckoned and we motored around the next morning anchoring off beautiful Playa Espadilla, that lies between the rocky headlands of Punta Quepos and Punta Catedral. With its white sands, bright green foliage, islets covered in birds and a deep turquoise sea this is one of the most scenic spots on the coast. Some went snorkeling, others went ashore but the most popular activity was body surfing in the big waves. In fact the waves were so large we decided to move to the southern end of the bay inside Islas Gemelas and right off the park itself for a more comfortable night.

On consulting *Charlie's Charts Cruising Guide* we found that author Margo provided some insight into this area's colorful past. Apparently Isla Mogote was a Quepos Indian ceremonial ground and a medicine man was the island's only permanent resident. These Indians were not hospitable to explorers and the first, Ponce de Leon, did not even disembark when he arrived in 1519; later the park's namesake, a Spanish soldier, was killed on the beach. It was Juan Vasquez de Coronado who, after landing in 1563, established the first mission in Costa Rica by the Naranjo River on the park's east side. There is also speculation that priceless treasure was hidden here by church officials who escaped Henry Morgan when he was pillaging Panama City in the 1600s, although others claim the treasure went to Cocos island that lies some 400 miles to the southwest.

Manuel Antonio Park was established in 1972 and covers 1,700 land and 136,000 maritime acres. With an annual rainfall over 150″ the park has lush rainforest and is home to a variety of wildlife. Although one of the smallest of Costa Rica's parks it is one of the most popular because of its setting so we decided to go ashore at 7:00am to avoid the crowds. We were spoilt by free forest walks and were surprised that the entry was $6.00 per person and a little taken aback when they charged us another $8.00 for *Bagheera*, anchored just inside the park limits! Charges in all parks had been recently raised, we were told, and we thought of friends who had planned to go to Cocos Island for three months.

We felt some of the money could have been spent on the poorly maintained trails, but enjoyed our walk to the top through an incredible variety of plants and trees that included black locust, monkey comb, bastard cedar, wild plantain, balsa, manzanillo and mayflower. These are home to nearly two hundred species of birds, including the rare white ibis, and one hundred mammal species. With four types of monkey, sloth, raccoons, coatis, armadillos, agoutis and a variety of lizards and snakes we had high expectations but saw little initially except leaf-cutter ants. Huge numbers of these ants moved in file, carrying in their mouths pieces of green leaves that were far larger than their own bodies. They travel long distances from their nests and their well-defined paths frequently crossed our trails. We carefully stepped over them so as not to disturb this great industry.

We had been chatting to a couple who had a guide. "Look!" he interrupted close to the end of our walk, and pointed to the top of the tree.

There were two white-haired sloths and we certainly wouldn't have noticed them from their movements. The Spanish word for sloth is *perezoso* which means 'lazy' and as they hang upside-down from the branches asleep eighteen hours a day they certainly live up to their reputation. Even when they are awake their movements, as we witnessed, are unbelievably slow and they live high up in the forest canopy to be away from predators. The guide explained that they are fascinating creatures: they support a miniature ecosystem by fertilizing the trees on which they live and provide a home for insects, part of their food supply. They grow to the size of a medium dog in adulthood, survive for up to thirty years and their almost human smiles exude contentment.

No sooner had we moved on from the sloths when Andy was calling out, "Monkeys."

Suddenly a troupe was nonchalantly swinging in the trees beside us. There were ten white-faced monkeys, one with a babe on her back, and they kept us entranced as they effortlessly glided between the branches, their perky faces, topped with smart black caps, peering down at us between the big green leaves.

We had just returned to Quepos in *Bagheera* when Micha arrived back after traveling inland. He had found a bargain flight to Guatemala for a quick trip and returned laden with brightly colored woven goods and great tales of the sights, good information for our future visit. It was New Year's Eve and with nine on board we decided to go ashore for dinner. There was just one other visiting sailboat in the bay, a 26' Westerly Centaur owned by Americans Mark and Lawrie, so we invited them to join us.

"Would you like us to collect you on our way to shore?" I asked.

We had seen them earlier paddling their dinghy with pieces of driftwood. Their oars had been stolen and they were in the process of whittling new ones. We had a great dinner of yellowfin tuna, wandered the streets with the locals then watched the fireworks before turning in. It was to be an early start the next morning, which was hard on those who didn't get to bed until 5:00am!

I'd finally been able to organize a visit to the Iguana Park and the adjacent Canopy Tour for New Year's Day, but it meant leaving the boat at 7:00am laden with luggage, as Duncan, Micha and Jamie would be continuing on to San Jose to catch their flights home. The ride to Orotina took 2 1/2 hours and was slow in places as the bus bounced over the potholes. But some of the sights were interesting, especially when we crossed a temporary bridge and found there were several crocodiles gazing up hungrily from the riverbanks below!

The Iguana Park, run by the Pro Iguana Verde Foundation, is a showplace of how humans can live off the forest and still preserve it for future generations by 'uniting human, animal and forest in a symbiotic relationship that may guarantee the survival of all three'. The local *campesinos*, who used to hunt the wild iguana are now learning how to raise them for food and a livelihood, and the project was able to earn a profit and release over 80,000 green iguanas into the wild in the first five years. It has been found that farmed iguana can produce more meat per acre while leaving the forest intact, than cows on the same acreage of cleared land.

"How about iguana for lunch?" asked our guide with an encouraging smile. Those of us who were adventurous all agreed it made a very palatable meal, tasting like flavorful chicken.

Equally important is the scarlet macaw program. Although a large population of these birds used to stretch from Mexico to Peru there are now only three groups left in Costa Rica. One group, with two hundred birds, lives in Carara Biological Reserve next to the Iguana Park. The exotic macaws have been heavily poached so the project encourages the locals to breed and raise birds for legal sale. This removes the need to poach, increases numbers, particularly as macaws will only rear two babies, and protects the established local macaw population. We passed breeding cages on our hike to the canopy tour but were really thrilled when we saw several flying in the wild.

The two-hour delay for the canopy tour was well worth the wait although it was rather different from the walkway between trees that I had

Iguanas everywhere!

expected. Instead, we climbed steps to platforms strapped to tree-trunks that were over 150 feet high. Each one donned a harness to allow us to swing on cables from platform to platform. Duncan went first, followed by Micha who made most convincing Tarzan noises as he flew through the air. Next Jamie swooped across, followed by Vicky, Cynthia and Andy. Meanwhile, I was peering down from the small platform to the ground that looked a very long way away.

"You go next," I said to Rob.

"I'm not going before you," he grinned back, sensing I might back out.

The guide was very patient as I donned the harness and gloves. He explained that I could control my speed by holding the wire behind my head, but warned me not to go too slowly as I might get stuck in the middle of the wire and have to 'walk' myself back with my hands. Finally, I was hanging free and he gave a small push. Once moving I was fine, my full concentration was on not ramming into the tree ahead! Nervousness gone, I happily 'sailed' through the treetops, slowly descending through the forest's canopy and all too soon it was time to take the vertical rope down.

Duncan, Jamie and Micha rushed off as they had been offered a ride into San Jose on a tour bus. It was hard to believe that the Christmas holidays were already over. They had flown by, but we still had the bonus of having Vicky, Rob and Cynthia for another ten days.

We headed to Unita, entertained by bottle-nosed dolphins along the 30-mile run. Rob caught several bonito, which we let go, then a boobie bird attached itself to our hook. It took awhile to get it free, then to our frustration, it came back, diving despite our calls, and got caught again. Finally Rob was triumphant, he had caught a travally for dinner. We took care coming in around the extensive reef and anchored off the new Parque Nacional Marino Ballena and adjacent campsite. Despite putting out both bow and stern anchors to face the swell it was a very rolly night, particularly when the tide came in over the reef, and we set sail early next morning for Drake Bay.

We arrived in this lush bay for lunch and anchored at its southern end close to the wilderness resorts. Having read that the river had a wonderful freshwater pool we headed off in the dinghy to Rio Drake but the bar was turbulent and looked very shallow. Perfectly timed, a local boat rushed ahead of us showing us the way in. The scenery was lush along the narrow stream with many of the trees covered in bright yellow blooms, but it was the 'Jesus Christ' lizards that held our attention. Dashing from the bank they rushed ahead of the dinghy, literally walking on water. Small, but large crested, they appeared in great numbers and darted back and forth so unexpectedly with their legs moving so quickly that we soon all collapsed with laughter. Finally we found deep fresh water and had the most refreshing of swims, soaking the salt out of our hair in the blissfully cool water. Then it was time to attack the laundry!

With an annual rainfall of 220″ the Osa Peninsula is one of the lushest regions in the country and 108,000 acres have been set aside as Costa Rica's second largest park, Corcovada National Park. The park is renowned for its biological diversity. The varied vegetation includes giant mahogany trees reaching over 80 feet high, the unusual garlic tree and strangler figs. There are over 360 types of birds, with the country's largest population of scarlet macaws, also toucans, parrots, hawks, kites and several types of hummingbird. There are also 139 species of mammals with large populations of jaguar, ocelot and the rare Baird tapir.

We wandered through the village along the muddy road chewed up by horses' hoofs. The well-kept gardens were a mass of tropical color and in the jungle gardens of the wilderness resorts Andy finally found orchids. An avid orchid grower at home he had been hoping to see them in the wild, but to this point had been disappointed. Here they grew in profusion, both wild and cultivated varieties, and together with the bromeliads were a glorious sight.

After crossing another river by a suspension bridge we were besieged by squirrel monkeys who happily sat on our heads, nibbled our hair and posed for pictures!

At dusk brilliant green parrots flew to the trees overhead. Then the exotic toucans came to roost, outlined clearly against the deep pink sky.

Walking back we could hear them calling from tree to tree, jerking up their large yellow beaks as they did so.

It was a 3:00am departure for Golfito, Costa Rica's most southerly Port of Entry and a nine-hour trip, sailing most of the way. Our guests amused themselves reading, playing games (with Cynthia delighted that she devastated her Dad at backgammon) and watching for wildlife. We were rewarded with more bottle-nosed dolphins seeking us out to play and a leatherback turtle sleeping on the surface. It was a massive six feet long and had five high ridges across its back. Apparently they can weigh up to 1,600 lbs.

The Peninsula de Osa is one of the most remote regions along the Costa Rican coast, little changed from the 1500's when Drake sailed its shores and reputedly buried large treasures of the gold that is found in the area. Twelve miles from Bahia Drake lies the flat-topped Isla del Caño,

Cheeky squirrel monkey in Bahia Drake

now one of three marine parks that protect local sealife and fragile coral formations. It also has some interesting features with its near perfect stone globes and a cow tree grove in its center. These trees are also known as milk trees because they exude a white liquid and are thought to be the remains of a Pre-Columbian orchard. But we were happy to leave it astern as this massive lightning rod has the reputation of getting struck by lightning more frequently than any other place in Central America and it had been constantly covered in black clouds.

Golfito is a shallow, almost completely enclosed bay and we were careful to enter inside the channel. A former banana port, the town is now struggling to survive by tourism and the government has built a Free Zone at its northern end. Although bananas and coffee used to be the mainstay of the Costa Rican economy they now form only 19% of the GDP with commerce and tourism now at 40%. It is a pretty bay to enter with colorful houses, some on stilts. Ashore we found the town run-down but by walking along the low road and returning by the high road were able to stock up on supplies, particularly much needed produce, as we wouldn't be near another store for several days.

For $5.00 a day we could leave the dinghy, dump trash and use the showers of the small Banana Bay Marina. There were some American boats alongside the docks, mainly with crews who were using the inexpensive facilities to work on their vessels and everyone gathered in the marina bar at night. We also enjoyed the attractive Samoa del Sur restaurant in town that is owned by vivacious Albert, a French circumnavigator. After cruising around the world, he explained the family had decided to settle here and had built the distinctive restaurant with its two high-peaked palm thatched buildings. No sooner had we started discussing his displays of shells than he was driving us up to his gracious home, its approach lined with royal palms.

On arrival, Albert called for his grandchildren to find their pet San Blas monkey.

"Dee Dee," they called, running to and fro in the beautiful garden. "Dee Dee."

Suddenly Dee Dee was swinging down from the telephone wire and leaping up for a cuddle. After admiring Albert's magnificent shell collection he dropped us down at the Port Captain's office to clear out. But in the end it took two full days to complete clearance procedures with Customs who were located in the Free Zone, Immigration, who wanted numerous copies of crew lists, and the Port Captain who, after several attempts, I finally located in a coffee shop! After a refreshing swim at

Hotel Las Gaviotas at the southeast end of the bay we left the harbor at 6:30pm en route for Panama. It was a spectacular night.

"I can't believe how clear the stars are," said Cynthia gazing at the sky, "they are so much brighter than at home."

"And have you seen the stars in our wake," I added. Our trail was a luminous blue from the dense phosphorescence, and the small droplets of water that were thrown up by the propeller formed starlets as brilliant as those overhead.

"That's the joy of being on the ocean," said Andy smiling contentedly, "there's nothing to clutter the wonders of nature."

9. Pacific Panama and The Panama Canal

"**W**ow, Panama's a skinny country," commented Cynthia as she looked at the chart.

"Yes, isn't it," I replied, "But it's at an amazing world crossroads."

S-shaped Panama is just 30-miles wide at its narrowest point but as it forms a strategic land bridge between North and South America it has had a huge influence on the movements of humans, birds, animals and plants. The country is crossed by the Panama Canal, which provides the vital economic function of linking the Pacific and Caribbean Oceans, saving 12,000 miles of arduous voyaging around South America.

Although it is natural to think of Panama as lying from north to south, the isthmus actually stretches from east to west and is bordered by Costa Rica and Colombia. Two mountain chains form the country's spine and like all Central American countries it has large, flat coastal lowlands, many covered in banana plantations. Although there are 725 miles of Caribbean and 1050 miles of Pacific coastline, it is the islands (over 1600 of them) that have become the favorite cruising grounds. The enchanting Caribbean San Blas Islands, inhabited by the colorful Cuna Indians, are particularly popular and on the Pacific side cruisers often stop at the pretty Las Perlas Islands en route from the Canal to the Galapagos Islands.

We knew little about cruising the western Pacific shore and were grateful that cruisers had recently told us about the Gulf of Chiriquí. While exploring this often-missed region we came across some of the most enchanting anchorages of the entire trip between the Pacific Northwest and the Panama Canal.

After leaving Costa Rica we stopped briefly to snorkel at Islas Ladrones then made our Panamanian landfall at Isla Parida, anchoring off the northeast end of the island by the lovely promontory of Punta del Pozo. Once ashore we wriggled our delighted toes into the powdery white sand and investigated the high piles of shells brought in by the winter storms. Most were broken but a few provided some colorful momentos for our guests. They also offered a variety of homes for land hermit crabs, and there seemed to be hundreds scurrying around.

We were greeted by a local, who introduced himself as Filo. His family was camping among the palm trees during the school holidays. He told us that the buildings around the point had been built and abandoned by a Canadian couple who had also arrived by boat. The attractive development spoke of dreams for an ultimate holiday retreat and cruisers' sanctuary. Tremendous care had been taken with the main house, cabins and gardens, and there was a large entertainment room decorated with baseball hats and flags that begged a bunch of noisy yachtsmen. Relinquished also were the expensive generator, all their personal videos and visitor's book. Although abandoned just a few months before, the development was already being reclaimed by the jungle and we felt saddened that after so much hard work things hadn't worked out as planned in this lovely haven.

As usual we enjoyed a sundowner in the cockpit. "Isn't it wonderful," Andy commented, "that it's still light at 6.30pm."

We had just changed onto Panamanian time, and were now three hours ahead of Vancouver, the same as Eastern Standard Time. It suited us much better than Central American time. Being dark at 5.30pm ends exploring, diving and beach barbecues far too early. It was a quiet, calm night with a sky again brilliant with stars, quite the opposite of the day before when there had been thunder, squalls and sheets of rain. We were now in the intertropical convergence zone (ITCZ) where hurricanes are extremely rare but squalls and thunderstorms can be expected even in this, the dry season. In the mid-May to mid-December wet season, heavy rain, lightning and violent winds are a daily occurrence and the sweltering humidity that we experienced after our last transit of the canal at the beginning of June is not easily forgotten.

The anchorage at Isla Gómez was just around the corner, a true tropical paradise with its lush vegetation, white sand beach and swaying palms silhouetted against the bright blue sky and turquoise ocean. Even the diving was good with the water much clearer than further north. Finally, there was abundant coral and we had to watch for bommies (coral heads) when anchoring. Cynthia, a newcomer to snorkeling, was enthralled by the tropical fish and full of enthusiasm to explore the underwater world.

The name Panama means 'abundance of fish' in a local Indian dialect, and fish we hoped to both view and catch in the next few days. There was little reason to be disappointed as we visited many of the islets around Isla Parida, Isla Bolaños and the Secas Islands to the east. Rob, Vicky and Cynthia contentedly spent hours face down in the water while Andy regularly went in pursuit of edible fish with his speargun outside the Parque Nacional Marino Golfo de Chiriquí. He successfully brought back trevally, and also found clams, oysters and conch for dinner.

"The conch will make a wonderful stew," he enthused pointing to the pile in the dinghy.

Cynthia looked horrified. "Yuck, they look like over-sized slugs," she exclaimed screwing up her face. "I know they have a nice shell, but.....!"

"They taste just like squid," Andy continued reassuringly.

"I've never eaten squid!" she retorted laughing.

"They're really very interesting animals," said Andy, trying to spark her interest on another tack.

"Look at their huge claw-like foot. They can use it as a door to seal their body into the shell and they also dig it into the ground to propel themselves forward."

As they watched, the conch were performing amazing athletics, showing their strength by pushing their shells into the air, although the hard, slippery surface frustrated their efforts to move around.

Delicious aromas came from the galley. Andy was in his element creating an appealing dish for Cynthia. Conch is tricky to prepare as it quickly becomes tough. We either eat it raw as an hors d'oeuvre, sliced very thinly with a lime marinade, or if cooked, either heat thin slices quickly in butter or stew them for a long time to tenderize. A pressure cooker would be useful for this, but we would seldom use it so do not carry one on board.

This time Andy had made a curry sauce and Cynthia did very well, although afterwards she admitted she didn't think the stew tasted of anything else!

The discussion of conchs and their habits led to the question, "If *homo sapiens* were to disappear from earth who would take over as the most intelligent on the planet?"

Suggested were termites, ants and the octopus. Vicky, Rob and Cynthia decided on ants and termites because they have great organization, are hard working and always on guard. They know how to build homes and roads which lead to food and building supplies, and how to return to their nests, they reasoned. Andy, however, argued that it would be the intelligent and highly skilled octopus. They build hide-aways that involve opening and closing doors, and have the great defense of spraying ink into the water in front of predators thus 'blinding' them, he countered. It was typical of discussions we had with our boys when circumnavigating and we missed their interesting comments on this trip. An exchange like this used to go on for days on board, as they furiously researched for more ammunition with which to bait their father!

Our guests were nearing the end of their stay and a decision had to be made about reaching a mainland center where transportation could be found. David, Panama's third largest city that lies half way between Panama City and San Jose, was an obvious destination but it was a long way up river.

While visiting one of the two other cruising boats in the area, they had told us that they had done the trip up to David's port of Pedregal but cautioned of shallows—and they were in a catamaran that drew only three feet! In view of our seven-foot draft they suggested taking a local guide. Filo offered his services as a pilot, but said it would take two days each way, which would entail a costly fee and considerable fuel. This was not appealing so he found us Carlos, a relative, who said he would do the round trip in a day in his own panga for $80. It was a great solution and reasonably priced for a party of five so we arranged a time for departure two days later.

While our guests packed their bags I wrote letters for them to take home, and added packets of local coffee. *Bagheera* was again off Isla Gómez, voted the most beautiful anchorage in the area, and this time we explored around the far side of the island in our inflatable kayak. There were green parrots and orchids, and the bromeliads were so prolific that 'host' trees were laden down with the weight of their growth. Carlos came to *Bagheera* in the afternoon with some live lobster and while paying we admired his other catch, an impressive grouper that weighed at least 100lbs and took up half of his *panga*

Although Andy had hunted all week, eating-sized lobster had eluded him and we had promised Rob, Vicky and Cynthia a lobster feast on their last night. The five lobsters were consumed with gusto, as could be seen by the debris on the table and cockpit grating—nothing that a few buckets of water wouldn't remove! With local corn and homemade beer bread it was a grand last dinner and we retired early in preparation for a dawn departure.

Carlos' boat was smaller than expected but with our cockpit cushions it was manageable for the 2 1/2-hour trip to David, especially as the ocean was a glassy calm for the open run to Boca Brava. Then, at high speed, we wove our way along the winding channels that bisect the mangrove swamps. There were frequent entrances to the open sea. The last was buoyed and a small ship was entering. In view of the information we'd been given about the shallow depths this was confusing, but apparently the entrance can become untenable in bad weather. There were ten yachts in the marina in Pedrigal, several American, two Canadian and one Spanish.

We had the distinct impression that the Port Captain thought we were a little crazy to take the trouble to come to clear in. However, it was necessary to get the Gilkers' passports stamped by Immigration to show that they had entered the country legally, to avoid problems when they crossed the border by bus to catch their flight from Costa Rica.

The town was humming and the new French-looking hotel recommended by the marina office was well located. We enjoyed an inexpensive but excellent lunch in their air-conditioned dining room. It was civilization again, the roads were smoothly paved and supermarkets packed with goods. There was also an active open market with shirts at $1.50 apiece and boxers for 99¢, all great for boat wear!

David is the capital of Chiriquí Province and is at the center of a rich agricultural area. The tack shops caught Vicky and Rob's attention as they own and train racehorses and the rows of beautiful saddles were impressive. This area is home to the Chiriquí Indians and the women were easily recognizable in their full, brightly colored skirts.

We were sorry that it wasn't convenient to go to close-by Boquete on the fertile slopes of Barú volcano. Friends had enjoyed the cool fresh climate in the hills, visits to coffee plantations and the hot springs. Apparently it is such a healthy environment that many residents have lived to be well over 100 years of age.

Our departure back to the boat was delayed as Carlos collected large bags of rice to take back to Isla Parida and we were becoming concerned about the huge cumulonimbus clouds that were building in the sky ahead. All the way we expected to be caught in one of the many downpours around us, but Carlos managed to miss them all and we could enjoy the brilliant rainbows before coming alongside *Bagheera* as darkness fell.

It was now January 12th and we planned to transit the Panama Canal in about two weeks. This gave time to enjoy some more of the pretty island anchorages and with wind often up to ten knots and with a positive current *Bagheera* flew along between them. Isla Cavada is memorable for its dense schools of fish and Islas Contreras for its lush vegetation. In the distance we spied the large island of Coiba, a prison island that is also a national park protecting both marine and coastal ecosystems. Guide books caution about escaped prisoners and friends had some 'unusual' visitors swim out to them when they anchored off its shore so we gave it a miss.

Bahia Honda on the mainland could provide a protected anchorage for a number of boats. A development had been started to the north, and the friendly locals informed us there were plans to complete a hotel. They gave us pineapples that were sweet and juicy, and much yellower in color than those in Costa Rica.

Tiny Isla Talon lies in the center of the bay only a short dinghy ride away. To our surprise, next to the whitewashed church and behind the laundry, there was a smart concrete phone booth, courtesy Cable and Wireless. As we waited in line I watched the children at play by the village well and a little girl particularly caught my attention. Cute as a button, she was dressed for a party in a multi-layered, frilly dress, its whiteness sparkling against her glowing dark skin. Her smile was enchanting, induced without doubt from her enjoyment of being a typical kid, jumping in the deepest, most muddy puddles in her oversized gumboots! We were interested that most people on the island were of African descent (originally brought from the West Indies) and learnt that Panama's population of almost three million is incredibly diverse. Over 65% are Spanish-Indian mestizos, 14% African, 10% Spanish and 6% Indian with Chinese, Middle Eastern, Croatian and Swiss immigrants also leaving their cultural stamp.

Soon it was our turn for the phone and in no time I was talking to friends who were flying into Panama City the following week and would be our line handlers on *Bagheera's* transit through the canal, as five on board is required. Phoning from Panama couldn't have been easier, despite this remote location. Dialing 119 linked us immediately to 'Canada Direct' and any call we wanted to make on our Canadian calling card.

Isla Cebaca was our next intended stop but an untenable southerly swell persuaded us to continue sailing. Andy remarks in the log at 16:30 that there was thunder, rain and windy squalls and that he took a wet t-shirt picture of me! By 18:30 I note the storm is behind us and it's cool at last. At 21:10 we were sailing off Punta Mariato and touched the most southerly latitude of our sabbatical year.

Cruising guides and Sailing Directions warned of a strong southerly set to the current, tide rips and blustery winds around Punta Mala, which translated means 'Bad Point'. With the help of a good current and an excellent breeze we rounded the cape early, at 7:30am, just before low tide, which is just when one is supposed to! Then came a close beat across the Gulf of Panama to the island of San Jose, at the southwest corner of the

Las Perlas Archipelago. It was initially a great sail but then the wind died and it was tricky getting into the rocky anchorage after dark. Although intending to go ashore to meet a former cruising couple who welcome sailors to their home, after an uncomfortable rolly night we decided to leave at dawn and make the most of our time in the island chain.

The archipelago was named Las Perlas after the large pearls that were once found here. There are 183 islands; 39 are of a reasonable size. The most important are mountainous Isla del Rey on which the principal town, San Miguel, is located, and Pedro González, San José and Saboga. We, however, planned more snorkeling, so gently cruised up the islands in the light breeze when we felt like it. There was no shortage of pretty white-sand beaches, and clear turquoise waters with schools of interesting fish in the coral.

At the northern end of the group lies Contadora, well frequented because of its attractive resort. We anchored beside some lovely homes next to the small airstrip and were entertained by the frequent planes. Astern the sea was a translucent aquamarine alive with small fish and at one point *Bagheera* was surrounded by jumping manta rays.

Since it was too shallow to anchor off the resort, we moved to a beach nearby next morning, and soon realized it was the nudist one as the guests began arriving! The ambience at the hotel was relaxed and we enjoyed talking to guests. There were mainly Panamanians, also Americans and Canadians, some on 'bargain' package deals. Spider and white-faced monkeys gazed cheekily as they swung between branches, dexterously using their tails as a fifth leg; another area held noisy blue and yellow macaws, and parrots. The water was crystal clear for a snorkel on the way back to the boat and we decided it was so pleasant we would stay another night and make an early start. At 4:00am it was blowing hard and very uninviting compared to staying in a comfortable berth! By 8:00am the wind was perfect for a good sail, so we headed out for the 50-mile passage to Panama City, although as the day wore on we again ended up motoring.

The calm gave a good opportunity to catch up on the history of the country and procedures for going through the Canal. According to our travel books Roderigo de Bastidas arrived in Panama in 1501, just a year before Christopher Columbus visited the San Blas islands. However, it was Vasco Nuñez de Balboa, who scaled its mountains in 1513 and found the Pacific Ocean, that sparked great international interest in the country. Panama City became the center of trade, particularly for the rich spoils from Peru. From here goods were transported overland to Puertobelo on the Caribbean side to be shipped to Spain. These valuable shipments inevitably attracted pirates and in 1671 Panama City was looted and burnt down by Henry Morgan. By the 18th century the Caribbean had become so dangerous that Spanish ships started to sail directly from Peru to Europe, around Cape Horn. With Panama bypassed the country went into decline and, in 1739, it became a province of what later was to become Colombia.

Several countries considered transportation across the isthmus. In 1846 Colombia signed a treaty allowing the United States to construct a railway across the isthmus which was made profitable by the Californian gold rush of 1848. As early as the 16th century the Spanish had talked of building a canal but it was the French who gained the concession close to the end of the nineteenth century. They wanted to build a sea-level canal, but difficulties with the project and thousands of deaths due to yellow fever and malaria led them to sell the concession to the United States. Columbia's rejection of the agreement led to a revolutionary junta, supported by the U.S., which declared Panama independent from Colombia in 1903.

Construction of the canal began in 1904. It was completed ten years later by 75,000 employees and is heralded as one of the greatest engineering feats of the 20th century. Since its opening to commerce on August 15th, 1914, U.S. control over the Canal and Canal Zone was a continual source of conflict between the U.S. and Panama. Finally, in 1977, a new treaty was ratified in which both parties accepted that the U.S. control of the canal would be phased out and that the Panamanians would take full control on December 31st, 1999. Since the handover the Canal continues running on schedule with over 1000 ships a month transiting and the huge expansion of the Gaillard Cut is well underway.

I came up on deck late morning to find Andy very concerned. "Look," he pointed ahead, "at all those ships anchored off, but I've seen no movement at all through the waterway itself. I hope they're not on strike!"

Later we learned that ships go up both sets of locks in the morning and come down the otherside in the afternoon, hence the lack of traffic at midday! But on the completion of the expansion of the Gaillard Cut two-way traffic will be possible throughout the Canal 24 hours a day.

We checked in with the Flamenco Signal Station on Channel 12 to get permission to proceed to the Balboa Yacht Club. Then on channel 6 the club gave us the number of a mooring buoy to tie to and soon the club launch was leading the way. Tides are 15' here and all transfers between the boats and shore are made by launch as this is just inside the main channel. We signed up at the Yacht Club office. The club looked just as it had in 1987—ready to fall down yesterday! Only the bar was operating but the atmosphere was as vibrant as ever.

It was stunning to see so many boats and great to get together again with a bunch of cruisers. Most were couples heading for the South Pacific but over the next few days we chatted with a Canadian family who were staying in Panama, whose children were on the same correspondence program that we had formerly used. We also met the crew on a British Nicholson 55, a yacht we last saw in Australia in 1988 taking part in the Tall Ship's events; enjoyed some lively Californian lads on an Irwin 26' who were planning to sail the same route as us; and were approached by a 75 year-old, last seen in California, who was trying to get sponsorship to become the oldest circumnavigator.

One couple kindly gave us a chart book of the U.S. East Coast. They were doing what we all dream of—earning their way as they cruised, by carrying on regular business from the boat. Most of the time they communicated with the States by fax using a Mini-M system or by e-mail. Occasionally, however, it was necessary to make a telephone call when it was more economical to use a landline.

"I will never forget the time in Iles des Saintes," Janet told us. These are charming laid-back French islands south of Guadeloupe and we could immediately envision the scene. "I had to make a conference call to a company in New York," she continued, "and in the middle of a tense discussion one of them suddenly said aghast, 'is that a chicken I hear in the background?'"

The contrasts are wonderful—a Caribbean island scene with a girl scantily clad in a bright bikini and pareu, with hens freely roaming the dirt road, on a payphone giving technical computer software expertise to a group of businessmen formally attired in dark wool suits seated around a boardroom table on Wall Street!

The Panamanians had just taken over the running of Canal operations from the U.S. and we were impressed with the job they were doing, particularly their concern for cruisers. Canal transit procedures were streamlined and efficient, especially as our 1987 crossing was on their computer. The Panamanian admeasurer came to *Bagheera* the next morning; he had been doing the job for 35 years, he informed us. The Port Captain, from whom we obtained our *zarpe* for the Canal transit and the San Blas Islands, was most pleasant and keen to know of any suggestions to improve Canal transits for yachts. He asked us if the cruising fees were in line with the other countries we had visited. At $67 for the cruising permit we assured him that they were quite average. (Most countries in Central America cost us around $100 for cruising permits and immigration.) We paid the transit fee of $500US (the charge if under 50') and the $120 damage deposit, (required in case of a breakdown) in cash, which was easily obtained through a bank machine as the U.S. dollar is the main

Panamanian currency and at par with the Balboa. The damage deposit was returned immediately after the transit. (Recently the damage fee has increased to $800 and the charges can be paid by credit card.) A transit could be made with two days notice but we opted for a later date to give our friends time to acclimatize after their arrival.

Although only a few of the machines worked, laundry at the club was a bargain with $1.00 per wash and 50c for a forty-five minute dry. I had made sure that we didn't fill the aft cabins with gear this time and soon berths were made up and provisions bought from American-style supermarkets, the Costco in Panama City, and from a well-stocked local produce market in Balboa itself. As we looked at the various stalls I had a flashback of buying crates of produce in 1987 when we were heading off across the South Pacific. At that time I had stocked up for six people for four months!

Wilson, Caroline and Ute arrived that night and were delighted that I was at the airport to greet them, particularly when they found out how hard the club is to find. I was pleased that not only were their personal bags small and soft, they also had a large heavy sailbag that contained our new autopilot. We had been using the windvane since Salina Cruz and hand-steering in the calms. It would be bliss to have the autopilot functioning again.

Our guests lapped up the scene over a breakfast of tropical fruit the next morning, already in bathing suits and lounging in the sun.

"We are going through the Canal the day after tomorrow," I informed them, "So thought it would be fun to go over to Taboga Island for a couple of days. It will just be a two-hour sail if the wind holds up."

"Sounds great," Wilson and Caroline agreed simultaneously. We have years of cruising history together with particular memories of Gulf Island gunkholing in British Columbia when our children were young.

Being on a sailboat was a new adventure for Ute. "A short trip sounds a good way to start," she nodded. "Just tell me where to sit so I won't be in the way!"

"I'd like to have a look at the freighter that arrived yesterday," Andy commented as he started the engine. There had been a massive fire in the center of this new-looking German ship and many of the high stacks of containers were now charred twists of metal. We were amazed that the bridge was unaffected but imagined the enormous heat and fearful scene at sea whilst the fire raged. Our pilot later told us that the fire occurred in their last port in South America, due to a defective refrigeration unit that was part of its cargo. I shivered at the thought of a fire on board and was comforted that we had purchased new extinguishers before departing Vancouver.

Taboga is known as the island of flowers, and the colors and aromas of the exotic blooms were overwhelming as we walked along the main path through town. The homes are also colorful and well kept and there are several old ruins, a reminder that Taboga has a long history. It was settled by the Spanish in 1515 and its small church is reportedly the second oldest in the Western Hemisphere. We wandered through the attractive graveyard that dates back to the 16th century. Due to the enormous tidal variation ships could not anchor close to the mainland and the island, with its deep-water harbor, became the center for shipping during the colonial era. It was even visited by Henry Morgan after he had sacked Panama and El Morro. The small island by Hotel Taboga, at the end of the low water sandspit, was the headquarters of the Pacific Steamship Navigation Company.

A fruit juice on the patio of the old colonial Chou Hotel made a refreshing stop. Below, the fishermen were returning in their colorful boats and laying out their catch on the beach. Andy chose some mackerel for dinner, a bargain at three for a dollar, and we were treated to another feast in the cockpit.

The hill gave us a steep hike next morning but the rewards were seeing huge blue-backed butterflies and some fascinating poison arrow frogs. It was Saturday and back at the beach passenger-ferries and motor boats were arriving in droves. Jet-skiers roared past the dinghy as we returned to *Bagheera*. Andy hates these machines with a vengeance (although our sons love them!) and declared it was time to head back to the mainland. We gave our guests a taste of snorkeling at close-by Isla Taboguilla and a panoramic view of Panama City as we returned.

Panama City now stretches about six miles from the original site to the Canal entrance and it is by far the most modern, international city in Central America. It is the country's hub, where all agricultural goods are sent for shipping and the center for the principal industries—offshore banking, the Colón Free Zone (second largest duty-free zone in the world, after Hong Kong), the Panama Canal and merchant shipping. The U.S. is Panama's largest trading partner, taking over 45% of its exports and providing 40% of its imports.

Marine Traffic Control informed us by radio that evening that our advisor (trainee pilot) would arrive any time after 6:00am. Despite the early hour everyone was full of enthusiasm but 07:00 passed then 08:00 with no advisor in sight. By this time Andy was convinced we'd been forgotten so called again. Rod finally arrived at 08:30 and immediately instructed us to cast off. Within no time *Bagheera* was passing under the strategic Bridge of the Americas, that joins North and South America, and approaching the first lock.

Rod was constantly on his handheld radio. "We'll be lying alongside a tug going through the locks," he finally informed us. "That ship ahead will go in first."

We were pleased, as being alongside a tug that is tied to the side of the lock (sidewall) is the easiest and safest way for a yacht, particularly in the turbulent 'up' locks. The alternatives are to go center chamber, using the four 125′ lines that are required on board to keep in position, or to go sidewall oneself, which is not recommended as the walls are rough concrete. The last time *Bagheera* transited with six other boats and was rafted to one of similar size. This usually works well but there was a nerve-racking moment when our partners forgot to keep tension on their lines and we swung close to the wall.

The crew on the tug was extremely friendly and this time we could watch unconcerned as the whirlpools swirled around *Bagheera* as the locks rapidly filled. The total length of the Canal is 51.2 miles and the first two Miraflores Locks raised us 54 feet, although this depends on the height of the large tide. Then a mile north, after crossing the Miraflores Lake, we were raised another 31 feet in a single lock at Pedro Miguel, close to the popular Pedro Miguel Yacht Club. It is then a 31-mile ride at 85 feet above sea level to the Gatun Locks through the 8.5-mile Gaillard Cut. This had been the most difficult part of the Canal to build, as it required cutting through solid rock and as we passed huge cranes were at work widening the cut for two-way traffic even for the largest vessels. Gatun Lake is one of the largest artificial bodies of water in the world, formed by damming the Chagres River. The water was low, caused by El Niño Rod told us, exposing rotting trees from the old forest and islands that were originally mountain peaks. On the Atlantic side the three Gatún Locks lie joined together. Each lock chamber is 1000′ long and 110′ wide and about 52 million gallons of fresh water is used for each ship transiting the Canal, fed by a gravity flow system through the locks and out into the ocean.

The Canal runs in a northwest to southeast direction with the Atlantic entrance approximately 27 miles west of the Pacific entrance. I will never forget looking at the chart for the first time, on our last transit. I had come on watch at 4:30am and seeing the Atlantic on the west side of the large-scale chart and Pacific on the east had made me wonder if I was really awake!

Permission to transit requires the ability to average 5 knots, and 8 knots is required to complete the trip in one day. Although we cannot maintain this speed we had done well and Rod asked us if we would like to continue right through. He was quite surprised when we declined, saying we wanted to spend the night in the lake anchored off the jungle.

At the Gatún locks looking out to the Caribbean

The day had been cloudy, which was perfect as temperatures weren't oppressive, unlike our previous transit, and there was a pleasant breeze that night. We contemplated a swim, but mention of crocodiles decided us against it! Instead we were lulled to sleep by the howler monkeys, then woken at dawn by a lively symphony given by the varied and colorful bird life.

Our new advisor arrived at 10:00am, and leapt on board with a wide grin and a huge bag of ice as a gift. This West Indian left no doubt he was an extrovert and a talented pilot. Reuben had trained at New York University and claimed he was tri-lingual—American, West Indian (heavily accented English) and Spanish!

Heading towards the locks, cruise ships passed and we were suddenly the focus of attention when several passengers called out "Hi Canada." and cheered.

As we waved back Ute, our newcomer to boating, commented, "They won't have any idea of what the canal is really about going through in a cruise ship. Transiting in a boat is definitely the way to go!"

This time we went center chamber. Soon *Bagheera* was at the front of the first lock and we were gazing down the three locks with awe and following the Canal out to the Caribbean. As a ship pulled in behind, Reuben advised that we cover our solar panels.

"I've seen some mashed by the turks head the line-handlers on shore will be throwing to collect your lines," he explained. "Windgenerators are vulnerable too."

Once attached ashore Wilson and Caroline adjusted the tension of our lines on the foredeck, easing the ropes out as we dropped to sea level. Andy and Ute handled the aft lines and I was at the helm following Reuben's calm but precise directions. Seven miles of motoring later we had finished our transit and Reuben leapt off onto one of the many vessels that belong to Canal Commission. He disappeared with a big smile and a wave, another successful transit completed. He enjoyed coming on yachts and meeting cruisers, he told us, although many of the other pilots preferred being on a ship which is more comfortable than a boat, particularly when there is no shade.

As we headed over to find a spot at the Panama Canal Yacht Club (2010 update: yachts now use the new Shelter Bay Marina) the cockpit was alive with conversation. Not only were we soon heading for the famous chain of the San Blas Islands but after calms for much of the last 3000 miles there was also a decent wind!

Andy and Liza

Duncan, Colin and Jamie

Vancouver, B.C.

Bagheera.

The Canadian Gulf Islands

Portage Bay, Alaska

Creek Street, Ketchikan, Alaska.

Totems at Nan Sdins on SGaang Gwaii (Anthony Island), Queen Charlotte Islands, B.C.

Golden Gate Bridge, San Francisco

Greeted by Sealions

Majestic pelican

Los Arcos, Cabo San Lucas

MEXICO

Typical fishing vessel

Puerto Angel

Ensenada

MEXICO

Our lively 'bag' lady

EL SALVADOR – *La Union*

COSTA RICA

Playas del Coco

Typical flaming sunset

Bahia Brasilito

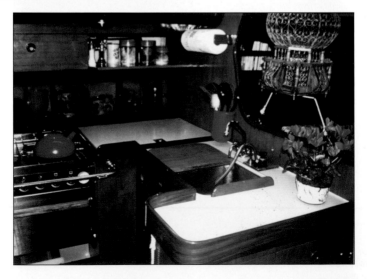

Caribbean
Central America

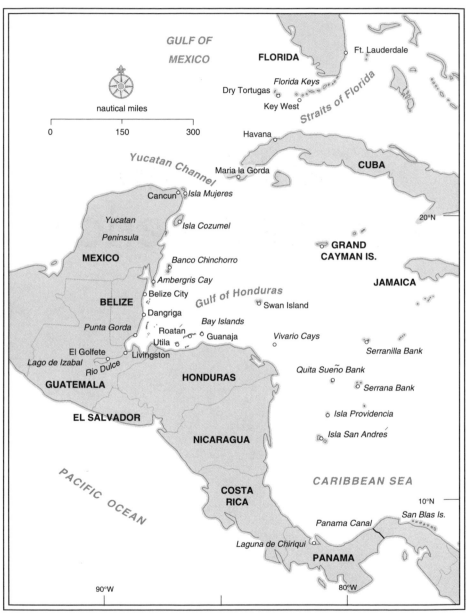

Caribbean Central America

10. Panama and North

Portobelo, Isla Grande, The San Blas Islands and San Andrés

Everyone loves Caribbean cruising in the winter trade-wind season—so long as they are sailing in the right direction! Blowing predominantly from the east (sometimes NE or SE) these winds give exhilarating reaches in the north/south island chains and we looked forward to being comfortably whistled north in *Bagheera* through Central America and up to the United States.

The picture dramatically changes however if one heads into wind, when the strength and regularity of the trades, together with their influence on the current and seas, give an extraordinarily uncomfortable ride. Long passages to windward can be a nightmare. Most who have attempted to sail east in the southern Caribbean against the prevailing wind and current vow never to do it again. Such was the experience of the crew we met in Acapulco when they delivered the boat from Panama to Bonaire.

Six months previously we had warned our guests that the next part of our trip, although not far, would likely be rough. The route from the Panama Canal to the San Blas Islands is in a northeast direction, not only into wind but also bucking a strong current.

"No problem," they had all agreed over a wonderful seafood dinner in Vancouver. "It will be great just to be in the sun!" Now we were facing reality in Panama and as it was blowing over 30 knots Andy and I felt it prudent to wait another day!

There were numerous sailboats in Bahia Limón, west of Colón. They were part of the British Blue Water Rally, making a quick 20-month trip around the world, and many had their yellow Q (quarantine) flags flying, indicating that they had just arrived. Despite the large breakwater the anchorage was choppy so we continued to the Panama Canal Yacht Club. Fortunately a Swiss boat was leaving and we Med-moored *Bagheera* off the Yacht Club grounds.

"Look at the kids playing in the trees," Andy commented wistfully. "Just like our boys did when we were here before." He echoed my thoughts exactly.

Two children were on a catamaran moored beside us. They had just been in the San Blas Islands.

"Did you stop on the way?" I asked.

"Yes, we stopped at Linton Island," the boy told us. "And it was really scary," the girl added." A monkey attacked my mom and me and tried to run off with our dinghy."

"Really?" I replied, not knowing whether this was a kid's exaggeration or a tall tale.

Later her mother told us that a monkey had jumped into the dinghy with them and had bitten her arm several times. After they had leapt overboard to escape the attack the monkey had tried to start the engine! Subsequently they were told by other cruisers that this monkey was dangerous and infamous in the area, also that he actually could pull an outboard cord and drive!

We decided to give Linton Island a miss but several people suggested Portobelo, the old port of the Spanish Main. Another recommendation was Isla Grande. These stops would nicely break the 80-mile trip to the San Blas Islands and we decided to complete the last 40 miles with an overnight passage. After a quick shop at Reyes supermarket and stops by taxi (Colón has never been a safe city for walkers) at a printer to photocopy some charts and at a travel agent to book our visitors' flights out of the San Blas Islands, we were ready to leave. There had been squalls and torrential rain during the day but the barometer was rising and the front appeared to have gone through. During a pleasant evening in the yacht club restaurant we spoke to the lads on *Desdemona*, last seen in Balboa, and agreed to leave together at 8:30am the following day.

It was still blowing hard as we headed out of the harbor and even before reaching the breakwater *Desdemona* was falling behind, not able to power into the rough sea. They soon radioed to tell us they were heading back.

"We'll just see what it's like outside before making a decision ourselves," Andy replied.

The waves were huge as *Bagheera* pounded her way out of the break-water into the open ocean and the wind was gusting to 32 knots from the northeast, right on the nose. All was quiet on board, our visitors too stunned to speak! However, away from the shore the seas settled down to a manageable 8-10 feet so we decided to motor-sail the 20-mile trip to Portobelo and use a deeply reefed mainsail and small genoa to help us along and steady the boat.

Caroline sat to windward in the cockpit, the most relaxed of our guests. Wilson stood holding the bimini strut, watching the seas ahead.

"It's the eighteenth wave that's generally the biggest," he concluded, ducking yet again from the frequent spray.

I stayed at the helm trying to steer the most sea-kindly course, but soon Ute came to sit beside me. The motion was too much for her and despite taking medication she wasn't feeling well. I got out the bucket, just in case!

Andy was below, nonchalantly completing some chores and reading at the chart table. He came up on deck after a couple of hours, stretching out on the leeward side of the cockpit with such a look of contentment that it sent Ute wild.

Her pallor was a delicate shade of green but she had enough pep to expound with disgust, "Can you believe that Andy and I are on the same boat!" At this point she would happily have traded a sailboat for a cruise ship!

As soon as we reached the calm waters of Portobelo five hours later, she quickly recovered, particularly because there was so much to look at in this stunning bay. Named Puerto Bello (beautiful port) by Christopher Columbus in 1502, during his fourth trip to the Americas, this natural harbor became the trading port for the Spanish fleet. Gold, silver and other goods from Peru were transported over the Camino Real from Panama City and stored here until the bi-annual trade fair, a large and boisterous event that in its heyday lasted up to 40 days. Galleons laden with goods for trade arrived from Spain and an estimated 45 armadas returned to Europe between 1574 and 1702, their holds heavy with metals worth over 30 million pesos. These wealthy shipments soon attracted pirates, in particular the British, and the harbor was fortified with three levels of defense. Trailing down the lush green slopes, the ruins of these battlements make the entry fascinating.

There were 25 boats in the bay. Some were anchored by the fort on the north side but we decided to anchor among those on the south side, close to the other two fortifications and the town. While looking for a place to leave the dinghy when exploring ashore we met some former cruisers who welcomed us into their home. They had sailed down from the U.S. west coast several years previously, and had settled in Panama. They hoped to open the first hotel in the area, as the sleepy town is gaining popularity among tourists. They have already written a book on the history of the region, completing much of their research in Spain.

Portobelo was declared a Historic Monument in 1976 and we found it a classic jewel. The impressive 1630 Renaissance-style Customs House had just been beautifully restored. It had been damaged twice, once from an attack in 1644 and later by an earthquake. Behind the San Felipe de Portobelo church stand the ruins of the seventeenth century hospital and the church itself houses the famous Black Christ of Portobelo. Many miracles are attributed to this black-wood statue and there is a pilgrimage to Portobelo every October 21st, when participants dress in the same royal purple as the statue's clothes.

The battlements themselves are immaculately maintained. Next to the Customs House the 1756 San Jeronimo Fort and Battery is well preserved and has an impressive display of canons aimed at the bay. The secondary fortifications of Santiago Fort and Battery are also relatively intact and a hike up the steep, bright-green slopes behind gave a panoramic outlook over the bay and a great aerial view of *Bagheera* at anchor.

Lunch was delicious plantain (the green banana-like staple) soup, rice, octopus and pickled sweet plantain. With its ethnic mix a variety of food is available in Panama. We particularly enjoyed the spicy food and found the national dish *sancocho*, a tasty vegetable and chicken stew, both palatable and inexpensive.

We took the dinghy to explore the Santiago Trench Fort at the entrance of the bay. The moss-covered ruins spoke of a battered life. Built in 1586 it was destroyed by Sir Francis Drake in 1597, then attacked by William Parker in 1602 after it was rebuilt. More recently it was denuded when many of the stones were used to build the Gatún Locks.

In 1739 Portobelo was destroyed by an attack led by the British Admiral Edward Vernon. Subsequently the Spanish decided to stop using the Panama route, as the armadas were too vulnerable to pirating, and instead sailed the long way around Cape Horn. Now, after centuries of oblivion Portobelo is just beginning to wake up again.

It had been a full day and we were just getting tea below when Andy rushed up the companionway steps to hail a vessel that was passing close-by.

"What's happening?" I called up to Wilson.

"Andy seems to know the people who just arrived," he replied. "Something about Seaview."

It transpired that old friends of Andy's from Seaview Yacht Club on the Isle of Wight in England were on the Blue Water Rally, and Andy had noticed their club burgee through the chart table port. It was great to get together that evening and enjoy their enthusiasm for cruising around the world.

Just 12 miles to windward of Portobelo lies Isla Grande. Friends had enjoyed this 'hippy' island; the Lonely Planet travel guide wasn't so positive. By visiting during the week we missed the crowds and associated problems, and loved the ambience of the island, with its dirt track lined with colorful homes, white sand beaches and lively West Indian residents. As Andy gazed at his perfect retirement job—fixing a stack of outboard engines that was assembled under some palm trees—three yachts approached from the east, surfing down the channel on frighteningly large swells. They arrived safely but a shrine in the bay told a different tale of other less fortunate mariners.

We dressed in tropical sarongs for a delicious dinner ashore and then, after preparing the boat for sea and ensuring our guests had taken seasick pills, left at midnight for the final leg to the San Blas Archipelago. It was another uncomfortable trip, with a dog leg out to sea, as it was necessary to go outside Escribanos Bank. Terrible gasoline fumes made me feel queasy; but it wasn't until dawn that I discovered that the cap had come loose on the spare outboard-fuel jerry-can on deck. With clean air and the sun rising, my spirits lifted, especially when palm-covered islets began to dance along the horizon. Soon *Bagheera* was approaching Chichime Cays and at 8:00am the anchor descended into the most brilliant of turquoise seas.

Our guests had fared well and were awed by the setting, but there was little time to reflect on our surroundings as *Bagheera* was already surrounded by dugout canoes.

It is said one should never return to a place of magical memories. Our previous visit had been one of the highlights of our six-year circumnavigation. Not only does this 370 island chain offer spectacular cruising and diving, we had been impressed by the traditional culture. The Cuna (or Kuna) are said to be descendents of the feared Caribs and are fiercely proud of their heritage. Known as 'Cuna Yala' to the indigenous people and 'Comarca de San Blas' to the Panamanian government, this thin strip of mainland and offshore islands is an officially recognized, virtually autonomous region of the Republic of Panama.

We had enjoyed the outspoken people when they came alongside *Bagheera* in their sailing dugout canoes and admired the immaculate palm-frond villages ashore. The boys became friends with the children, each talking in their own language but having no problem in communicating. They played with local toys made from seedpods, pleaded with us to buy one of the green parakeets that were everywhere as pets, watched dugout canoes being hewn and became friends with the local medicine man.

135

The women wore the distinctive dress of blue and gold sarong skirt, red and gold headscarf (if married) and mola blouse with puffy sleeves. The molas form the back and front panels of the lower blouse, so unusual and intricate that they have become popular souvenirs of primitive art. The appliqué designs are cut from many layers of brightly-colored cloth, are sewn with the tiniest of stitches and represent all aspects of life whether old or new. No one knows exactly where the molas originated but it is speculated that the designs are similar to those originally painted on the body. The attire is completed with a gold nose ring, a black line painted from the forehead to nose-tip, arm and leg bands of geometric designs made of yellow and orange beads, with hammered silver or gold necklaces worn for special occasions.

Although the islands are just as beautiful as ever, we were saddened by the changes in the culture. Inevitably times move on. As we were leaving in 1987 the first television aerial was being erected. Now there are hundreds and much interchange with mainland Panama via the many commuter planes. Tourist hotels have sprung up on the islands, as has the number of visiting yachts. On our previous visit we saw just three other cruising boats in two weeks, this time there were over 200 in the six days we spent just in the archipelago's western end. Many cruisers had been several weeks enjoying the wonderful anchorages that the chain offers. Typically, after completing boat work in Trinidad, they sailed along the coasts of Venezuela, the ABC Islands and Cartegena in Colombia before reaching Panama, enjoying Caribbean cruising outside the hurricane belt. Soon they would go through the Canal and on to the South Pacific, reaching French Polynesia after the cyclone season had ended there in March.

We were used to each woman having just a few special molas for sale but now bucket-loads were being emptied on deck as we were anchoring. Instead of the friendly interchange we had previously enjoyed with the Cuna women this time there was an aggressive spokesman, Lisa, who was dressed in jeans (and we heard later was actually a man). She spoke English well and was a forceful salesperson who had her own internet site and definitely dealt in dollars; coconuts appeared no longer to be the local currency! As we traveled the islands we noticed that many of the younger women were not wearing the traditional dress, childrens' toys were made of plastic, the only green parakeet was on another yacht and most of the locals now had outboards rather than sailing their dugouts.

However, it was our guests' first visit and they were enchanted by this area that epitomizes the tropical dream with sparkling white sands, azure seas and overhanging palms. Two other boats in the anchorage left mid-morning, then an 80′ ketch gracefully made its departure. It was a yacht we knew from the Virgin Islands in the 60s and as she sailed towards the horizon she passed a contrastingly small sail that was coming our way. It was *Desdemona*. The lads had sailed direct from Colon and were delighted to make their landfall after a turbulent passage.

Later, Craig, Steve and Rick came over to dinner, laden with pasta and garlic bread. Ute and I were on dinner duty that night and our coq-au-vin, beans and cabbage combined for a great spontaneous dinner, with papaya and Fundador brandy (our favorite) to round it off. It was a lively evening, celebrating everyone's safe arrival in the San Blas Islands after weathering a rough ride. Craig went up further in our estimation when he offered to do the washing-up. He and Ute did a fine job.

We visited several islands and again enjoyed meeting the local people. One extended Cuna family came on board and stayed during a torrential squall. When they sailed their canoes away we were amused to see the grandmother hiking out on her dugout!

Another family took us inside their cool bamboo home. Immaculate

Grandmother on board

clothing was strung on beams under the palm-frond roof, the sand floor swept until it shone and ten hammocks, strung at random, were the main furniture.

In one village we came across bead bracelets for sale displayed on a stick. Most were the traditional orange and yellow with blue/green borders but Caroline found a red one that appealed. Great care was taken as they wound the canilleras beads around our arms and looped the retaining string underneath so that the bracelet would stay in place. Occasionally a daughter would click impatiently if her mother made a mistake and in turn gave us a big smile!

Everyday the pile of molas that our guests had purchased was growing. As several already adorn our family-room walls I'd been reticent to buy more but in Ciedras Village there was one that I could not resist! Not only detailed and beautifully stitched, it was heavy from the many layers of cloth and the only one displayed outside this home. Its owner hovered shyly inside her dark doorway but indicated she wanted $50 for it. Both back and front panels had attractive designs but this was expensive so I said I would come back.

An hour soon passed as Ute, Caroline and I walked around the town looking at more molas and taking photos. It is the custom to get permission and pay a $1.00 per picture, but seeing the proud look on the children's faces as they gave their parents the money was worth the fee. Later I painted several of the children's fingernails with polish and was soon surrounded by lively chatter, the ice broken and shyness gone.

The mola was still beautiful when I returned! I tried to bargain, but the older woman held out. If I wanted it, I had to pay her the full amount.

"It is wonderful," I said smiling in admiration as I paid. Someone behind me translated.

Her eyes lit up. "It took me a full year," she replied.

"It will be much enjoyed," I assured her.

Meanwhile Andy and Wilson had just caught us up.

"Where have you been?" we asked them.

"We went to get permission to visit the island from the chief, who is called a sahila," Wilson told us. "He was most welcoming and even declined the usual $5.00 visiting fee."

"We thought it must be because of all the spending you ladies have been doing!" commented Andy. I showed him the mola and it met with approval!

They had also been introduced to the goldsmith whose main product was nose rings, although he had also made several delicate rings with fine butterfly motifs for fingers. Business was obviously good. His new television antenna was just being raised and behind his workshop there were two large brand-new outboard engines.

Wherever we looked as we sailed away there were sandy islands and islets smothered in clusters of palms. Sheer numbers make these hard to identify, especially as the formation of new sandbars make a mockery of the ancient charts. In addition, our visibility was quickly reduced by one of the frequent rainshowers. Piloting through the shallow waters took some concentration, with Andy frequently looking out from the bow.

Shelter is also deceptive, as an anchorage that appears open to the ocean can in fact be quite protected by a reef. We are used to this in the tropics but our guests often found the roar of the surf pounding on the outer reef quite intimidating, especially with winds always over 20 knots. Other places that appear to be protected can become quite rolly and we were happy to be at Green Island for a peaceful last night in the islands. There were three other yachts, British, Swedish and American and a large ketch on the other side of the bay. A brilliant full moon shone that night, but at high tide we unexpectedly started to pitch.

"I think I'll put more chain out," Andy commented around 2:00am, after peering out of the forward hatch, "so our guests will be comfortable." It was a routine operation and I immediately started drifting back to sleep.

Meanwhile Wilson and Caroline were galvanized into action, woken by the noise of the chain rattling out over the windlass. In seconds they were on deck, having uncharacteristically extracted themselves from their berth in seconds flat.

Wilson called out, "It's OK, I'm here, are we moving?"

We have an all chain anchor rode for tropical cruising but at home it is customary to have rope with just a few feet of chain by the anchor. To hear chain means that the anchor is almost up!

It was a grand gesture but the fact that Wilson remembered nothing of it the next morning was the cause of great hilarity over breakfast. It was also a reminder that it is easy to be disoriented when not fully awake.

Ashore, much of the island is covered with a coconut plantation. Although the natural palm trees are tall and willowy, those planted, in common with much of the Caribbean and Pacific commercial growth, are dwarf stock to facilitate picking. A fascinating find on the beach was a Portuguese man o'war jelly fish. Its bright pink inflated bladder, or sail, stood out dramatically and it was photographed so much it should be flattered! In the island's interior Andy found white orchids in bloom and many white lilies. The ground cover had purple flowers, just like the English vetch. Together with the pale green new growth of the common foliage these blooms made a colorful display on board.

The snorkeling was superb with varied corals and gorgonians, as well as a great variety of colorful reef-fish. As I swam back to the dinghy I was surrounded by a dense school of sprat, the next moment the sea was pure aqua and the next a deep blue. Andy and I had gone by ourselves so I took our guests later to enjoy a quick view 'bottoms up' from the dinghy. Then we headed to Corazón de Jesus to verify their flight the following morning.

Being in the software business, Wilson was concerned when the travel agent in Colón had booked their flight without using a computer. To be on the safe side he had booked another flight with a different airline in Portobelo. Now he wanted to check them out.

Ashore we found two islands joined by a bridge.

"The airline office," we were informed by our self-appointed guide, " is on Río Diablo (Narganá). Come this way, I'll take you there."

We noticed that most of the people on these two islands were dressed in western attire. Apparently this is due to the doctrines of the fiery evangelist Anna Cooper who came here in the 1920s. Although there were many who objected to her teachings from the bible, an imposing church and the people's way of life indicate her success as a missionary.

We were grateful to be shown the right building, as it certainly didn't look like a travel agent. As we ducked through the doorway and our eyes were getting accustomed to the gloom we were introduced to a man who had a school-type exercise book on the small table beside him. He seemed disinterested, so our guide interceded.

"Sign the book if you want to fly out tomorrow," was our interpretation of the instruction!

"But which airline is this for?" asked Wilson. "We have reservations."

"It doesn't matter, you just put your name down and a plane will come to collect you," it was explained.

"What time is the flight?" Wilson finally asked, aghast that his reservations didn't seem to count.

"7:30am." This was right between the two flights he had booked!

The night was short with frequent awakenings and all too soon a conch horn sounded; it was the village wake-up call. At 05:35 Wilson and I departed by dinghy for the airport, located on yet another island. It was pitch black and he held the flashlight high so we could see the white surf on the reef close-by. We unloaded the luggage onto a dock. At the end there was a small hut but it was in darkness and firmly locked.

"No problem," commented Wilson, when we searched further and found the runway. "At least we will be first in line!"

I went back to get the others and we all returned with the pinprick of Wilson's flashlight guiding us in. Soon the sky was brightening and there were signs of life from Río Diablo. Dugouts started coming, laden with people and bags. At first Wilson was pleased that there were others arriving but when a twenty-foot boat docked with seventeen on board he became worried that there were now too many passengers for a small plane. Finally the man with the 'textbook' was walking down the dock. This looked promising, until he entered a door at the far end of the building, which left Wilson at the back of the line!

Andy and I waited outside, hysterical with laughter by this time. We had already learned that the windsock was up—the signal that they needed another plane to land! Finally the others came out smiling.

"We knew all would turn out well," Wilson told us, "when we were 7th, 8th and 9th in line, the same placing as in 'the book'!"

All went like clockwork. Two planes arrived and there was plenty of room for all the passengers. Our guests took off and landed in Panama City exactly on the schedule of the flight they had booked in Colón!

Wilson's first e-mail to us after returning home read, "Hard to come to terms with wearing shoes and socks. When I look at the computer I keep thinking, I wonder if there is another way!"

A quick trip up the jungle river across on the mainland gave an opportunity to do laundry under a shady tree and soak ourselves in the cool water. It was hot; we even found an iguana snoozing in the middle of the path that ran alongside plantations of pineapples, bananas, papayas, sugar cane and mangos. There were brilliant red/orange passionflowers along the riverbanks and canoes were going past on their way to collect fresh water. One man was paddling so we gave him a tow.

We had planned to stop at Holandes Cays on the way out but on seeing a Canadian Beneteau anchored at Green Island we diverted. They were easterners but we had friends in common and had a relaxing day with them and several other cruisers from the twelve boats that were now in the anchorage. While Andy fitted the new autopilot I caught up on my journal and e-mails, then we dove and gorged ourselves on red crab brought by a local fisherman.

On the VHF we heard that a boat had gone up on a reef. They were not the only boat having problems with navigation. High on the outer reef there was a ship hard aground. Apparently they were trying to sell their cargo of fuel hoping to lighten their vessel enough to be towed off.

Despite our initial disappointment we left the San Blas Islands on a positive note. The beauty of its tiny palm-covered sand cays, the spectacular diving and sea life, and the unique and colorful culture of the Cuna Indians still render it an irresistible destination. Although life is gradually changing for many of the islanders (we understand less so for those living on the isolated mainland coast), they have a proud heritage and peaceful lifestyle where chores are equally divided between men and women (it's a matriarchal society!), and there is plenty of time for leisure.

We had also been impressed by the diversity of Panama. It offers not only some great cruising destinations, including the Canal, but also fascinating cultures and great historical sights. As we saw both from the coast and when travelling inland the country has dramatic forests, waterfalls and vast tracts of virgin jungle and reforestation is underway for many areas that had been cleared. There are fifteen national parks that cover over 29% of the total territory—the greatest percentage of land protection of any Central American country. Its position between the two continents has led to a remarkable variety of animal and plant life and the country is the highway for migratory birds. In addition, we were amazed to learn that over a hundred animal species, which include reptiles, fish, amphibians, mammals and birds, are found nowhere else in the world.

It was time to head north and there were various options. Along the coast to the west of the Canal, Laguna de Chiriquí offers wildlife and plenty of island anchorages. The problem of sailing this far west is a likely beat to windward when the time comes to head north. The winds along the coast can often be northerly as compared to the more typical northeasterlies farther offshore. In our initial plan we had hoped to explore this area but when we looked at continuing along the inshore route we found that for the most part the coasts of Costa Rica, Nicaragua and eastern Honduras do not offer particularly gratifying cruising. Depths can be shallow and the climate hot and humid year round; there can also be an adverse counter current.

With this in mind and the fact that we had also made substantial miles to the east by coming to San Blas we decided on an outside passage, the common choice. Our destination was the Colombian island of San Andrés about 200 miles to the north. Although the seas were still lumpy we were soon easing sheets and romping along, *Bagheera* effortlessly completing our usual 150 miles a day. With abundant tuna, dolphin fish and mackerel to catch the time passed quickly. This remote island is fringed by a long barrier reef. We arrived at the entrance to the channel at 02:00 and easily found our way in through the well-lit markers that also showed clearly on radar.

Anchoring close to some catamarans, and after a few hours of sleep, we went ashore at the Club Nautico. Not only was the club extremely hospitable, they refused payment for use of the club for one night and served wicked margaritas. We were amazed by the sophistication and excellent facilities in this duty-free town. There were several supermarkets with a wide variety of produce brought in from the Colombian mainland and

The immaculate oldest church on San Andrés island

although obviously a tourist area for the mainlanders the town had character and color.

An interesting tour showed a pretty tropical island with both traditional and newly built holiday homes. The beautiful white-sand beaches and deep turquoise ocean were best seen, we were assured by our young guide, from the bell tower of his church. It was the oldest church on the island, simply built with white clapboard and a peaked red painted roof. The wooden steps were steep but the view from this elevation was stunning.

Our guide pointed out the school next door.

"Although Spanish is the official language, many locals speak English," he told us, "and there are some bilingual schools such as this one that I attended."

The island has a colorful history, particularly as its location was right in the path of laden galleons as they headed for the Yucatan Channel on their way to Spain. Several of its caves reputedly held buccaneer Henry Morgan's booty. We were taken into one; it was dark and unimpressive.

"Probably just a decoy," was our guide's dry comment.

What did catch our eye was a hand-painted sign on a ramshackle stall at its entrance that read 'Viagra se vende aqui'!

Providencia, also Colombian, is a daysail north, and can be a tight haul to windward. Its jagged peaks that rise to 1,200 feet can be seen 20 miles distant and we viewed them through the binoculars. Although we had wanted to stop at the island and enjoy its rural community and old-world charm a 'norther' was on its way. Unlike the eastern Caribbean where weather is generally settled during the winter months, the western Caribbean is affected by northerly winds that often reach gale force in strength. Associated with cold fronts that move down from the continental U.S., the 'northers' can march through as often as weekly from October through April, with the greatest frequency in December and January. Their effects are particularly found in the Yucatan, but they are felt all the way down to Panama and generally last three to four days.

Next morning the weather fax from NMF (USCG Marshfield, MA) showed the cold front had been delayed, also confirmed by a Caribbean weather guru on the radio.

"Great," said Andy. "We will have plenty of time to get to the Bay Islands and stop for a snorkel on the way."

There are several cays en route north that offer excellent diving but limited protection for the night, as they are barely awash. Popular stops include the Quita Sueño, Serrana and Serranilla Banks, which are particularly convenient for those heading to Swan Island.

The passage to the Honduran Bay Islands takes one around the shoulder of Central America where the north-south coast of Nigaragua joins the east-west coast of Honduras. We moved quickly to the Vivario Cays, sheets eased and riding a two-knot current. There was a huge deserted structure ashore with pens, presumably for fish or lobster, but we saw none that were worth catching while we were snorkeling, although the water was crystal clear and the reef attractive. There was a short storm during the night, when we were again underway. Visibility was greatly reduced by rain both for the naked eye and on the radar. Nothing to worry about, although it was rather startling when a cruise ship 'leapt' out of the murk.

Then we were roaring down-wind under a starry sky with sails comfortably 'wing on wing', the sail plan that had taken *Bagheera* most of the way around the world. The hills of Guanaja, the most easterly of the Honduran Bay Islands came into sight. As I looked through the binoculars I realized that there were no tops to the trees. Honduras had been badly hit by Hurricane Mitch three months before and the stark skyline had us anxious to learn how these islands had fared.

11. The Bay Islands of Honduras & Guatemala, including the Rio Dulce

When we lived in Antigua in the 1960's this region of the Gulf of Honduras was referred to as the 'unknown Caribbean'. Most who sailed between Florida and the Panama Canal bypassed Honduras, Guatemala and Belize, although during the early '70s a few adventurous charter operations tried their luck, in particular Caribbean Sailing Yachts. But the area never really caught on and even today we found very few boats in this fascinating region of contrasts.

Geographically and culturally, the attractions of the Gulf of Honduras are untold. To the southeast, the charming Honduran Bay Islands reminded us of the undeveloped eastern Caribbean of the '60s. To the southwest, in the bight of the Gulf, Guatemala's Rio Dulce not only offers a spectacular jungle gorge, but also ranks as one of the best hurricane holes in the western Caribbean. Guatemala is the most scenic of the Central American countries and a boat can be safely left at one of the many marinas in the Rio for inland travel and visits to Mayan ruins. To the north, Belize features the second largest barrier reef in the world, surpassed in magnitude only by Australia's Great Barrier Reef.

Although the Honduran mainland coast is not very hospitable to sailors, the Honduran Bay Islands are a cruiser's paradise. Stretching 75 miles, 20-30 miles offshore, they consist of three main islands, Guanaja, Roatán and Utila, along with several small cays, notably the Cayos

Cochinos. Utila to the west is low-lying and perched on the edge of the 100-fathom line, while Roatán and Guanaja are hilly, both rising straight out of the ocean depths and ringed by a fringing reef. Blessed with a climate cooled by the trades, a variety of excellent anchorages and an English and Spanish speaking populace unspoiled by tourism, the islands exude an old-world charm.

Rising to 1,300 feet, Guanaja can be sighted several miles off and there was plenty of time to assess the effects of Hurricane Mitch on the vegetation while heading over to the only sizeable community, the Guanaja Settlement. As *Bagheera* approached the south side of the island, the many cays became visible, several topped by homes. Andy finally found the quick-flashing green light on Pond Cay that marks the entrance to the channel. It had been difficult to spot with the town behind. Once through we headed over to Guanaja Settlement's west side to anchor.

"It seems strange that the town is on a cay, with the island so deserted behind," I commented.

"It must be because the terrain is so steep," he replied. "But I agree and the houses are so crammed together many seem to be toppling into the water."

Later we learnt that many of the original waterfront properties had been completely washed away during the hurricane. What we were seeing used to be the second tier.

Several *cayuco*-sized waterways crisscross the town, which is actually on two cays with the unusual names of Hog and Shin, giving homes access by water as well as by the narrow walkways. As we made our way to the Port Captain's office the town exuded character with its busy shops and wooden homes often perched on stilts, and we were drawn by the cheering spectators to the lively basketball game at its center.

The Port Captain was looking at his watch as we entered. It was 3:30 on a Friday afternoon! After studying our documents carefully, his face lit up.

"Your exit papers from San Andreas say your landfall is Roatán," he commented.

"Yes," we replied. "The officials insisted on putting Roatán. Does it matter? We're leaving for Roatán on Sunday, but understood this was also a Port of Entry."

He was beaming now. "Leaving on Sunday, no problem. Enjoy Guanaja and clear in at Roatán next week." He left the office with us, pointing out the good variety of stores on the way to the bank.

"The Settlement has a considerable shrimp fleet and is quite prosperous," he informed us. "You should be able to get anything you want."

First we needed some Honduran lempira. The bank was busy and as we waited in line a couple rushed up, greeting us by name! They had last seen Andy while he was on a business trip to Antigua but they had left their Caribbean yacht charter business to try their luck ashore. Tragically they had just finished three cabins on the northeast coast when Mitch hit. It had been a terrifying experience having to shelter in a ditch with their bird, dog and five cats, while huge waves pounded over their homes and 180-knot winds flung the debris over the hill. Only concrete foundations and water tanks remained.

The hurricane's path was quite extraordinary," they told us. "It was originally forecast to hit Jamaica and the Cayman Islands, but it deflected south and the eye tracked backwards and forwards off Guanaja for three days. Unbelievably, while we were being devastated the west end of Roatán was barely affected."

The next morning we woke to strong winds, heavy rain, constant lightning and thunder, although nothing compared to hurricane forces. On the radio there was great debate by the weather buffs as to whether the cold front had hit, or whether these conditions were caused by a trough which had slowed the front down. Whichever, it was great to be at anchor and not on the high seas. An English woman ashore suggested we go round to El Bight, as it is a sheltered anchorage with good holding and pleasant beaches. She had originally arrived by boat and told us that there was quite a community of former cruisers ashore there.

Touring around the bay on arrival we found the many wrecks quite eerie. A German sailboat was up on the beach with no keel but there was a power cable to it. Did someone still live aboard, we wondered? Derelict fishing and transportation boats had been run up the beach and were rusting away. There was a wooden sailing vessel for sale with an extreme bend in its mast, and a fiberglass boat on its side; although the mast and fittings were intact the Aries windvane had been stripped.

There were two other international yachts at anchor, one German and the other Canadian, from Vancouver. Walking ashore we were beckoned up to a home to have tea and were surprised to find that we had several mutual friends in common. Michael and Angela were obviously avid gardeners but we were fascinated that plants were bursting with growth.

"Weren't you affected by the hurricane?" Andy asked.

"We battened everything down and put the shutters over all the windows," Angela replied, "but most of the wind went overhead, although the leaves were stripped off everything in the garden."

"But it looks wonderful now," I commented. "I've never seen hibiscus with so many blooms, and the leaves look so healthy and shiny."

"We had a huge amount of rain afterwards and then sun. Plant life rejuvenates so quickly in the tropics and our garden has never looked better, although the palms and fruit trees have suffered."

They came for a sundowner on board and brought spectacular apricot-colored double hibiscus blooms. Later, we were warmly welcomed at the local Hotel Manatee, where many of the settlers had gathered; mostly Germans, British and Canadians we noticed.

"Sorry, supplies are limited after Mitch," the German owner apologized. "There's only beer, rum and soft drinks available."

The restaurant was doing good business with goulash, rice and potatoes. Many of the locals had stayed here during the hurricane and they joked, "Although the roof on the top floor was blown off our biggest concern was running out of rum!"

The barometer was still at 1020. The front had supposedly passed to the east and the forecast was 25-30 knots of wind. We decided to leave as it was only a short trip of about 20 miles to Roatán and it was deceivingly calm in the anchorage! Transiting through the reef was tricky and the passage between the islands in the big, sloppy waves extraordinarily uncomfortable, but soon we were in the lee of Roatán.

The largest of the Bay Islands, Roatán is 28 miles long and between two and four miles wide. The north coast is surrounded by reefs that rise from the deep ocean bed, but the few passages that give access to protected anchorages are not accessible in a 'norther'. In contrast the south coast has several fine inlets that cut back into the steep hills. Protected by a shallow reef, they offer a choice of many secure anchorages.

A trip to Pigeon Cays at the east end of Roatán had originally been on our itinerary but these formerly picturesque sandy spits had been devastated by the hurricane so we continued along the south shore to Port Royal. This 2 1/2 mile bay, backed by lush vegetation, brilliantly colored water and protected by a string of pretty sandy off-lying cays, offers a variety of anchorages.

We decided to head to the west side where there were several other boats and the first one we came to was *Cygnus*. I had been talking to Carol on the radio since Costa Rica so we exchanged excited words of greeting with curious appraisals as to what we each looked like. It can be quite a shock to meet the body of the 'voice' when it doesn't fit one's mental image; I'm always amused when people say that I look just like my voice!

We'd barely finished anchoring when a powerboat came alongside.

"Hi, fellow Canadians. Would you like to go down the coast for lunch?"

"Sounds great," we chorused.

A quick batten-down and lock-up and we roared off to Jonesville, coming alongside the Hole in the Wall pub. Standing on stilts, perched over the water like many of the locals' homes, this great bar and restaurant exuded atmosphere. During a huge buffet-style late lunch we met several other yachties and ex-pats. One of the group was the owner of the small marina in Oak Ridge, where we hoped to do a good scrub-down and laundry before our next guest arrived, so arrangements were easily made.

'What an amazing arrival this has been.' I noted in my journal before turning in. 'It quite made up for the uncomfortable passage.'

The following day the owners of the powerboat, Terry and Patrice, took us ashore to their attractive home. Like many of the expatriate houses around the bay it was perfectly designed for the tropics, with a rewarding garden developing before their eyes. Doors, frames and much of their furniture had been fashioned by Honduran carvers from the mainland, and the woodwork, artistry and subtle coloring were stunning. Each guestroom portrayed a different theme with fishes, lizards and gorgonians all depicted in real-life scenes.

Their three tame parrots were full of character. Andy took one on his shoulder and while the bird nibbled his ear bright green droppings appeared down his white shirt! The other birds were obviously jealous of the attention and started to quarrel on the back of Patrice's chair.

"Shush, that's not good Valentine's Day behavior," she admonished them smiling, and they immediately stopped!

As we were heading for the pass en route to Oak Ridge we heard *Segue* call *Cygnus* in the VHF, "What's the name of the Canadian boat? They're going to go aground!"

"Thanks for the warning, but we're OK," I called back. "We checked it out while diving yesterday."

We had noticed that several coral 'bommies' projected beyond the buoy and had noted the extent of the outer reef, but we appreciated their concern.

The port of Oak Ridge is just five miles down the coast and after entering the channel at right angles, as instructed, we continued into the bay for the night. Not only was *Bagheera* soon hard aground in the mud, we were immediately surrounded by canoes and while some kids frantically bailed their boats others were chanting, "Give us a dollar."

As we back off the gooey bottom I had a flashback of the wonderful welcome and gifts of fruit or fish that we had been given on previous travels and was saddened. Finally I told them. "I'm happy to pay you for a service but you shouldn't expect me to give you money for nothing."

One of the boys clinging to our topsides turned to his friends, "I told you so. That's what my mum said!" There was instant laughter, then many suggestions for work and services poured forth. 'They could get us ice, their mother would do our laundry, they could clean or paint or take the garbage?'

It was nearly dark so I suggested they come back early the following morning. Unfortunately by the time they showed up it was mid-afternoon and we were just raising the anchor. But they proved willing by suggesting they take the garbage so I gave them some lampiras and a huge box of Corn Flakes, left over from the Christmas invasion. As we motored around to the marina we could see a cluster of canoes astern with kids holding out a hand for their ration, their faces alight with their engaging smiles.

We were interested that these black children spoke English, albeit a patois, when Spanish is the Honduran language. The reason was easily explained. Although Columbus visited Guanaja on his fourth visit to the New World in 1502, the Spanish settlements never prospered and the area became a refuge for the many British, as well as some French and Dutch pirates who preyed on the treasure fleets of the Spanish Main. Henry Morgan made his base in Port Royal in the mid-seventeenth century and at that time it is estimated that there were 5000 pirates in residence. Later more British arrived to work the mainland forests, contributing to a further white English-speaking population.

The Spanish shipped the indigenous Maya and Aztec islanders to work in the plantations of Cuba and mines of Mexico, so the British introduced black Caribs, a racial mix of Carib Indians, Africans and Europeans, from the Caribbean island of St. Vincent. Many of their descendents now live in picturesque fishing villages, with clapboard houses perched on piles, like the one close-by. Wandering down its main pathway later we realized that the abrupt steep hills were indeed the reason that these communities are right at the water's edge. We found Oak Ridge one of Roatán's most attractive towns and after the heat of the day were energized by the laughter of happy kids swinging on hammocks, playing ball games and hopscotch.

Local transportation is mostly in large canoes, *cayucos* that weave in and out of the mangroves along coastal canals. With its sizable shrimper fleet the harbor was busy and many colorful *cayucos* buzzed back and forth as *Bagheera* headed for the marina. Other cruisers came to give us a hand as we wriggled through the mud to get alongside the dock. With much heaving and engine revving we were finally within reach of fresh water. Full of enthusiasm Andy flooded the deck and, as ports were still open, much of below! The washing machine ashore was soon put to use. The laundry dried quickly in the tropical breeze on the clothesline strung between palm trees and I could get the cabin ready for our next guest.

A taxi took me along the crest of the hills on the only road that runs the length of the island. Although green and lush there was not much cultivatation, but new homes and a few hotels were springing up. After a satisfactory shop at Alden's supermarket in French Town I went to the airport where Nancy was already waiting, having caught an earlier flight. It was great to see my next door neighbor and as we drove back to the boat she filled me in on the news from home. As usual there was a large bundle of mail, some interesting, and the inevitable bills that didn't fit into the category of being automatically paid.

On the Northwest Caribbean Net the next morning we were given the latitude and longitude co-ordinates for crossing the bar at the entrance of the Rio Dulce for the greatest depth, 7'3" they assured us, which sounded promising. We also learnt the Balboa Yacht Club in Panama had burnt down.

"Just as well," commented Andy. "It couldn't have stood much longer!"

The sea was glassy calm for a motor to French Harbour, the second largest principal town in Roatán after Coxen Hole, and the center for a large, modern fishing, shrimp and lobster fleet. A dive relieved the intense heat. Below all the fans were on 'high' and to catch the last drop of breeze windscoops were rigged once we had anchored.

We had been planning to go to the well-known French Harbour Yacht Club. Although we were beckoned to the dock, the club was closed as it was changing hands. Instead, we took a cab to Coxen Hole to clear into Roatán as required. The town seemed somewhat chaotic but was developing some character and Warren's supermarket supplied our provisioning needs. There were a few tourists in the handicraft shops, although we observed that most trinkets came from other countries in Central America.

The officials were pleasant and efficient and we could clear in and out simultaneously, although having been told the clearance fee was $30.00 it was somewhat of a shock when Immigration, Customs and the Municipal fees totaled $91!

With no wind forecast we needed fuel so I took the dinghy over to the Fantasy Island Resort after we had moved *Bagheera* out into the bay. What a contrast in tempo, but the American power boaters at the dock needed fuel themselves and said none was available.

When I turned on the radio for the net in the morning the conversation was already about our fueling needs.

I laughed to Nancy, "And people are always asking me how I can live in such isolation on board!"

As suggested we proceeded to the northeast corner of the commercial inlet and found gas but no diesel. Continuing further by dinghy we finally saw an outlet, although we had to walk out to the main road to pay the bill at the Texaco station. Its module, including the mini market, looked just like those in the States and I felt transported to another world.

The west end of Roatán is a cruiser's and diver's paradise. A turquoise bay edged by white sands laced with palms, it became our favorite part of the island, although not a sheltered anchorage for a 'norther'. After passing uplifted coral we could suddenly see the beautiful bay where nine yachts lay peacefully bobbing at anchor. To add to the charm *Bagheera* was surrounded by dolphins. They were swimming at the bow, then there were more out to sea, then more still on the shore side. Large and light in color, as always they were an exhilarating sight.

A dinghy came rushing out of the pass. After a quick foray with the dolphins they came over to lead us into the anchorage. It was Bruce and Jennifer from *Tabula*, with whom I'd also been talking for several weeks on the 'Central American Breakfast Club' radio net.

"You must pass the entrance stake very close to port," Bruce instructed, "then immediately turn hard port to avoid a coral head."

The water was exceptionally clear and it seemed we must go aground, but all was well and Andy was most relieved when we finally anchored in ten feet, even if it did look like two!

"What a beautiful area," sighed Nancy. "The surreal colors give the impression that the reef goes on for ever."

Such clear water demanded an immediate snorkel and it was fabulous being able to see the beautiful coral gardens, fish and acres of queen conch that were over 25' down, as though they were just in front of one's eyes.

During a sundowner on board Bruce and Jennifer told us how they had left South Africa to cruise the world in a ferrocement boat, but finding interesting work on arriving in the United States they had stayed to build up the cruising kitty. Now they are happy to have their fiberglass Palmer Johnson and an open-ended timetable. Succulent barbecued chicken and wahoo (fish) ended a great day at a party ashore. Nancy and I even managed to get Andy dancing despite the predictable instant 'bad knee'!

We enjoyed the pretty flower-filled village on the hill and walked the sandy beach road lined with dive shops and restaurants that rambled around the bay. It was time to get going but we were finding it hard to leave this idyllic setting. The weather made our decision with a 'norther' hitting earlier than predicted. Although forecast to be slow and weak it rushed down from the States in two days and was vicious. The dark skies and rain squalls did not bode well for a visit to the recommended Cayos Cochinos, especially as we had heard that one was not permitted anchor but had to tie to mooring buoys that are quite suspect. Instead, we pointed *Bagheera* to the west to visit Utila, the third large island in this group.

Utila is low lying and swampy with its rise, Pumpkin Hill, a landmark. The large Bay of Puerto Este was sheltered although we had to search hard for the channel markers. It was pouring with rain.

"I thought this was the dry season," commented Nancy.

"It is in the Eastern Caribbean," I replied, "but here the wet season is from October to February with March and August the hottest months."

Despite the weather we enjoyed the atmosphere ashore as we waded though puddles along the concrete path. Although some of the houses are old, many are beautifully kept with well-tended gardens. Enthusiastic groups of young people could be seen in the numerous dive shops along the shore, eagerly discussing the day's activities and plans for tomorrow. We decided to stop at the busy Mermaid Restaurant and found they served a delicious tuna special. As we dinghied back to *Bagheera* the rain finally stopped, the skies cleared and later the stars appeared for a perfect night.

An early start took us to the popular diving areas to the west past Suck-suck and Pigeon Cays, more simply known as Up and Down, that are picturesquely crowded with more clapboard houses on stilts. Although it took a while to find a sandy spot to anchor, the reef diving is excellent here with large coral formations, dramatic drop-offs and many beautiful fish, a true representation of the extension of the Belize barrier reef to the north. Apparently this is the cheapest place in the world to get a diving certificate and what a great place to do it.

There was a good 15-20 knot breeze from the northeast and a two-knot current with us for the passage to the Rio Dulce. Often surging at over eight knots, *Bagheera* made a rapid passage along Honduras' spectacular mountainous, but almost harborless, north coast although beam seas sometimes tossed her about unexpectedly, causing Nancy to get a few bruises. Nancy had never been sailing until a charter to Tonga five years ago and has subsequently joined us in the Virgin Islands and Pacific Northwest. Her enthusiasm, together with her help with the 'housework' below, more than makes up for any lack of expertise.

In the past, men were in greatest demand as crew because of the muscle power needed on deck. Modern rigs with furling gear have changed all that; Andy and I can easily handle the deck routine without help. Now having someone to help below is the best asset, especially as one tends to cook more gourmet dishes when one has guests. If we have several visitors on board we alternate duty days. Cooking and galley duties one day and clean-up duties both below and on deck the next. When there are six on board each couple has every third day off. It works really well. Otherwise, we find everyone feels they should be helping so no one relaxes and the boat quickly feels over-crowded.

The Caribbean coast of Guatemala is short and were it not for the Rio Dulce and enticing inland travel most sailors would probably pass it by, instead heading straight for the southern cays of Belize whose lights we had seen on the starboard beam during the night. The fact that many who visit this river stay for months, even years, had piqued our curiosity. It would be a struggle to cross the bar at the entrance with our draft, but we were determined to try.

There was plenty of time to get organized before the afternoon high tide when the trades are at their strongest and the sea piles up against the outpouring river. Over a foot may be gained at this time, we had been told, with waves giving an additional lift over the hard sand. Jerry cans of fuel were loaded into the dinghy to give extra weight for hauling *Bagheera* on her side, a pulley was attached to the end of the boom and halyard prepared for heeling the boat from the top of the mast. Although our confidence had been boosted by information given on the radio that there was 7'3" clearance over the bar, our guides and other cruisers informed us otherwise, with those drawing 6' crossing with the odd bump and those drawing 6'6" having a struggle. To reduce our estimated 7'2" draft (we'd raised the waterline more than once!) to even 6'6" would require *Bagheera* to be heeled over so that the toe rail was in the water, hard to accomplish with only an 8' 6" inflatable dinghy.

The co-ordinates for the bar were prominently placed on the chart table and we motored the ten miles across to the entrance marker located at latitude 15° 50.18'N and longitude 88° 43.80'W early. We seemed so prepared and conditions were perfect, but I still had a sense of foreboding as we headed 200 yards to the west of the buoy and planned as instructed to come in on 225°T.

Just as we were approaching the shallows a local boat roared up asking us if we would like a guide. I wanted to try by ourselves first but uncharacteristically Andy jumped at the idea, negotiating the $30.00 asked to $20.00. He rationalized that if we refused now they could charge an extortional fee if we needed help later, which made sense.

Juan came on board, standing at the bow with Andy. He kept insisting that I should go left, which worried me as everyone had told us, 'If in doubt keep right'. With a feeling of helplessness I turned port again and *Bagheera* went hard aground with an abrupt thud. We were now in 4 feet of water; all the more frustrating as it seemed to be a complete set-up.

We tried everything to get free, heeling the boat with the dinghy, rocking it and spinning the wheel but to no avail. We suggested they take the halyard from their larger vessel and pull us over from the top of the mast, but instead of pulling *Bagheera* on her side they roared forward at full throttle.

Desperate they would break the mast, we shouted and shouted for them to stop. Unaware, they continued revving their engines. We were sure that any minute the mast would snap, as we were being dragged into even shallower water. They finally stopped when the depth sounder read three feet. Whichever way they pulled us after that the sounder read 3-5 feet. In despair we agreed they should fetch a bigger boat.

It was a relief when they left, and we could catch our breath. Then suddenly, as we were discussing what to do next, the promised waves came in, getting bigger by the minute. Although we were banging the bottom it was not too jarring and as I turned the boat back on our original waypoint

Bagheera *hauled over to the gunwales*

course, and accelerated slowly and wriggled the keel, the depth increased to 5'8" to 6'. When Andy went out in the dinghy and pulled us over with the halyard we started to move through the mud. Then *Bagheera* leapt forward, momentarily free from the bottom at last.

Before I could throttle back, Andy was calling out. He was being towed backwards in the dinghy and sinking as water rushed over the stern! We helped him on board quickly; *Bagheera* was again plowing through the mud and we needed to keep up momentum. Finally, she was free, in deep water at last.

The officials came on board as soon as we had anchored in Livingston. They gave us a decal and instructed us to come ashore soon to pay fees and pick up the paperwork.

Several boys lined the dock, each wanting to be our boat boy. We have learnt from the Eastern Caribbean that when there is such competition it is prudent to pick one and pay him a nominal fee to look after the dinghy. We chose Elmer who we recognized and had seemed efficient out at the bar. Unlike most kids he had fair curly hair and freckles. There were many different ethnic groups to be seen as we walked up the main street of this town with its attractive stores, restaurants and lovely hotel. Most were Black Caribs but the Mayan women were distinctive in full striped skirts and loose lace tops. The officials were charming and, although it was now evening, all paperwork was completed with no extra charges.

The mist was rising when we lifted the anchor at dawn and entered a truly magical jungle gorge that twists and turns for over six miles. Dramatic 300-foot cliffs are highlighted by lush vegetation dotted with blooms of orchids, bromeliads, passionflowers and the large red bottle-brush Zapotón. As hoped at this time of day the trees were crowded with birds, their calls echoing as they swooped down the steep limestone walls.

Thatch-roofed dwellings straddle the water's edge, young kids gazed as we passed, cute and curious, while their mothers slapped laundry on the rocks with great gusto. The river was a hive of activity, Mayan dugout canoes following the traditions of their heritage, some fishing, others taking freshly baked goods to market. As Livingston cannot be reached by land, faster boats crowded with people also rushed by, as did canoes carrying school children smartly clad in uniform.

We anchored by sulfur springs and after a hot climb to a stalactite cave had a relaxing soak. Then, all too soon, the river opened into El Golfete, 'little gulf', the lake that would take us to our final destination.

A side channel led us to Salvador Laguna for the night through carpets of water hyacinths. It gave a tranquil anchorage and we had a number of local visitors. The informative display at the Manatee Park was enjoyable as was getting some exercise walking along its lush rain-forest trail the following morning. As usual there was a good breeze to sail the ten miles down El Golfete and soon we were viewing marinas through the binoculars, trying to identify them from our guide. Beyond stood the picturesque old Spanish fort of Castillo San Felipe, and Lago de Izabal that provides further cruising opportunities.

Mario's Marina is popular with those who like to stay aboard long term. We decided to visit for a drink at the bar, hoping to get some advice about inland travel, only to find everyone was arriving exotically dressed for a masked ball!

"Welcome to the Rio," was a frequent greeting after we had paid the entrance fee.

For those looking for a place to winter in their boat this is a nurturing, friendly community, and the active cruiser's net every morning at 7:30 on Channel 69 is highly informative about the many local events whether in the marinas or ashore, and for inland travel.

With three days left to organize a tour of Guatemala and to prepare the boat for friends, who would be staying on board while we returned to Vancouver to complete our taxes, the boat was a hive of activity.

As is usual at such times I completed chores ashore while Andy serviced the boat. Then Nancy and I loaded, stowed and organized *Bagheera* back into a habitable state. With a travel agent in Mario's our trip was easily arranged. *Bagheera* was taken around to Hacienda Tijac, a small marina and shoreside cabins with an attractive international atmosphere, also conveniently close to Fronteras for shopping and our friends' arrival. The town has excellent stores and market, we told them in our copious notes.

Nancy and I also visited the Casa Guatemala Orphanage by dinghy, armed with gifts of clothing. Several enthusiastic volunteers from around the world greeted us and a Dutch girl offered to give us a tour. The facilities were basic but adequate we felt, although there was a shortage of Spanish books. Another problem, an older French Canadian woman told us, was getting funding for a full-time co-ordinator to keep a consistent program in place, necessary as volunteers generally only stay for three months. Interestingly, we learnt that most of the children were not actually orphans but had been sent by their families who lived in remote locations where no schooling was available.

Rather than take the bus to Guatemala City and fly up to Tikál to see the Mayan ruins we had been able to arrange an economical direct flight on a small plane with Russell, an American now living in Guatemala.

"No wonder we couldn't weigh more than 500lbs in total," I commented on seeing its size. As you can imagine a total of 500lbs for three people with their luggage had been a challenge!

And so began a stunning week of inland touring. It is hard to put into words the magic of Tikál, the grandest of all the classic Mayan cities. Designated a UNESCO World Heritage Site in 1979 Tikál is to Guatemala what the Pyramids are to Egypt, a grand national symbol and source of pride.

Its exotic temples and thousands of other buildings in the process of being excavated, hold great mystique having lain lost for so long smothered by forest. Tikál National Park encompasses 222 square miles of jungle. About six square miles of central Tikál have been mapped revealing over 3000 buildings: temples, palaces, ceremonial platforms, residences, shrines, ballcourts, terraces, plazas, even a structure for the ritual sweat baths. There are also 200 stone monuments, *stelae* and altars and it is estimated that as many as 10,000 earlier platforms and buildings lie beneath. Excavations reveal over 1,100 years of continuous construction. More than 100,000 tools, ceremonial objects, ornaments and other items have been unearthed with particular treasures, especially jade, found in the tomb of Ah Cacau, one of Tikál's greatest rulers.

We found the brilliant orange of dawn and cool of dusk the most rewarding times to climb these temples of kings and to see a profusion of wildlife. The birds are deafening, their colors brilliant. Over 300 species have been recorded and we saw two types of toucan, many different parrots, yellow-breasted black-headed trojuns (related to the quetzal), swallow-tailed kites and woodpeckers besides the large Petén, ocellated, colorful turkeys that look rather like peacocks, that wander the grounds. The coatimundi (*pizote*), related to raccoons, are the great scavengers. Howler and spider monkeys frequently swung by our path. Agouti lurked in the brush, foxes crossed ahead, and our guide told us that deeper in the forest jaguars are common.

The heart of Tikál is the Great Plaza, a large grassy area with two grand temples at either end and ringed by terraces, palaces and ball courts. It is not only awe-inspiring to sit 160 feet high at the top of Temple II, the Temple of the Masks, and gaze across at Temple I, the Temple of the Giant Jaguar, it is also overwhelming to contemplate how this city, with a peak population in the 8th century AD estimated to be over 75,000, could have so mysteriously disappeared.

The old capital of Antigua is also a jewel, a beautiful city set amidst three magnificent volcanoes. After the great earthquake of 1773 destroyed the city, the capital was moved to Guatemala City but many returned to Antigua and the result is a charming town that has retained its Spanish

Colonial character of old homes, together with stark stone ruins. A tour by Elizabeth Bell, an American married to a Guatemalan who has been in Antigua for 30 years, gave us an insight into the country, politics, people, culture and history and an idea of how the town formerly looked, and the active restoration work in progress on buildings and paintings. She also showed us an example of the colorful, ornately designed carpet of sawdust (alfombras) that would line the streets for the famous Easter parade during Semana Santa (Holy Week). This is a busy time in Antigua when people don robes of purple to accompany the religious processions in remembrance of the Crucifixion.

The one-story buildings along the cobblestone streets are painted in bright yellows, blues and pinks. From the street little can be seen as life takes place in the central courtyard but if both wooden entrance doors were opened wide anyone was welcome to enter the courtyard; if only one was open, visitors could just go into the entrance. It was in these courtyards that we were first introduced to the Mayans' brilliantly colored dress. Colors and designs vary according to the region and some intricate fabrics and clothing were on display. Prices were high, however, as Antigua has become a tourist destination, so we saved our money for visits to the highland markets.

The name Chichicastenango sounded intriguing and reports from those who had been to this famous market in the highlands made a visit to this isolated town irresistible. We loved every moment, from the smoky fires and subdued atmosphere amongst the vendors the night before to the amazingly colorful vibrancy of the market itself. At 7:00am on Sunday morning clouds of incense rose from the top steps of the Iglesia de Santo Tomás while the bottom steps were covered with exotic tropical flowers. Chichi's main square was packed with vendors. The outer stalls were mostly tourist oriented with blankets, linens, carved masks and clothing in a huge variety of colors and design, while in the center lay products for the locals, yards of cloth for their skirts, fruit and vegetables, hardware and notions.

We were laden with purchases and glad a minibus could pick us up at our hotel and take us to Panachel on Lake Atitlán. Surrounded by volcanoes, the lake was a picture-perfect blue as we descended the steep road. Although this town is nicknamed Gringotenango (place of foreigners) we found some lovely colonial homes and gardens, with the climate allowing interesting mixes of bougainvillea, passionflowers and roses.

Our visit across the Lake to Santiago turned out to be the most intriguing part of our trip. Squeezed between two impressive volcanoes, Santiago is known for keeping to the traditional lifestyle of the Tzutuhil Maya. Sitting next to us was Dolores, a Guatemalan woman who spoke English, having spent several years in the United States. We admired her blouse, a work of art of finely embroidered animals and flowers.

"It took me three years to make," she told us, "and the designs are typical of this area."

She was originally from Santiago and gave tours of the town. Having told her we wanted to focus on the Mayan culture we were surprised when our first stop was the Catholic church. Once inside she pointed out that it was lined with wooden statues of Mayan gods. Apparently the non-Christian Maya had no place of worship and the Catholic Church needed more congregation, so this shared arrangement works all round! All the effigies were beautifully dressed, apparently changed each year and the god of fertility, decked in purple, had a place of honor near the altar.

Several back streets and uneven cobblestone roads later we entered

Mayan fertility god

what appeared to be someone's home. Here resided the effigy of Maximón, who is based both on the Catholic saints and Mayan deities dating back to the conquest by Pedro de Alvarado in the 16th century, although the image dates back to the 11th century. His large head is carved from the branch of a 'Palo de Pito'. He is dressed to be someone of 'means' shown by his elegant hat, fancy trousers, coat and many silk scarves. He likes cigars, considered a symbol of earth, and there is always one in his mouth. He understands the problems of ordinary men and women and will do favors for things he likes, such as candles, liquor, cigars etc. As far as we could gather, after a good evening of partying with these offerings, sins are forgiven by morning! Although shunned by other towns, Maximón is revered here and is paraded all over town on the Wednesday of Holy Week.

Maximón is supposed to change homes every year, Dolores told us, but as not many people have enough room it had been in this house for three years. That an effigy of Jesus Christ lay in a glass box at the far end of the room seemed not to matter at all; we were realizing that here, as elsewhere, Christianity and ancient religions can co-exist. Lastly, she took us to another home with effigies, where incense burned and men were chanting to a guitar, praying for a good crop of corn. The room was ornately decorated and even the men were wearing 3/4 length striped pants with embroidered designs of the town on the bottom.

As we walked back to our hotel, Dolores told us how life had been very troubled for the Mayans during the 36 years of civil war with suppression, hardship and frequent killings during dictatorships, military rule, coups and guerilla wars. Since peace accords were signed in 1996 life has improved dramatically and now the Mayans, who comprise 44% of the 12.6 million population, are starting to move forward with education and jobs becoming available.

"Finally, we can show we are proud of our culture," she concluded smiling. " You know it has withstood five centuries of European occupation and domination."

The lake was steaming with tendrils of mist, while the sun blazed on the volcano behind, as we walked to the ferry along the lakeside cliff early the next morning. Below, many Mayan women had gathered, sociably busy with laundry, their flat-bottomed boats neatly caressing the curves of the beach. Those alighting from the ferry were colorfully wrapped in woven shawls and many effortlessly carried large baskets of goods on their heads.

In all of our travels, Guatemala is one of the most exotic countries we've visited. With increased tourism many amenities are springing up.

The inexpensive minibuses, transporting from hotel to hotel, are a much simpler and less fraught way of traveling than riding the local 'chicken' bus, although we had a most comfortable trip from Guatemala City to Fronteras on our return to *Bagheera* in a local bus that even had air-conditioning.

Recently a new road has been opened from Guatemala City to Flores to visit Tikál, so it is no longer necessary to fly or take a tortuous 15-hour ride along rutted roads. Do go soon before it gets too crowded. Sit atop the 200-foot high Temple 1V at dawn to enjoy exquisite peace, then glory in the wondrous sight of Tikál's temples, vibrant again, as towering through the canopy of gracious trees, their peaks are bathed in a golden gift from the new sun.

12. Belize and
The Yucatan

With taxes and businesses in order in Vancouver we returned to *Bagheera* in the Rio Dulce full of enthusiasm for our next six months of cruising. Provisions had already been bought and stowed by friends Nick, Rosana and ten-year-old Renata, and we left at 6:00am for another magical ride through the jungle gorge.

"Remember to be back by 12:30pm for the tide," Andy cautioned as Rosana, Renata and I climbed into the dinghy at Livingston.

Again the officials were charming and the paperwork to clear out of Guatemala was completed in under an hour, although they managed to relieve us of another $60. There were many attractive choices to spend the remaining quetzals extracted from everyone's pockets on the way back to the boat but the anchor was weighed in good time for the 1:30pm high tide.

Optimism was high about crossing the bar successfully, with a survey of depths completed by a cruiser two months earlier. But no such luck! Although we used the co-ordinates of the deepest channel (Lat. 15° 49′300, Long. 88° 44′775 and Lat. 15° 50′150 Long. 88° 43′775) which showed just a small section down at 6′5″, *Bagheera* was soon hard aground. Using the halyard from the masthead, Nick tried hauling us over with our dinghy but again it took a larger local boat to get her toe-rail in the water and achieve the necessary reduction to our draft.

"Thank goodness for a well-built boat, cast iron keel and robust rig," was Andy's only comment when *Bagheera* was happily back floating in the Caribbean Sea.

Two hours later we were in Belize and for such a small country it made a big impression. Not only did we find the azure waters, exotic snorkeling and hundreds of islands stunning, we also loved our trips ashore in this pristine Central American democracy that has a British heritage, peaceful coup-free history and its own fascinating Mayan ruins.

Geographically, Belize forms the southeast region of the Yucatan Peninsula, a narrow strip of land squeezed between the ocean and eastern Guatemala, with Mexico's Yucatan to the north. Just 8,867 square miles in area, it seems much larger in attractions and diversity. Although in the heart of Central America it is, in several aspects, quite different from its neighbors. Along its eastern shore the country is blessed with 174 miles of reef, the Western Hemisphere's largest barrier reef and second in the world to the one in Australia, with three easily accessed offshore atolls. Behind the reef calm seas give exhilarating sails in the 15-20 knot tradewinds, although depths have to be watched carefully, and the coast offers hundreds of usually deserted anchorages.

Inland, Belize has its own Mayan temples that, although smaller than those of Guatemala, Honduras and the Yucatan, are poignantly beautiful. The tropical forests to the west have scenic rivers and limestone caves, and intriguing diverse animal and plant populations with several species that are on the endangered list. That Belize cares for its natural and cultural resources is evident in the immaculate way the country is kept and we were told 40% of the land is protected in some form.

Northerly winds and an adverse current necessitated motoring to reach Moho Cays, a group of five islands, before dusk.

"Can we go ashore?" asked Renata. She had been very patient during the long day on the boat so we went to South Moho Cay in the dinghy, a sandy island that is shaded with tall, stately palms. A local couple welcomed us and as we explored Renata was full of enthusiasm.

"Those termite nests are huge," she pointed, "and look at all the shells over there on the beach."

The large queen conch shells are very decorative with their shiny bright pink apertures and we searched without success for one that did not have a hole in the back. The holes are made by locals to release the body of the mollusk from the shell for eating, and obviously all of these had been collected for food.

"Don't worry," I assured her, "we will find many more."

The grassy bottom under the boat looked promising conch country and Renata was ready to go snorkeling at dawn. Although there were no queen conchs, we were rewarded with hundreds of brilliant orange fighting conchs that lay cunningly hidden in the sand.

Heading north up the coast *Bagheera* was soon inside the barrier reef, evidenced by her motion in the calmer seas. There are several recommended anchorages on these southerly outer cays that are 20 miles offshore in the south, but we would miss them as we were heading for Placencia, one of the few communities on the coast, to clear in.

The river at Big Creek, west of Placencia Point, is narrow but well buoyed as it is an important citrus, banana and fishing port. As we circled around looking for a spot to anchor, a large shadow appeared underwater beside us.

"Look Renata, it's a manatee," said Nick excitedly.

"We saw similar animals in Australia," I told Renata and that Duncan had read that they are related to elephants!

Manatees are commonly found in the inner mangrove islands, but in our time in Belize this was our only sighting. These were grayish brown in color and about ten feet in length. The average adult weighs 1000 lbs, with a vast 3,500-lb maximum recorded. They have big bellies, small flippers and an efficient paddle-shaped tail. The two pectoral flippers that are commonly used for steering are very flexible and we found it fascinating that they could also bring plant food to their mouths.

At Customs Andy and I filled out the necessary forms, then had to wait for the paperwork to be completed in the back office. Two Guatemalans walked in, and after glancing at Andy one said,

"I recognize you. Have you been in any of the yachting magazines?"

Somewhat surprised Andy answered. "A few, as Liza is a writer."

The man went to the desk to sign the book under our entry. When he got up he came straight over to me. "I know who you are now," he told me. "You are Liza Copeland and I have your book *Just Cruising* on board."

We had run into several people who had the books but it was most surprising to be talking to a Guatemalan who kept my book on board his game fishing boat!

"I bought it on a visit to the United States," he explained. "My dream is to take the family cruising in the Mediterranean as you did."

We went to Immigration together. The taxi driver wanted $20, but agreed on $5.00 when he realized another taxi was on its way! As Canadians we didn't need visas but one was necessary for Rosana, a Brazilian. She had fortunately acquired this in advance but it was a reminder that we should always warn our guests of different nationalities to check both visa requirements and time limitations.

Situated on a long sandy spit, the fishing village of Placencia is fast becoming a backpackers' haven and favorite place to charter for dives on the outer reef. It was warm ashore as we wandered under the swaying palms down a concrete path close to the crescent-shaped beach, even hotter returning along a dirt track which gave views of the mangrove covered islands to the west. Built on coarse river sand between these two routes lie colorful houses on stilts that comprise the bulk of the town.

Enticing aromas led us to the bakery. School was in progress and a couple of grocery stores providing the basics were doing good business. Fish could be purchased, we understood, at the fisherman's co-op, and fuel at the dock, although as yet no one had appeared to serve Andy who had been waiting with our jerry cans.

There were nine other boats in the protected anchorage east of Placencia. "I had expected more from the radio check-ins on the Northwest Caribbean net," I commented, "but it will be fun to get together with other cruisers and find out where they have been."

Almost immediately Keith from *Wingstar*, a Canadian boat first seen in Guanaja, was over to invite us to sundowner drinks on board their spacious Fraser 51. Here we learnt that most cruisers had spent a month or two in the Rio Dulce and were now on their way north before the hurricane season. We were particularly pleased to meet Denis and Arleen from *Tiger Lilly*. A retired meteorologist from Toronto, Dennis had not only been active in the net providing weather information, he had made a point of teaching cruisers how to read the weatherfaxes that many were receiving through their SSB radios onto their laptops. We had met several new cruisers recently who depended on others' interpretations of the weather and decisions for passage-making, and had been concerned about their lack of independent judgement that is so fundamental to safe boating.

It was estimated that there were a mere forty yachts cruising in Belize. When we pored over the chart that night and saw the hundreds of islands north of us, we realized there would probably be few other groups of boats such as this one. The problem of cruising the area for us lay in the shallow depths. Although reasonable in the channel close to shore up to Belize City, between the inner cays and outer barrier reef it is extremely shallow with numerous patches of poorly charted reefs that would be hard to pilot through with our draft of over seven feet.

Although the many inner mangrove cays have excellent anchorages it is the outer barrier reef that provides the clear water, wonderful growths of coral and tropical fish that we all wanted to see.

With Andy at the bow it was a tense motor through the Blue Ground Range, with the depth sounder flashing down to 8.5 feet, then on out to

South Water Cay. Not only was it tricky to weave through the shallow patches, the water was frequently murky so that although the sun was high there was no advance warning of reefs.

"Maybe we should go back," said Andy, after an hour with often only a foot of water under our keel.

"But we haven't gone aground yet," Nick and I chorused, "and it's still early in the day." We continued on slowly, finally arriving at the outer reef mid-afternoon.

"What a magical spot, I'm so glad we came," said Andy coming back from the foredeck after the anchor was down. "It's even a sheltered anchorage and surprisingly deep, relatively speaking of course."

South Water Cay, just north of one of the passes through the reef, is a true tropical paradise. Although there are three resorts, they are small and informal, barely intruding on the peace of the palms as we walked to the spectacular sandy spit with its brilliant turquoise water.

During a drink ashore that night we discussed Nick and Rosana's departure plans, sad that they had to return to Vancouver two days later.

"It's such a shame to have to leave this spot," said Rosana. "This is just how we had imagined Belize."

"I wonder if you could get a ride back to the mainland on a resort boat?" I suggested. "then take a bus to Belize City."

"Yes, I think that launch anchored off is for passengers," Andy agreed.

"I'll check tomorrow morning," decided Nick.

With no difficulty we arranged with Jennifer in the Zoological Institute that Nick, Rosana, Renata and I could go to Dangriga on their passenger boat. It could also bring back Alison, my eldest stepdaughter and her family who were arriving from Vancouver later in the day. This was a perfect arrangement not only because their launch would travel many times faster than *Bagheera*, but also because Dangriga was an open roadstead so not a viable anchorage. As well as buses there were many inexpensive flights to the capital. Plans in order, we could finally go snorkeling!

The mini reef right off the beautiful beach was picture perfect and just below the surface. It took me back to the early days of snorkeling with our sons when Renata grabbed my hand; we pointed out, identified and treasured the sights together.

"It's so beautiful," she said at last, taking out her snorkel for a quick break.

"I can't believe the number of fish, and the coral is spectacular," I agreed.

A woman swam over. "I just wanted to tell you that this reef is protected by the Audubon Society," she told us smiling at our enthusiasm, "and to ask you to be careful not to touch the coral with your flippers." The Society is very active in Belize we noticed subsequently, managing several areas that were established under the National Parks system of 1981.

Dinghying through the channel to the outer reef and drifting along in the strong current we found everything much bigger and grander. It was also much rougher and even our mini reef became more turbulent in the afternoons and far less of a haven.

Some hospitable Guatemalans invited us to join them for snacks on the beach, then Rosana cooked a delicious final dinner of beef and eggplant Brazilian style. It had been great having the Fletcher family on board, another sailing memory for them on *Bagheera*. Not only had they cruised with us previously, they had also taken the boat by themselves, and a special memory was bringing *Bagheera* back to Vancouver from the Queen Charlotte Islands.

It was a smooth 40-minute ride in the resort boat to Dangriga, through the Tobacco Range and across the inner channel.

"Any chance you could deliver some cars for me as you'll be in town all day?" asked Jennifer, who besides running the resort also has a car rental business.

"No problem," I replied enthusiastically. "It'll be a great chance to look around."

"Despite being Belize's second largest town, its not that big," replied Jennifer laughing. "But it will also give you a chance to go to the store and market."

I'd soon not only been through town but also to the airport, much to the Fletcher's surprise, and stocked up for the next week. I noticed that many of its 8000 inhabitants were Garifunas (black Caribs). Their ancestors had been deported to the Bay Islands of Honduras from St. Vincent by the British in 1797, I was informed, and Dangriga is now the center for Garifuna folk culture, with a festival every November to re-enact their first arrival here in Stann Creek in 1823.

Approximately 7% of the country's population of 250,000 is Garifuna, with 11% Mayan, 30% Creole (descendants of the African slaves and British pirates) and 44% Mestizo (Spanish and Indian). Added to this mixture are Swiss-German Mennonite farmers, Chinese and Lebanese traders and increasing numbers from Europe, North America and neighboring countries. We found the mix of cultures fascinating and loved the laid-back atmosphere in this country. The national language is English, which makes life easy, although with the Creole patois we didn't always recognize it as such, and wherever we went people made us welcome.

The Maya and Carib Indians were the earliest inhabitants and Belize boasts important sites of some of the earliest Mayan settlements, such as Cuello that dates back to 2500 B.C.. While some Mayan sites have been excavated; hundreds still lie shrouded by jungle. By the time Columbus arrived in the western Caribbean in 1502 the great Mayan civilization had been gone for several hundred years. Like the other nations of the New World, what is now Belize was claimed by Spain but the lack of gold in the swamps and jungles of the coast quelled any desire to conquer the area.

Instead, the sheltered waters became a safe haven for pirates and it wasn't until 1638 that Peter Wallace, who had originally left England to hunt down pirates, founded the first settlement by the Belize River. The abundant mahogany and logwood soon became more profitable in the European markets than bounty from the high seas. Subsequently, Spain frequently attacked Belize but in the Treaty of Paris in 1763 Spain agreed to recognize the settlers' rights. Attacks did not cease, however, until the historic sea Battle of St. George's Cay in 1798, which is well documented in Belize City. With British Naval support the Spanish fleet of 32 ships was defeated.

A short time later in 1821 all Central American countries gained their independence; both Guatemala and Mexico then claimed the country. England rejected these claims. Mexico gave up her claim in 1893 but it wasn't until 1992 that Guatemala finally renounced hers, encouraged by Britain's assistance in building her a Caribbean port.

In 1964 British colony status was granted to British Honduras with internal self-government established. In 1981 the colony of British Honduras officially became an independent nation called Belize, a far more exotic-sounding word in Mayan than its translation of 'muddy waters', although the British still keep a small military presence there for defense.

"Maybe I should phone to make sure Alison's arrived," I said to Jennifer. I had suggested they relax at the Pelican Beach Resort and we would make contact there."

A few minutes later Steve was on the phone. "I can't believe this," he said after an initial greeting. "Here I am lying on a Caribbean beach finally away from the office, and I'm given a cell phone!"

"We came in a really small plane and flew over the reef," six-year-old Christopher told me excitedly about the trip from Belize City, when I went over to pick them up.

"And I've been swimming since the minute we got here," continued five-year-old Sarah.

"Great!" I responded. As we walked out to the car I explained to Alison that there would be a boat ride to get to *Bagheera*. Alison had been concerned that Christopher might be seasick, as he had felt queasy in a boat at home, and had hoped we could start in a calm anchorage.

"Yes, Nick and Rosana met our flight in Belize City and told us, so I've already given the kids medication," she assured me.

Unlike the morning, the sea was now quite choppy, especially at the shallow entrance to the creek.

"You remember how much you like Splash Mountain," I said to Christopher, recalling his trip to Disneyland. "Well, we're now going on a boat ride that will be just like that but much longer."

"Goody!" he cried, climbing into the launch enthusiastically.

Much to my relief he bounced on Alison's knee, full of beans, all the way to South Water Cay. In fact the only one to suffer was poor Alison who was sitting on the hard wooden seat. A bouncing seven-year old is no lightweight!

When we were home in Vancouver I'd helped Alison with Christopher's seventh birthday party. It had an underwater theme and the house was decorated with colorful tropical fish.

"On my real birthday I'll be snorkeling on a reef with live fish just like these," he told everyone and of course he was. It was another reason we had wanted to stay at South Water Cay where our mini reef was perfect for beginners.

"We've been practising in the pool with our masks, snorkels and flippers," Sarah told me.

"And I'm going to take my new underwater camera," said Christopher holding up one of the disposable units that take amazingly good photos. Not only could he take pictures of many colorful reef fish, Andy also found him a small shark!

It was a superb week of family cruising with Steve not seeing another cell phone, and Christopher never feeling seasick. Our Guatemalan acquaintances from the border arrived and we spent a delightful evening on their boat drinking piña coladas and eating an endless array of delicious canapes—seafood, cheese and our favorite Spanish chorizo sausage. We were interested to learn that their friends export pineapple juice and broccoli to Canada and our hosts gave us a bottle of 25 year-old rum from their family's distillery.

With several on board to keep watch and relay messages between the bow and stern, threading our way through the coral patches became more routine. Snorkeling by day on the outer reef, then returning to the sheltered mangrove anchorages of the inner cays for the night worked well.

Of all the cays, Rendezvous was our favorite. A tiny islet with just thirteen

Tricky piloting out to Rendezvous Cay

palm trees, it stands all alone on the barrier reef surrounded by a sapphire sea. We had it all to ourselves with not another boat in sight.

"It's a Robinson Crusoe island," said Andy to the kids.

"It's not very big," said Sarah.

"But there's a beach all the way round. Let's see how quickly we can run around it." The kids and I completed the circuit in no time flat!

Again the snorkeling was lovely, particularly off the southern end where the deep blue backdrop caused by the drop-off highlighted the coral formations and the many varieties of fish that darted between the purple fans. On the outer reef the diving was even more sensational with huge staghorn and elkhorn trees of coral standing twenty feet high, enormous angelfish and five-foot long barracuda whose wicked arrays of pointed teeth, although harmless, always make me a little wary.

Bagheera couldn't enter Moho Cay Marina, close to Belize City, until the tide was high the following morning but despite a strong east-south-easterly wind, near-by Peter's Bluff gave good shelter for the night. With the help of the marina work boat, a quick haul over by Steve who was manning the dinghy and my weaving *Bagheera's* wheel we quickly ploughed through the sandy channel and med-moored to the wharf.

The marina has pleasant surroundings and within minutes the kids found large green iguanas en route to the marina office and restaurant. There was even a washing machine—irresistible! Hauling a large bag of laundry on deck I noticed Andy talking to a man on the newly arrived boat to starboard. The newcomer looked up and we suddenly realized we knew each other, having met at many boat shows! It was Nigel Calder, who writes technical books and cruising guides, including one on this very area.

"How nice to meet actually out cruising," I greeted him, delighted.

"That's the job I have to do, too, over the next two days," he commented looking at my bundle, "while Terrie, the kids and our friends go inland." I was impressed, not only was he extremely talented he was also practical!

Meanwhile Steve and Alison had contacted a friend of Jennifer's and rented a car for a day of sightseeing. As it was already available Carlos suggested we collect it that afternoon. The vehicle was perfect for us all and we asked him directions to town.

"Why don't I give you a tour?" he suggested with his charming smile.

"Why not," we replied, "but how much?"

"Ten dollars would be fine."

"Done!"

He was full of information about the history of Belize, and the current political and economic situation. The government was stable and a good one, he told us. Belize has an extensive government social structure, good medical facilities and an impressive educational standard with a 90% literacy rate. Having previously heard reports of this city being rundown and unsafe, even of gunfire, we were pleasantly surprised.

"There has been a problem with drugs," Carlos agreed, "but the present government is doing a good job cleaning that up. You don't have to worry about walking anywhere by day but like all cities there are some areas where it's not wise to walk at night."

Reputedly built on a base of mahogany chips and broken rum bottles, Belize City has been the country's main seaport for over three centuries. Although periodically hit by hurricanes, many of the old wooden buildings have survived as has the brick cathedral, the courthouse and large Governor's house, the residence of the Governor General before independence and now a museum that gives a pictorial history of the country through several centuries.

A mixture of old and new, the town has a definite charm.

"Look at all the fishing boats," Alison pointed out to the children as we crossed the swing bridge over Haulover Creek that runs through the center of town. We had seen these brightly-painted wooden sloops with their attractive gunter rigs, sailing the cays and often heavily laden.

Carlos finally left us at the Fort St. George Guest House, located in an attractive residential neighborhood of colonial buildings with ornate balconies and trim. There we had a relaxed dinner on a cool deck bathed in the fragrance of tropical blooms.

Next morning everyone was up early for our day of inland travel along the Western Highway, one of the two main paved roads in the country. After forty minutes on the most immaculate road seen in Central America we arrived at the Belize Zoo. It was 8:30am, the zoo's opening time, and we spent two hours entranced by the animals and birds that live in this natural setting with fencing often completely hidden by jungle growth.

The zoo began in 1983 when local animals were tamed for the filming of *Path of the Raingods*. Sharon Matola, a marine biologist and animal trainer, was in charge of the seventeen animals that took part and when the budget ran out she founded the zoo for the animals that had become too tame to return to the wild. Currently there are over a hundred indigenous animals, with a research center and educational programs that actively promote awareness and conservation.

So many were interesting, such as the Baird's tapirs, Belize's national animal, but the highlights were the ocelots who loved to socialize at the fence, and the jaguars.

"Granddad," Christopher said to Andy excitedly pulling his hand. "That jaguar looks just like Bagheera in the Jungle Book."

"A magnificent animal," Andy agreed. "A perfect Bagheera."

He was blue-black, powerful and sleek, just like Rudyard Kipling's panther, and symbolically just right for our boat.

"Here comes another jaguar," Sarah pointed out, "but it's a different color." Equally striking was the golden and black spotted coat, apparently the more common coloration.

'They are the largest cats in the Americas," one of the wardens stopped to tell us. "We call them tigers here."

Ten minutes further down the main road we found the recommended JP's Watering Hole, a favorite pub of the British soldiers and still used by the small detachment today. It is packed with military memorabilia and amusing quotes, although the sign 'Officer's Mess' over the washroom door was a little confusing!

This pub opens out into a comfortable restaurant that overlooks a wide valley and distant hills. The breeze blowing over the ridge was deliciously cool after the heat of the zoo. It was easy to relax, dream of 'the old days' and wish for a hammock for a siesta—but we had a full day planned!

Back in our car Belmopan, Belize's new capital, passed in a flash. Planned and finally built after Hurricane Hattie destroyed much of Belize City in 1961, its population is small although gradually growing as embassies as well as government departments move there. From here one can reach Dangriga by skirting the Maya Mountains, along the rough Hummingbird Highway.

Lunch was at Caesar's Palace, recommended by Carlos, under huge bougainvillea trees brilliant with cerise blooms. An attached gift shop enticed us to buy local souvenirs, including bowls made from the beautifully patterned local zericote (ziricote) wood.

The high, single-lane Hawkesworth suspension Bridge, built in 1949 and designed after the Brooklyn Bridge, took us over the Macal River to San Ignacio and into its bustling high street. Confused, we stopped to ask the way to Xunantunich, Belize's most excavated Mayan ruin and our final destination.

"You are going exactly the wrong way," the local woman told us with a twinkle in her eye. "Go back and you will soon see the ferry. You children will really enjoy it," she said to Christopher and Sarah.

We had to get out of the car for Steve to drive onto the small platform and the children were fascinated, as the ferry was hand-cranked across the river. A drive up the hill brought us right to the charming ruins. Although miniature in comparison to Tikál, Xunantunich, Mayan for 'Maiden of the Rock', was the perfect size for Christopher and Sarah. Running across the Central Plaza to El Castillo they easily climbed the steep steps to the top of this 130' tallest man-made structure in the country. From this height the panoramic view stretched across the lush Mopan valley and beyond the border into Guatemala.

On the way down, we stopped to look at the impressive Sun God frieze and had the eerie feeling that he was looking back at us! While some of the carvings here are the original, plaster casts are preserving others. Xunantunich was built in the Late Classic period, between the 7th and 10th centuries and is believed to be the coastal river-trading center that connected Tikál to the ocean.

With only two other groups visiting it was immensely humbling to stroll across the bright green grass, immersed in the past without intrusion. Glancing in the information display room on the way out we were pleased to see that unlike Tikál, the Mayan historical notes were written in English as well as Spanish. Now we could learn about this magnificent empire that disappeared within a very short space of time.

The Maya rank as one of the three great civilizations of the Americas, along with the Aztecs of Mexico and the Incas of Peru. Although their his-

Exploring Xunantunich

tory can be traced back 4000 years, the Classic period of the Mayan civilization began in the third century AD and lasted for about 650 years, with a short renaissance in the 10th and 11th centuries under the Toltecs.

Extending through the Yucatan, Guatemala, Belize, Honduras and El Salvador this original stone-age people reached great sophistication in architecture, astronomy, agriculture and mathematics. They devised a calendar more accurate than ours, developed a decimal system with 20 instead of 10 and used zero in their calculations, as well as inventing a unique hieroglyphic script. Interestingly, they never used the wheel or metals in a practical application. They also had gruesome practices such as sacrificing the young and holding gladiator contests, and were involved in frequent bloody warfare.

At the height of their civilization over forty cities held an estimated one to three million people, and the graceful temples housed the kings and queens who were their rulers. No one knows why the Mayan civilization started to decline in the 9th century AD but all building of temples and stelae stopped, use of the calendar was abandoned and the population drastically decreased. Overpopulation, drought, over-use of the land and barbaric rituals are all possible explanations.

With the Kinsey family gone and a good weather forecast we headed for Belize's atolls, anchoring the first night in the Drowned Cays, where we were entertained by a large number of white egrets. Pounding against ocean swells and a two-knot current *Bagheera* passed through the barrier reef at Tobacco Cay. Then, with sheets eased and sails full she romped across to Glover's reef in the calm waters of the atoll's lee. There was one other boat in the anchorage at Southwest Cays. We had met in Placencia on *Wingstar* and they immediately came over in the dinghy.

"Would you like to come over for a drink and conch fritters later?" they suggested.

We agreed to go over at 5:00pm but first had to sample the beckoning seas that were crystal clear and teeming with fish. Like the other atolls Glover's has an outer wall of coral that rises straight from the ocean depths enclosing a shallow lagoon. The Southwest Cays are two of the few coconut-covered cays in the southeast rim right by the atoll's southerly entrance.

"What wonderful coral," Andy commented of the coral walls that in places plunge 2000 feet. "And I can't believe the number of lobsters."

Ashore, the small resort was being rebuilt after Hurricane Mitch and on another cay there was a Canadian camp with canvas tents and bright yellow kayaks lined along the sand. String bags bursting with fruit and vegetables hung decoratively around the open-air kitchen and the energetic cook was producing enticing aromas. Although warned about the bugs, the short trip back to the dinghy was one of the few times we were attacked. Despite repellent they were vicious and we were itching for days.

Nigel Calder had given us a sketch of one of his favorite anchorages at the north end of the atoll. The water here is an brilliant patchwork of blue and turquoise and we felt just as we had in the Indian Ocean—in the middle of nowhere. Besides spectacular fish and coral there were huge spotted eaglerays that effortlessly glided over the smooth sandy bottom.

"It's hard to tell whether the front will come down this far," Dennis told the 'fleet' on the radio. "It depends on the high over Texas."

We had also been watching the weatherfaxes closely. Bad weather in the atolls presents two problems. Although protected in the easterly tradewinds, most anchorages are open to 'northers'. It is also difficult to get back inside the main barrier reef, except by the single large shipping channel, as the few other passes can become too rough for a safe transit.

"There should be plenty of time for a visit to Lighthouse Reef," analyzed Andy.

"Good. I'd really like to see the red-footed boobies on Half Moon Cay. Apparently they're white."

It was blowing hard when we anchored off the pretty beach of the Half Moon Cay National Monument. I lowered the outboard motor to the dinghy by using the handy pulley system but most unusually it wouldn't start. Since purchasing the Mariner 9.9 in Singapore ten years earlier it had been unbelievably reliable, but it was not only getting old, it had undergone a few salt-water dunkings.

"It seems to be electrical," Andy diagnosed. As he worked for an hour I cleaned the mildew from the deckheads below. Already it was beginning to 'run' throughout the boat. The problem turned out to be the ignition cutout switch on the side and Andy was able to bypass it.

At a small dock ashore a man was at the top of his mast fixing the rig of his local boat. He was out with guests from Cay Caulker, a popular back-packers venue close to the mainland.

"It was a rough ride getting here," he told us. "As the forecast doesn't look good we're going back tomorrow."

Walking along the conch-lined path we were welcomed by the warden. He informed us that the sanctuary had been established in 1982 and that the lighthouse was over sixty years old. He also asked for $10 Belize each to visit the birds. Neither of us had thought to bring money ashore but seeing that *Bagheera*, was a mile out from shore because of the reef, he graciously waved us on.

It is a lovely walk by the sparkling water, then through the forest of zericote, fig, gumbo, limbo and palm. Ahead, the visitors from the fishing boat were looking at an eight-inch ball of white fluff lying on the path.

"It's a baby booby that's fallen out of its nest," they told us as we moved closer.

Viewing from a wooden observation platform, the trees were full of boobies, also frigatebirds with their long hooked beaks. After arriving in November the boobies build and renovate old nests and six weeks later the baby chicks pop out of their shells. From white, the young boobies turn a gray-brown and three years later gain adult plumage. Most adults are brown with a white tail, but a few become a beautiful white tinged with gold and have black edges and tips to their wings, in stunning contrast to their red feet and blue-pink bills. While most boobies in the Caribbean are brown, virtually all the nesting birds on Half Moon Cay are white.

The waves were up by the time we returned to the boat; we were not going to be able to make a trip to the famous Blue-Hole. Over 450 feet deep, this perfectly round hole is a favorite of divers and a spectacular sight from the air. Once a cavern on land it has two layers of underwater stalactites and stalagmites, discovered by Jacques Cousteau during *Calypso's* visit in 1972.

Instead we headed for Long Cay where the water was crystal clear and we were rewarded with spectacular trenches of coral, huge deep-purple fans and fire coral in mixtures of green and yellow. Teeming fish perfected the scene, especially those with fluorescent gray/blue stripes around their bodies that flashed in the rays of the sun. We spent the evening with *Skol* and were delighted to find we had mutual friends who would soon be visiting.

An early morning forecast showed that the front that had been stalled for a few days was starting to move south towards us. We decided to head up to Turneffe Atoll but, in case we needed to continue further, pulled the dinghy on deck for a faster trip. I watched the depth sounder carefully as we departed through the passage; we had touched bottom three times when entering.

"It's an amazing drop-off," I told Andy. "We were just in 15 feet, now it's 83 . . . and now it's 230 feet!

The southeast wind and 2-knot current gave a fast run with constant speeds of 7-8 knots and the occasional surf over ten. When the wind clocked around to the east, then northeast, we decided to keep going to Ambergris Cay.

"Forty-eight miles in 6 1/4 hours—not bad," said Andy grinning when San Pedro on Ambergris was in sight.

The buoy at the entrance to the pass was hard to find through the binoculars with the wind now at 18 knots and seas building. Just for an instant there was a flash of yellow. Now we could furl the sails and head in. The pass sounded tricky in the cruising guide, with a reef dead ahead and a jog to the north required, but at low water the coral was quite visible, although Andy also had to keep an eye on the breaking waves astern as I helmed our way in. Soon two anchors were down. The weather fax showed that the front would pass overhead around 6:00am. Our timing was perfect. Almost immediately a torrent of huge raindrops bounced noisily on the deck, the wind increased to 25 knots and lightning flashed from dusk to dawn.

Dave from *To Boldly Go* opened the Northwest Caribbean Net the following morning. "Any boats under way? I hope not!" In fact one boat arrived from the north later, after a grueling night at sea despite being with the wind, but the most adversely affected was *Skol*, who, although safely at anchor in Long Cay, had been struck by lightning. Having been struck ourselves previously, we felt for them. It takes so much work to check everything on a boat—electrics, electronics, the rig, compass, engine etc. In our case, we had to replace a huge amount, but updating equipment that was five years old was some consolation. On *Skol* they had been talking of selling the boat and now had a massive amount of repair work to do.

The white caps in the harbor convinced us to stay, along with eleven other boats that were mostly American and French. It gave us time to catch up on e-mails and visit this attractive fishing town that is exploding with tourism. Belize's largest cay, Ambergris stretches 25 miles down from the Yucatan border, separated from Mexico by a mere 6-foot wide channel thought to have been dug by the Maya.

Ambergris Cay was named after the gray waxy substance excreted by sperm whales and used in perfume, which was found on these beaches by early explorers. It was settled mainly by Mestizo refugees fleeing south from the War of the Castes in the Yucatan. From copra production the people turned to the sea, exporting conch, lobster and fish. Reduced catches and the cost of land with rising tourism and expatriate developers have created a problem for the local people, although we understand the government is making available some land to the north.

For tourists this laid-back town with its clapboard houses, and immaculate, hard-packed sand road lined with colorful shops and restaurants makes a delightful destination. As with all of Belize the people were exceptionally friendly and despite the weather we spent much time ashore.

It was also quite uncomfortable on board. "I baked Denis a birthday cake," Arlene told everyone on the radio. "I didn't think to gimbal the stove as we were in harbor and it came out with a 20° tilt. I'll have to prop it up the other way to ice it!"

"I've taken more seasick pills in the last three days at anchor than in eight years of cruising," commented another. "Ugh."

"I know what you mean," a third agreed. "I'm not a drinking person, but today I had a 'bloody Mary' for breakfast and have had two coffees with brandy this afternoon—that's how I feel!"

A clear blue sky greeted our awakening on the fourth morning. As we had already cleared out, *Bagheera* was soon underway. Several local boats left with us. We were now following La Ruta Maya and imagined being one of thousands of canoes that traded along this coast in the height of the old Mayan civilization.

Four hours later we entered Xcalak, easily lining up the leading light with the lighthouse for a safe entry. Mexico's southerly port of entry had seen better days before being devastated by a hurricane in the 1950s. Sleepy, with laid-back officials who didn't even mention the need for a fishing license or charge fees, it is a great place to enter Mexico. We left with several other boats the next morning for a stop at Mexico's atoll Chinchorro, a marine park, and enjoyed a day visiting back and forth, exchanging books, information and many stories.

Four mahi mahis were landed on the overnight passage to Isla Mujeres, opposite Cancun, which compensated for several fish heads we had hauled in, the body taken by sharks. We had decided to bypass several small, and shallow, anchorages behind the reef and also avoided Cozumel; friends had warned us on the radio not to clear in here.

"We were charged $50 to hire an agent," they told us. "They don't discriminate between yachts and big shipping."

Not only a pleasant island, Isla Mujeres has a large sheltered anchorage and several marinas. The bay was filled with cruisers lapping up the last of Mexico and waiting for a good weather forecast before starting a three-day passage across the Yucatan Channel to Florida. There were parties every night. We caught up with the Calders before they left and Terrie helped us organize an inland visit to the Yucatan.

First stops were to colonial Valladolid and the underground limestone cave of Cenote Dzitnup where impressive stalactites hang over the pool. There are many of these *cenotes* in this region and they were the Mayas most dependable source of water. Next was the Mayan Site of Chichén Itzá. The Yucatan was the center of the ancient Mayan civilization and although lacking the mystique of the jungle setting of Tikál, Chichén Itzá (Temple of Kukukan in Mayan) with its mixture of both Mayan and Toltec architecture is a remarkable sight. First settled in the mid 6th Century and finally abandoned in the 14th Century, the buildings are extensive. Particular memories include the Group of a Thousand Columns, the ornate stonework of the Nunnery, a ball court with pure acoustics and the immense central pyramid.

The vast esplanade gives a great view of this square-based 75' tall El Castillo, a nine-terraced masterpiece of Toltec-Mayan genius. Built as a calendar of stone the eighteen separate terraces represent the eighteen 20-day months in their 'Vague Year' while the steps total 365, the number of days in the solar year. Similar to the outer structure lies an inner pyramidal temple whose chamber can be visited by climbing a claustrophobic staircase.

El Castillo in Chichén Itzá

Museum of Anthropology in Mérida

Outer walls are adorned with sculptures of serpents, rattlesnakes, prowling jaguars, warriors and coats of arms. The main attraction of the earlier inner pyramid is a reclining figure of a Chac-mool (messenger of the gods) with shells for fingernails, teeth and eyes, and a sculpture of a fierce red jaguar inlaid with jade pieces, with jade balls for his eyes and flint for fangs.

"The other amazing thing about El Castillo," our guide informed us, "is the light phenomenon that occurs on the equinox."

El Castillo is devoted to the cult of Kukulkan, (also the Mayan god of Quetzalcoatl), the plumed serpent that is the god of learning, creation and priesthood, as shown by the many sculptures such as the formidable serpents heads that guard the main stairway on the north side. The Maya also worshipped the sun and at each equinox a phenomenal event occurs. During the March equinox, triangles of light reflected from the sun create the illusion of a serpent creeping down El Castillo's steps. In September the serpent takes the same time, over three hours, to ascend to the heavens.

Bordered with dazzling red flamboyant trees, the old road took us to beautiful Izamal where a huge Franciscan monastery, built on the platform of a Mayan temple, and the surrounding town are painted the traditional sunny yellow-ochre. Horses and carts were common on the road to the bustling capital, Mérida. The center of Mayan culture in the Yucatan, we found it a charming town with its stately colonial buildings and narrow streets. Our timing was perfect for shopping at the lively Sunday market in the main square, listening to live mariachi bands and for free admission to the many museums. We particularly enjoyed the Museum of Anthropology with its well-preserved artifacts, many from Chichén Itzá. We had wondered about the ancient Mayan's strangely pointed heads and were interested to learn that forehead flattening was done both to beautify babies and to keep headdresses in place.

The new toll road, although pricey, allowed a quick and comfortable journey back to Cancun, particularly as it avoided going over 83 speed bumps!

"Look how empty the anchorage is," Andy commented on the ferry ride back to Isla Mujeres.

"Hi Bagheeras," Stella from *Wingstar* greeted us from the marina bar. "You missed the entertainment this morning!"

"Let me guess what happened," said Andy grinning. "There was a good weather forecast and. . "

"That's right," Keith butted in, "As soon as Denis lifted his anchor all the other boats slotted right behind like ducklings."

We listened to their chatter on the passage back to the United States, but one by one they faded away. Although partly due to poor radio propagation it was also because after several months of cruising, the chores and frenetic pace of civilization quickly take over.

Aboard *Bagheera* we weren't quite ready to leave. Kay and Joe, the mutual friends of *Skol*, joined us for a few splendid days of sightseeing, wining and dining. We had met Kay Pastorius in Newport Beach when taking part in the Cruisers' Weekend. She was selling her *Cruising Cuisine* cookery book at the same table we were selling our books and Andy had been impressed by her recipes. (Quite a feat I might add!) A fast friendship had been consolidated during our stay in San Diego.

When we finally left Mexico it was in the direction of Cuba. Having visited briefly in 1991 we were looking forward to seeing the changes in this country of contrasts and check out more of its coastline, another vast new cruising destination awaiting discovery.

13. Cuba

Maria la Gorda to Havana

'Cuba, the land of a thousand sepia myths; the land of rhythm and rum; of sugar and smoke; of cigars and crooners, croupiers and cashiers. A land of . . . waving canefields and dusty green tobacco; where heroes mingle on fading, curling photographs; and a sultry Nat King Cole can glance, casually, across to the young guerilla on the opposite page of our long discarded magazine memory. The silk, the rags, the microphone, the eyes, the beard, and the rifle—Cuba, the land of revolution and rumba.'

Simon Charles—*A Cruising Guide to Cuba*

Contentious, lush, historical Cuba is not only a fascinating country to visit, it also offers cruisers some 4000 cays and islets, and over 3000 nautical miles of coastline. Its untold anchorages give innumerable secluded palm-ringed bays, acres of deserted white-sand beaches, world-class diving and dramatic mountain views. Ashore the fertile countryside and colonial sites are outstanding and although sometimes initially reserved the people are lively, warm and hospitable when they get to know you. It also has unbelievably tedious officialdom.

Our landfall was María La Gorda (Fat Mary!), on Cuba's southwest shore, after tacking to counter the screaming 3-knot current that had whisked us too far north. The Yucatan Strait was busy with shipping but it was a pleasant 24-hour passage despite being on the wind. As instructed by the Guarda Frontera on the radio, at the required check-in when 12 miles offshore, we anchored in pristine turquoise water off a spectacular beach by the hotel on the eastern shore of Bahia de Corrientes.

In 1991 it had taken us several hours to clear into Cuba, mainly because of an extensive boat search and the time it took to examine the 14 photo albums we accrued during our circumnavigation! With tourism now the country's largest source of foreign exchange we hoped that procedures would be completed more quickly. Not a chance!

Eleven officials soon arrived in a resort boat that included a doctor, Port Captain, Customs, Trade and Public Relations Officers. The next day Immigration, Health/Quarantine, Port Captain, Trade and Public Relations Officers and two men who booked diving trips visited. On the third day the Customs Officer, Port Captain, and Trade and Public Relations Officer came to tell us we could conclude the final procedures ashore, where there were more documents, questions, our itinerary detailed and everything officially stamped!

During these visits much official and social conversation transpired, *Bagheera* was searched, fruit and vegetables that looked 'tired' were confiscated, as were the frozen chicken and eggs (subsequently returned, both frozen in a sealed bag). One onion had a tiny speck of mold. Instinctively I reached over to flick it off but quickly gathered by the reaction of horror that this was not the thing to do! It had to be taken ashore to be analyzed. All our equipment was listed and our budgerigar (parakeet) was discussed then also added to the manifest. To be fair, many of these procedures are common in other countries but few include them all. Finally the *Aduana* (Customs), who informed us he was the boss, came with our *despacho* (cruising permit). We were pleased to find that although a few places were off limits and others required special permission, for the most part we could cruise wherever we pleased en route to Havana.

During this process we were entertained by curious international and local visitors who swam out to the boat. They enthused about diving on the coral walls and in the underground caves that have made this area

The first of many Cuban officials on board

famous. During a lull between officials we snorkeled ourselves, and found the reefs close to the boat were excellent.

Two American lads came by in their dinghy and after we had been cleared by Immigration they returned for sundowner drinks, laden with gifts of ice, red cabbage and squash. The stories about their newly discovered cruising life were most entertaining and as they were off to Mexico with few resources on board, we lent them Nigel Calder's *Cruising Guide to the Northwest Caribbean*.

So began two weeks of exploring nearly 200 miles around Cabo San Antonio and along the north coast of Cuba to Havana. In 1991 when heading for the United States from the Caribbean we made our landfall in Baracoa at Cuba's eastern end.

"I didn't realize how large Cuba is when we were here before," I commented to Andy as we pored over the charts, "or how close it is to the United States at this end of the country."

"Yes, compared to the Caribbean islands we're used to, it's huge," Andy agreed, "and it must only be about 100 miles to Florida."

He was almost spot on. By far the biggest island in the Lesser Antilles, Cuba is the fifteenth largest island in the world and at 44,000 square miles with its thousands of islands is between England and Ireland in size. With a length of over 650 nautical miles and a width of over 100 miles at its widest point, it forms the northwest boundary of the Caribbean Sea and there are just 93 nautical miles between Havana and Key West, across the Florida Strait. Cuba's other close neighbors are the Bahamas to the north and Jamaica to the southeast, with Haiti 42 nautical miles to the east.

Much of Cuba is incredibly lush, with fertile flatlands that are ideal for farming; about 25% is mountainous. The climate is subtropical, cooled by the trades, and vegetation is divided between the lower hot zone and the temperate zone above 3000 feet. Pinar del Río Province, the region we were now to cruise, is a non-touristy, nature-lover's paradise with limestone hills and caves, rugged, pine-forested mountains and a tobacco-growing region that produces 80% of the country's crop. It is one of the prettiest areas in the country.

The land drops off dramatically at this western end of Cuba and the waters around Cabo San Antonio can be extremely rough, noted on the Cuban charts as Perpetua Rpte—perpetually rough. This is the narrowest point between the Yucatan and Cuba and, as the Gulf stream surges north through a 10,000-foot trench, speeds can be between two and seven knots. We were lucky to have a light northeasterly wind, the ideal direction whether heading north or south as it flattens out the seas inshore and gives a reach either way.

There are a few small towns along this stretch of the north coast inside the Archipiélago de los Colorados and we were mostly by ourselves anchored behind the Arrecifes Colorados, the reef that extends 120 miles to Bahía Honda, a daysail short of Havana. Many of the southerly anchorages have fishing docks, generally active with boats going to and fro. We had seen small dories out to sea with one or two men using hand lines, bringing to mind Hemingway's *Old Man and the Sea.*

"Wouldn't it be great if we could get some fish from the camp?" said Andy after a frustrating day with no fish conveniently attaching themselves to our trolled baits.

We were in Cayos de la Leña and right on cue a fisherman jumped into a wooden dinghy and rowed out. He held up a bag of six large, prepared lobstertails.

We were already drooling. Thank goodness our garlic hadn't been confiscated, was my immediate thought!

"What can we give you in exchange," Andy asked.

"I can't use money," he told us, "but how about a bottle of rum?" Unfortunately we had very little rum on board. This was obviously a mistake!

"What about clothing?" I suggested. He nodded reluctantly.

"No rum?" he persisted. I questioned him about his family and packed clothing for everyone from items left by our guests, then added our last half bottle of rum before towing him back to the dock. To our surprise he immediately handed the bag of goodies to his superior, who seemed satisfied and invited us to look around.

All was immaculate, from the neatly made beds, pristine kitchen and sitting room, and fish laid out to dry in the sun. Fillets had been finely sliced on the skin and salted, a method used on the Grand Banks in the fifteenth century that has certainly stood the test of time. The lobster traps were huge and although we couldn't figure out what lured the lobsters in, or even where they got in, the number of lobsters held in pens in the water verified their efficiency.

"They are collected every ten days and taken to the mainland," they told us.

Apparently it was a privilege to be at the fishing camps; signifying that individuals were trusted enough to enjoy a freedom not experienced by most Cubans. The many pictures of Fidel Castro, mostly laughing, and the positive slogans of encouragement on the walls were a reminder of the contentious political situation with the United States. We wondered if their television sets could pick up any American Channels and later saw they could.

Cuba's history has been one of turbulence—a long struggle for freedom, independence and social justice. The Taino, a branch of the Arawak Indians, were the main inhabitants when Columbus arrived in Cuba on October 27th, 1492. He described Cuba as 'The most beautiful land human eyes have ever seen', and initially thought it was part of the coast of Asia. Lacking gold, Cuba was initially ignored but subsequently became the main gateway for shipping bounty from Spain's New World. Havana, with its easily protected harbor, became the largest and most sophisticated city in the Caribbean.

When most of the Indians died working on the cattle ranches that were the mainstay of the local economy, slaves were imported from Africa to work the fertile lands. This is reflected in the population today. Of the present 11 million people, 60% are Spanish, 22% mulatto and 11% are of African descent. Unlike the United States, Cuba grouped African slaves in their tribes and much of their culture was retained.

Tobacco, sugar and coffee also became major industries and by 1820, after a slave revolt in Haiti, Cuba became the world's largest sugar producer. Meanwhile the British and French were challenging Spain's hold on the Caribbean and after Simón Bolívar led South America and Mexico to independence the only countries left under Spanish dominance were Puerto Rico and Cuba. In Cuba, even the Spanish loyalists were calling for home rule.

With over 200,000 deaths, Cuba's first war of independence ended after a ten-year rebellion which established Antonio Maceo as one of Cuba's great heroes. Cuban exiles in the United States instigated the second war and the martrydom of Jose Marti, a respected journalist, earned him the recognition of being another national hero. Then, with the mysterious explosion of the American warship Maine outside Havana's harbor in January 1898, the Americans joined the war, not so much on the side of the rebels but against Spain. Overextended in conflicts elsewhere, a limping Spain finally signed a peace treaty at the end of the year—and so began democracy for Cuba under an American governor. In 1903 the American naval base was built in Guantánamo Bay which is still in use today.

Gradually Americans took over most of Cuba's farmland and intervened in Cuban affairs, exercising a stranglehold on the Cuban economy. The Great Depression caused devastation to the Cuban economy and further social unrest, which was violently put down by President Gerado Machado y Morales. In 1933 Morales was overthrown and power was seized by an army sergeant, Fulgencio Batista, a despot who, with other leaders, ran Cuba into the ground. It took several years of guerilla warfare and many attacks for the government to be overthrown on January 1st,

1959 by Fidel Castro, a young Cuban lawyer. Castro quickly began reforming Cuba's economy, expropriating many of the larger land holdings and three American oil refineries which resulted in the trade embargo by the United States that still exists today. Low points in Cuban/U.S. relations were the CIA-supported Bay of Pigs invasion in 1961 and the 1962 missile crisis. Out of favor with the United States, Castro turned to Russia for support, although he maintained the Cuban regime was socialist rather than communist.

With the strong idealism of the revolution and Soviet subsidies, Cuba changed from a labor-based rural society into a highly mechanized industrial one, using its rich mineral resources. The people became the best educated in all of the Caribbean and Central America. But the collapse of the Eastern Bloc in 1989 and loss of Russian aid devastated the economy through the loss of the sugar cane market and no further supplies of grain, fertilizer, animal feed and the essential oil for mechanization.

On our last visit to Cuba in 1991 the country was at a low ebb; machinery was lying by the wayside rusting, factories were idle, sugarcane fields lay neglected and, although fruit was falling to the ground in the country, there was no means of transporting it to the towns. Saddened then by the state of affairs we were keen to return to see the country's reported amazing road back to recovery.

We had no grand expectations approaching Los Arroyos, a remote fishing port with a sizable fleet, but when allowed ashore we were pleasantly surprised. Although the straight road of uniform houses with cement fronts, wooden sides and back could have been characterless, the variety of palm-thatched roofs and red Spanish tiles with the profusion of flowers made it very attractive. Although old, everything was immaculate and newly scrubbed. The occasional truck passed with workers, otherwise transportation was by bicycle, horse, horse and cart or motor bike and sidecar.

"Fascinating," Andy murmured as he inspected one of the motor bikes. "It's an old look-alike BMW, 1750cc." Biking had been another of Andy's passions as a youth!

Since 1993 Cubans have been allowed to hold U.S. dollars. They are obtained through tourism, retail and gifts from overseas, a major source of Cuban's revenue. The dollar stores give Cubans an opportunity to buy goods not available from the State. Nearly all the houses had TV antennas and there were TVs for sale in the dollar store here, costs ranging from $65 to $400. Many shelves held beer, mostly European brands, and there were several racks of clothing.

"There are no labels to say where these are made," I commented to Andy. "But they nearly all have brand names. Pierre Cardin seems popular."

There was no bread to be seen, the reason we had given the officials for coming ashore. We asked the boss of the fishing camp who had come up to greet us where we could find some. "There isn't any available today," he told us, "Anyway, Cuban bread is terrible!" When we finally found some in another town the newly baked bread was delicious, but with no preservatives it soon becomes stale and has to be carefully checked when purchased.

Back inside the port, many were hard at work. Fishing boats were being replanked and lobster traps hammered together. In contrast, others sat around smoking and playing warri, an African board game commonly played in the Caribbean. We've always been intrigued by the quick, seemingly nonchalant way the locals play these silky-gray seeds while we have to laboriously count them around the board! The men were friendly, women a little more reticent, unlike 1991 when Cubans were scared to talk to foreigners.

Our documents were not yet ready so I wandered off to take photos, particularly wanting one of the huge sign that read "4th 1999 Aniversario, REVOLUCION."

Returning, I noticed Andy was taking his camera out of its bag. Within moments a guard came rushing out to him, yelling angrily, "No foto, NO FOTO!" Fortunately I had already taken several!

A pleasant young man came over and asked, "Why not?"

"I look subversive," replied Andy grinning, but also annoyed.

It had been an irritating arrival with a rude young official throwing his weight around on board and demanding we give him our papers. He was so unpleasant that we refused and he left highly annoyed. After our quaking subsided we began to worry that this could be an imprisonable offence and we turned to Nigel Calder's and Simon Charles' cruising guides for direction. Relief came when we read in Simon Charles' guide (written with the co-operation of the Cuban Government) that you should never give up your documents!

In contrast, the boss was pleasant and apologetic, but yet again the boat had to be searched on his arrival. It was the sixth time there had been officials on board in five days and although this was the only unpleasant experience, having officials lying on one's bed and searching through our underwear daily seemed rather unnecessary.

There were huge sighs of relief when they left. We could now gorge on our lobster, but soon the mosquitoes were gorging on us. "Where's the netting for the forward hatch?" Andy called up from below.

"Good question," I answered. "Probably shoved back in the locker with my bikinis!"

Before leaving for Santa Lucia we chatted with some Dutch cruisers who warned us about shallow areas inside the reef. "Are you heading down the Central American coast?' we asked them. "We have spent the last two months in shallows!" Again the difference between a draft of 6'0" and 7'3" was significant as we cruised the cays for the next 100 miles. It wasn't until we reached Havana that we saw Cuban Government chart books called GEOCUBA Cartografia for sale. Next time we won't cruise without them as the large-scale American charts lack detail and are out of date.

We might have passed Santa Lucía because of the odor from sulfur, but our Dutch acquaintances had informed us that the sulfuric acid manufacturing plant wasn't working. After stopping for a snorkel at Cayo Jutías, by the distinctive black and yellow striped lighthouse that gives great views from the top, we headed for the channel. Officials started calling us on the radio while we were at the outer marker telling us to come alongside the dock. There was a sign greeting yachts and we tied up as indicated, behind a small warship. This time the awaiting official couldn't have been more pleasant and even took off his shoes, neatly placing them on the side deck.

He dispensed with formalities quickly, but not quickly enough to avoid the deluge from a huge thunderstorm that filled his shoes! We emptied and propped them up to drain. He took it in good humor; what better excuse to join us for a beer! He informed us that the small town refines and ships mineral oils and that yachts often visit.

Walking early next morning we crossed a tiny park with a silver painted statue of the Madonna and Child then continued up the main street. It offered a small but active market (now allowed in Cuba), a cinema that apparently showed old British and French films and a dollar store. Children were going to school, smartly clad in bright white blouses and red skirts or shorts with wide straps. Education still holds a high priority in Cuba; schooling is free and available to all between kindergarten and the end of University.

Several times children approached us asking if we needed accommodation in a paladar. Cubans are now allowed to have people to stay in their homes, to subsidize their low state allowance (commonly equivalent to $10 a month). We loved being invited inside and relaxing in the typical wood and cane rocking chairs while we talked about life in Cuba. The food was generally good, if lacking in seasoning, but it was important to ask "Cuanta cuesta?" in advance. Cuba is fast catching on to world prices!

Several rusty fishing vessels surrounded *Bagheera* when we anchored in La Esperanza; there was no spare room on the jetty. With the 15-knot breeze and wave action the two officials, a man and woman, were having a hard time making headway despite rowing hard. Finally a fishing boat towed them over and procedures were quickly dispensed with in their immaculate scripts.

"Leave your dinghy in the compound by the Guarda Frontera watch tower," we were instructed.

"Do you think we have to leave it there because of theft?" I said to Andy, "It doesn't seem compatible with this regime. Maybe its because they want to keep an eye on us!"

"We're happy to get you diesel," the officials had told us. "It's 45¢ a liter and $35.00 U.S. to bring it from the fuel depot!"

"Mucho, mucho." Andy muttered under his breath, although the fuel was cheap the transportation was outrageous. We thanked them and said we would leave it for now. There had to be another way!

Although she spoke no English, bubbly Sandra had no trouble communicating that we were most welcome to visit her house. We had been told about Sandra and her mother Dora from the American lads in La Gorda and readily agreed. Living side-by side with room for a horse and cart, the family exuded warmth and hospitality. Dora's walls were covered with messages from other yachtsmen and with little room left we scribed our logo on the kitchen ceiling. All was immaculate from the tiled kitchen, dining room arranged for guests and a comfortable living room with TV. We organized a car to travel inland the following day. As we were leaving Sandra suggested we bring a jerry can ashore with us the next morning as she thought she could arrange fuel.

Before entering the security compound we waved at a family who were happily making charcoal. They had become used to us coming to and fro and laughingly posed for a photo. While launching the dinghy, we noticed that the huge binoculars at the top of the watchtower that constantly scanned the horizon by day were put to bed for the night. The wind was clocking around to the east and there was a spectacular storm to the south, the bursts of lightning flashing in circles, then falling and fading like fireworks.

Sandra greeted us effusively at 8:30am the following morning. The driver would be there with a car by nine, she told us. He finally arrived at 10:00am but no one was concerned. Visitors popped in and out. Sandra pressed hot rolls into my hands for the trip; her brother-in-law insisted on giving us eggs and fruit, rosy mangoes, soursop and several hands of sweet finger bananas. Her husband went up on the roof to clear off the pigeons, and her 4-year-old son came in with a hen, the mother of the best cock-fighting birds they told us proudly, that he thrust into Andy's arms while he rushed off with a friend!

Our trip inland was to include Viñales, Pinar del Río and the countryside everyone had mentioned that was so beautiful with its unusual landscape and thatched farmhouses. Immediately outside the town the land was neatly cultivated with fruit, vegetables, sugar and tobacco, with rice paddies on the lower ground. We stopped to take photos of the tobacco fields and A-frame drying houses. A great character decked in a straw 'cowboy' hat, open shirt and cigar hanging from his mouth showed us the racks full of leaves, and explained that they have to hang for four months to mature.

Then on to the wide fertile valley that houses the colonial town, both called Viñales. With its red soil and brilliant green vegetation, intersected by lumpy limestone, karst 'haystack' hills called Mogotes, this area's stunning scenery is similar to the Quilin region in China. Below, underground rivers have eaten away the bedrock, etching out vast caverns. Stalactites and stalagmites cast eerie shadows during our peaceful boat trip, subtle lighting the only accommodation to tourists. The end of the ride was dramatic, with the rocks forming an angular entrance to the cavern that was backlit by the sun.

The grounds are beautifully tended here at Cueva de Indio (the cave of the Indian). Andy was overjoyed by the variety of orchids, and the many trees, that were a mass of color and full of birds.

'Ssshhhh, ssshhh," whispered our guide. "There's the tocororo, listen." Cuba's trogon is the national bird and we could hear several calls, but search as we may in the old tree covered in yellow blossoms, these red, white and blue birds eluded us.

"It's a member of the quetsal family,' she informed us, "And it was chosen because its colors are those of the Cuban flag. It's also a fascinating bird," she continued, "because it can climb trees using its feet." She spoke English well and had worked as a professor at the university before becoming a tourist guide.

"Any chance of seeing the bee hummingbird?" asked Andy while we were on the subject.

"We call them zunzuncito or pájaro mosca, fly bird. They are only found in very remote areas now and are so tiny," she replied. "I've never seen one. It's the world's smallest bird," she informed the other couple on the tour," and they weigh about 2 grams (less than one tenth of an ounce). This is the time of year they lay their eggs. They have very long bills, quite out of proportion to their bodies, so they can get the nectar out of a flower but have to beat their wings so fast humans can't even see them."

The flower-filled town of Viñales had a relaxed atmosphere with its 1607 square filled with pungent frangipani and colorful bougainvillea. Surrounded by old buildings, a church with distinctive colonial tower and the round-arched Casa de la Cultura mansion that houses an art gallery, it is a fitting center for many cultural programs.

We lunched in a home on the back streets and chatted to German back-packers, newlyweds who had been bicycling around the country and were elated about their visit. Lunch was a choice of fish, chicken or pork with rice, fries, beans, tomatoes, plantain and a root plant, all beautifully presented. For desert there was fruit, watermelon and grapefruit so sweet it reminded us of the pamplemousse of French Polynesia.

"Where can we buy some grapefruit?" I asked our hostess. She rushed back into the kitchen and came back with three as a gift. An old, but immaculate, red Russian tractor was parked outside. Andy spent several minutes inspecting it. "Fascinating, fascinating," he exclaimed yet again!

To the south, the balcony of the Hotel Los Jazmines, once home to a successful planter, gives spectacular views of the lush valley with dramatic mountains behind. Further south lies Pinar del Río, a town with over 100,000 population that dates back to 1669. We were struck by the beautiful latticework and balustrading on the colonial buildings, although begging a coat of paint, in this bustling town full of cyclists. After driving around we decided on a tour of Fabrica de Bebidas Casa Garay, a distillery that makes Guayabita del Pinar brandy from fruit similar to a small guava. The factory wasn't working as it had run out of labels but the woman touring us was informative. The brandy only takes four to five months to mature and she was generous with free samples! The ornate but not very informative Museum of Natural History was disappointing, although they did have a stuffed Cuban trojun bird.

El Mural de la Prehistoria, just to the west of Viñales, was our last stop. On the cliff at the foot of the 2000-foot high Sierra de Viñales there is a gigantic mural. Inspired by Morillo in 1961, figures and background were painted, our guide told us, by local farmers. Our guide was an attractive girl in her early twenties and I joined her at the bar after the tour. She had also left the academic world because of the financial opportunities in tourism.

"I'm trained as a professor," she told me," but am now working hard on several languages, as tourism is the best avenue for both the country's and personal gain. Also when Cubans can again leave the country I want to be prepared and have money so I can see the world!"

Her sister had gone overseas to university in the '80s, sponsored by Russian money and now lives in the United States. They hadn't seen each other for eight years.

"But she writes and sends me clothes," she added. "Most people have relatives overseas who send them clothing or money."

I was impressed by her candidness and asked her about the political situation.

"Cubans now recognize they must embrace capitalism for the country to move forward. My generation understands that we must have private enterprise," she told me, "and that this requires hard work. The problem is that Cuba has a whole generation of people who have grown up indoctrinated by the communist idea that capitalism is wrong and they have no work ethic as everything has been provided for their basic needs."

As we dropped her off at a friend's house I slipped her a generous tip. "I really admire your working so hard," I told her. "But go and have some fun too." As she disappeared, her smile quite transformed her earnest demeanor.

Back in La Esparanza Sandra had found us some diesel and Dora had dinner waiting. It felt as though we were coming home. The next morning we came ashore with two bags full of gifts.

"Hold them low," Andy urged as we walked along the dock. "They can see us from the watch tower."

Although it had been impressed upon us that everything had to stay on board, I'd related that to equipment, not old sheets, towels and clothing our friends had left behind with the intention that they should be given away. This fell into the category 'one man's garbage is another's treasure'.

As Andy peeled off to the watchtower to clear out I headed down to our friends with both bags. There was great excitement as they opened the first one. I'd put some Christmas mugs and decorations on top and they were ecstatic, chanting, "You are Santa Claus, Santa Claus!"

All items were greeted with enthusiasm and several neighbors arrived to watch, enjoying their friend's delight. Sandra was especially pleased with the colored paper, pens, crayons and glue, as children's supplies were hard to come by.

They had just unpacked the second bag when Andy entered, breathless.

"They saw us bring the bags ashore and are not pleased. I said we were giving away old shirts in exchange for fruit."

Every new item instantly disappeared. We quickly said our farewells as the officials were heading over to check the boat. There were hugs all round, how sad we were to leave this wonderful family.

"Not much *frutas* for two big bags," commented the official as he looked at our fruit bowl, although fortunately it was piled high with our gifts from the day before.

"What is the time?" he asked. As I looked at my watch he pointed at his bare arm, "I no watch."

"I'm so sorry," I replied sincerely, but had no intention of giving up my only one!

It was getting too shallow for us to go up the inside of the reef but we had a relaxing sail outside up to Cayo Levisa, a mangrove island with a lovely white sand beach on its northern shore that has an informal palapa-style resort. Here we met some Americans who were cruising in their trawler. Over a dinner of freshly caught tuna, they told us that it was not difficult for Americans to visit Cuba legally.

"We called the U.S. Coastguard and they faxed us a form that gives per-mission to depart the 'security zone'," they explained. "It's not illegal for Americans to visit Cuba; we just can't spend money here. You can get sponsored for the entry fees by Cubans or even the Club Nautico in Marina Hemingway."

"Is this your first visit?" I asked. "What about going back into the United States?"

"No problem. This is our third trip here, and we love the fact that most Americans feel it's forbidden. It's our own paradise!"

Next morning we were awoken by a huge Russian-style helicopter tak-ing off with great gaffuffer. Up to watch the spectacle, Andy decided to feed our budgie; he was full of beans, heartily singing away to the sound of the local birds. Cornflake had really blossomed in personality on the trip, thriving on his close contact with us, with the cage hung over the gal-ley. We were particularly amused by his realistic mimicking of the noise of sending e-mail on the radio. By lunch he was lying in the bottom of the cage, dead. It was a shock, there had been no warning and he seemed so healthy. Then we realized he had lived far longer than any of our former birds, although if you have read *Just Cruising* or *Still Cruising* you may remember they did get up to a few antics.

"What are we going to do?" I asked, worried about future officials' questions with Cornflake listed on the boat manifest.

"Maybe we should freeze him," Andy suggested. "We can give him a burial at sea when we leave Cuban waters," he added, as I looked shocked.

This was an unusual use for a ziplock bag; I wonder how we ever man-aged to cruise without them!

The small crescent-shaped Cayo Paraíso, one of Ernest Hemingway's favorite getaways over fifty years ago, looked enticing but we continued along in the iridescent green water and out through one of the quebra-dos, passages through the reef, into the deep blue water of the ocean. Within a mile we were off soundings but could still faintly hear the breaking waves on the outer reef as the dramatic mountains of Sierra de los Organos and Sierra del Rosario faded astern. It took us two hours in the dark to negotiate our way into Bahia Honda through its narrow entrance. The buoys were unlit, did not even show on radar, and a dredger lay in the middle of the channel. We anchored off the Guarda's office and he rowed out at 10:00pm completing the paperwork by flashlight in his dinghy.

With excitement and anticipation we entered Marina Hemingway the following afternoon. Lying five miles to the west of Havana, this huge and well-run facility, has four channels over half a mile long for moorage. It also has stores, restaurants, laundry, experienced day workers and a yacht club that offers great benefits in joining, especially for a stay of over a week. The officials were efficient and while *Bagheera* stayed in the Marina no further checking was required—bliss!

There was of course one problem—where was our bird? I quickly whipped poor, stiff Cornflake out of the freezer and presented him.

"So sorry, so sorry," they commiserated and quickly indicated that I should put him back to keep him in his frozen state!

Havana is one the most engaging cities we have visited and we loved being regular tourists lapping up the crumbling beauty of the rich architecture and exploring the many facets of its changeable history. We took the bus into town from the nearby Hotel El Viejo y el Mar along an esplanade lined with gracious old homes, fascinating jagüey trees with their many aerial roots, and brilliant red flamboyant mixed with tabebuia trees heavy with golden blooms. The bus stopped in town by a market jammed full of goods for sale—tropical paintings, intricate lace and crochet-work, musical instruments, pottery, wood carvings and many pictures of Fidel. The market was oriented towards the tourist trade, as it is located right by La Habana Vieja, an area that was declared an UNESCO World Heritage Site in 1982.

Cuba's political, economic and cultural hub, Havana has seen great riches. It has also seen much poverty but fortunately was not damaged during the wars of independence and revolution. Many of the beautiful colonial buildings with their ornate stonework, grand columns, beautiful arches, high ceilings, wrought iron balconies, towering pinnacles and flower-filled central courtyards, have been or are in the process of being restored. Although glorious when finished, it is a massive task.

We decided to follow the walking tour of old and central Havana suggested in The Lonely Planet Travel Survival Kit that led us to the beautiful Plaza de la Catedral and on to the Plaza de Armas, again filled with stunning examples of colonial architecture. These buildings have been turned into museums, memorials and art galleries, while others appeared to be workshops. Peering inside the shutters we could see potters, seamstresses and a number of schoolrooms full of desks, pupils again clad in red and white uniforms and hard at work.

It was some time before it dawned on us that there were absolutely no

Havana—School is out!

shops! In Cuba all the basics are provided to the population by coupon, which they take to warehouses in the back streets.

As we continued the circuit we were impressed at the restoration work completed and in progress, and also at how much more there is still to do. Some buildings that filled a full block have been gutted, just crumbling walls left standing. In Centro Havana we gazed down narrow side streets full of old row houses; laundry hung drying high across the street, lines strung between the windows.

"It's so like northern Portugal," I remarked to Andy. "So attractive, but think what it would look like with a fresh coat of paint."

Similar but more detailed than The Capitol in Washington DC, the Capitolio Nacional stands proudly in its own square. Lined up in front, and gleaming in the sun, is always an impressive array of colorful vintage American cars, taxis dating back to pre-revolution days.

"What a collection!" exclaimed Andy, overjoyed. He stopped by a white one. "This is identical to my father's 1947 Ford that we had in Spain."

The old cars mostly operate as taxis. There was little traffic for a big city. Very few private individuals can afford cars but bicycles are abundant, as are the local buses. These frequently belch smoke but are an efficient, if crowded, way of traveling around the city. The few Russian trucks looked very different to western designs.

Huge and ornate, the Grand Theatre is home to the internationally acclaimed National Ballet Company. Several ballerinas were relaxing and chatting on the balcony behind. During the late 1940s and 50s during

Andy looking nostalgically at the 1947 Ford V8

Batista's time, opulent Mafia-owned casinos were opened in Havana, attracting the likes of Betty Grable, Nat King Cole and Frank Sinatra. We viewed fascinating pictures of these times on the first and ninth floors in the old Sevilla Hotel.

Over the next few days we continued to explore by foot and visit some of the many exhibits. The Museo de la Revolución was particularly interesting and we enjoyed a visit to the forts that guarded the entrance to Cuba's large harbor, the perfect haven for the treasure ships of the Spanish Main. Fort Morro, Castillo de los Tres Santos Reyes del Morro, the most famous, was built between 1589 and 1630 on the north east headland. It was captured by the British in 1762 but they buried the Spanish Commander, who was killed in action, with full military honors. Other than the museum the fort is quite plain with just a few canons lined up, pointing towards the entrance of the harbor, so we were pleased to be invited to view the shipping channel from the Harbor Control's Office where we learned that yachts are not allowed in this busy commercial harbor. When we were leaving they tried to sell us some black coral jewelry. Although a little disappointed that they had this ulterior motive, we were realizing that money from tourism is the key to Cuba's future prosperity.

Wanting to see a little more of the country I decided to go on a two-day tour to Trinidad in the south. We were a mixed group—two English girls, two Frenchmen, an Ecuadorian doctor who was supposed to be attending a medical conference, a Swiss couple, a Cuban who resided in Miami and myself. Communication was quite interesting with just our guide and the Swiss couple reasonably multi-lingual. We headed on the freeway towards Cienfuegos. The land was lush and fertile with sugar, citrus and cattle all efficiently farmed, although with the expense of fuel, ploughing by oxen is still a common sight. Cienfuegos itself is a gracious well-kept town. It sits on a beautiful bay and despite being beside a large industrial center it retains its old identity with two palaces and a neo-classical cathedral in its lovely main square. Interestingly many of the people here have blond hair and blue eyes.

We were then taken to Marina Jagua for a boat ride! Lunch was at a beachside restaurant and we were entertained by singers accompanied by guitars.

Cuba, of course, has a reputation for its music and one of the pleasures of Havana was live bands, often the jazz-related salsa, or harmonizing in dulcet tones, their music influenced by a happy combination of African rhythm and Spanish melody. That night we stayed in a converted *finca* (farm) and after delicious mojitos—rum, crushed mint, sugar, lime juice, sparkling water and ice, with a large decorative sprig of mint—were treated to a vibrant performance of country dancing with an excellent dinner of local pork.

Around the cabanas, mango trees were dripping with fruit, so laden some almost touched the ground.

"Is there a chance of buying any?" I asked Denora, our lively tour guide.

Music is played everywhere in Cuba

"No problem, just go and pick some for free."

The driver came out of the bus with me, found a plastic bag and stick and managed to pick some huge mangoes that were higher up. I was touched, not only was it a great haul of my favorite fruit, there were several varieties and degrees of ripeness.

The old town of Trinidad and close-by Valle de los Ingenios have also been declared World Heritage Sites. Trinidad was founded in 1514 by the first governor of Cuba but essentially remained a smuggler's backwater until the late 18th century when goods and slaves were brought in from Jamaica. In the 19th century, during the slave rebellion in Haiti, many French refugees poured into the town and built fifty small sugar mills in the valley. By the middle of the century this region was producing a third of Cuba's sugar. It is the wealth of that era that makes the area so attractive to visit today. Although the boom ended with the wars of independence, colonial Trinidad remained in a time warp, very similar in many ways to Antigua in Guatemala.

Riding along the valley we saw that many of the old mills and manor houses lay in ruins. A few of us climbed the 136 steps for a panoramic view of the fertile countryside from a 143-foot-high old slave-watching tower that stands on the Manaca Iznaga estate next to the Hacienda House. Embroidered linens and clothing for sale billowed in the light breeze and I bought some of the maracas, seed pods shaken for rhythm in bands, from the enthusiastic vendor.

A tasting of Canchanchara, another rum drink with honey, lemon juice and ice, and lively salsa band persuaded me to buy Cuban drums for our boys. Although the young drummer spoke no English he understood what I wanted and took no end of trouble to take me around town, bargaining for a good price and tuning them to his satisfaction.

During a coffee stop on the way back to Havana the Cuban/American passenger suggested that it would be nice if we gave the driver and tour guide a tip.

"Of course, we were planning to," we chorused. Both had worked long hours and put tremendous effort into making the tour a success.

"How much would be appropriate?" I asked.

"Well they get paid about $10.00 per month so I think they would be really happy with $1.00."

And here lies a major problem in Cuba, the two-tier level of costs, as every item purchased as a tourist is at world tourist price. Thus the coffee I was drinking was $1.50 and the tour had cost $115.00. To me it seemed an insult to give these hard-working people just one dollar, however if everyone gave 10% the resulting amount seemed so out of line with their monthly salary that it seemed unfair to anyone working outside tourism.

I was the last to be dropped off and was sad that it was not permitted to invite these two delightful employees on board for a beer.

"How were your two days?" I asked Andy.

"Never a dull moment," said Andy, a twinkle in his eye.

"Oh yes?"

"I hadn't even been back on board ten minutes after seeing you off at the hotel," he told me, "before the first Chica was knocking on the hull! The grapevine works pretty fast around here, obviously they knew you were going to be away!"

We had seen these lovely-looking girls wandering the marina. A disappointing aspect of Cuban life is the blatant sex trade found everywhere there were tourists. No doubt a reliable dollar earner, but sad to see.

After a last chat to various cruisers we had met around the docks, mostly Europeans and Canadians, a visit to the excellent market in Santa Fé and buying more of the irresistible Spanish chorizo and excellent $2 Spanish wine in the marina store, we went alongside the official dock to clear out. Procedures went quickly as over 400 American boats were imminently expected to arrive. One group was on a sports fishing tournament while the larger number of sailboats were participating in the Annual Tampa-Havana Cup. Although this would quadruple the number of boats, the marina with its long channels has endless capacity.

Outside the twelve-mile limit we gave Cornflake his burial at sea. Andy e-mailed the boys.

'We regret to announce that Cornflake passed away on May 16th. Chirpy on Saturday morning, supine by lunch, she died peacefully in her sleep.

Funeral arrangements had to be delayed and her remains remained in the freezer due to the insistence of the Cuban Authorities that we depart with whatever we entered. Today she was buried at sea with full military honors as befits an aviator of renown.

No flowers, please. D.'

United States East Coast

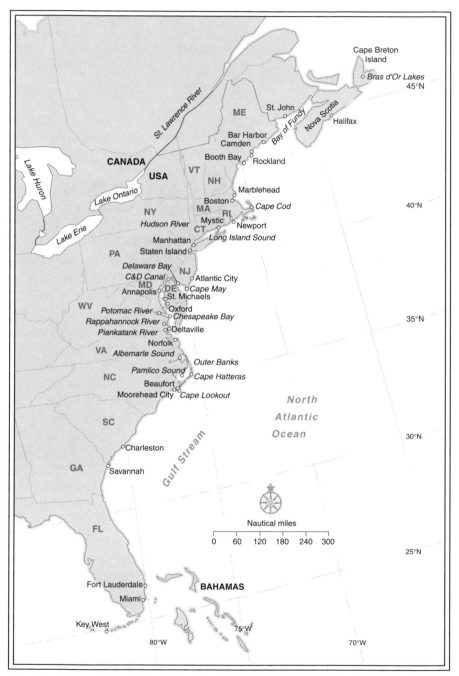

The East Coasts of the United States and Canada

14. Florida to New York

*B*agheera spent the summer and Fall cruising the east coasts of the United States and Canada, and the experience was unexpectedly rewarding. In planning our one-year sabbatical around North and Central America we had tended to focus on new destinations in Central America, not anticipating the incredible cruising diversity of the North American coastline, its wealth of fascinating history, and the abundant seafood along its shores. Our passage up the east coast took us nearly 2,500 nautical miles from subtropical Key West, along 14 American states to the cold Atlantic waters of Canada above the 46th parallel.

A sailboat like *Bagheera*, with a draft just over 7' and a mast height of 55' above water permits the choice of completing some of the passages within the protective bounds of the Intracoastal Waterway. We chose to go offshore for the 400-mile passage from Fort Lauderdale, Florida to Charleston, South Carolina, then transited the waterway to enjoy the backwater beauty of the Carolinas. At Norfolk, Virginia, we entered Chesapeake Bay where we found an abundance of cruising destinations, from quiet picturesque anchorages to resonant historic townships. At its northern end, the C&D Canal ushered us into Delaware Bay and thence back out to the Atlantic for an ocean passage up the New Jersey coast and a memorable visit to New York City.

Lying at the western end of the Florida Keys, the Dry Tortugas are a cluster of seven islands on a large reef that were discovered by Ponce de Leon in 1513. When I had first suggested a visit, Andy had not been keen.

"I think we should be getting north," was his preference. "I'm looking forward to the amenities in Fort Lauderdale to get some work done on the boat." I could tell he was already on a different agenda!

"But it would be a pity to miss Key West and Fort Jefferson looks fascinating," I continued, hoping to pique his interest in something military. It did the trick!

Surging north across the Gulf Stream we left the tropics.

"I feel sad in some ways," I lamented. 'It's as though our trip is almost over."

I need not have been concerned. Arriving at the Dry Tortugas as dawn broke, the picturesque keys epitomized the tropics and the massive fort was intriguing. We were surprised to find over a hundred boats at anchor off Garden Key, but later learnt that many were taking part in the rally to Cuba. Almost immediately a warden came to the boat and handed us an information sheet on this National Park, a wildlife refuge. It particularly alerted us to wrecks, with over 500 in the vicinity!

Open to visitors from sunrise to sunset, the brick fort is impressive to explore. We learnt its history from the documentary video and there are frequent information sites around the walls. The fort was built by the American government to control shipping through the Straits of Florida to the Gulf, and to protect trade from the Mississippi River bound for the Atlantic Ocean. Started in 1846, it was to be one of the world's most

Massive Fort Jefferson

effective maritime defenses with its 8-foot thick, 50-foot high walls and batteries of cannon, but building was halted by the Civil War. Ironically, during this period rifled cannon were developed that could easily demolish its walls, so the construction that had taken over 20 years and 160 million bricks became obsolete before it was finished and it was never completed.

From the high walls of the fort there are stunning views of the keys and the turtles in the moat. On our way back to *Bagheera* by dinghy we drifted by Bush Key for a closer look at the hundreds of sooty terns and pelicans crowding the beach.

Running for 124 miles in a southwesterly curve from Biscayne Bay, the Florida Keys are a coral and limestone barrier that protects Florida's marshlands and gives comfortable inshore cruising for shallow draft boats. America's only continental reef, it is enjoyed for its diving and fishing. Within an hour of leaving Fort Jefferson we had caught two mackerel and a trevally, had lost a dolphin fish (mahi-mahi), released a huge barracuda and seen several large turtles.

The strong flow of the Gulf Stream quickly whisked us up to Key West, the southernmost point of continental U.S.A. and the most famous key of them all. Once America's richest city from the salvage of Spanish wrecks, and home to Tennessee Williams, Ernest Hemingway, Robert Frost, John James Audubon and key lime pie, it is now a colorful tourist destination and the favorite island of flamboyant singer and writer Jimmy Buffet.

There is a deep-water harbor with several marinas and acceptable calm-weather anchorages. Arriving at 6:30pm we could see crowds ashore, and tourist vessels under full sail on sundowner cruises passed by. Unfortunately it was raining; there were also warnings of water-spouts on the radio.

I was below typing e-mails the following morning when Andy called down from the deck.

"You have to come and see this, there's a water-spout welling up about two miles away."

As I came up the companionway I noticed a cloud with an unusual dip on its lower edge.

"Look," I pointed to Andy. " It's right over that turbulence on the water and it's growing bigger."

As the wave action on the ocean became wider, higher and more confused the 'tube' from the cloud extended further down. Then suddenly the two fused together, an amazing phenomenon of nature. Also surprising were numbers of windsurfers and jet skiers rushing out to see it, far less concerned than we were of being close to the water-spout in the storm that on radar extended over an area of 5x10 nautical miles. For ten minutes the black column marched down the bay before separating from the sea and collapsing.

The water-spout

With the water-spout faded and wind abated, Andy went ashore to clear into the United States.

"We really should have finished those Cuban mangoes," he commented.

"I know, but as much as I love mangoes there are only so many that you can eat!"

He returned an hour later aghast. "As it's a long weekend we have to wait until Tuesday to clear in with Customs."

"I can't think of any country in the world that we had to wait for three days in an official Port of Entry except Cuba! Can't we even go ashore?"

"Yes, we can. I was able to clear in with Immigration and he didn't mention any restrictions."

We had only planned one day in Key West and this was an irritating delay.

"At least we can finish the mangoes at our leisure!"

We went ashore later in the day and enjoyed the charming, if touristy, town with its old colonial and southern architecture and busy waterfront full of well-kept traditional sailing yachts. In particular the replica of the famous nineteenth-century racing schooner, *America*, gleamed in the sunlight with its glossy black hull and varnished spars.

We were just getting back in the dinghy when we were hailed. It was the lads we had met in Maria la Gorda when clearing into Cuba.

"You're here already," I exclaimed. "Did you see much of Mexico?"

"We had a great time. Here's your cruising guide back," one replied, "and we met some friends of yours in Isla Mujeres."

"I guess some people still haven't left," I commented.

"No, these people had just arrived, they were Peter and Ann Deeth."

"Good heavens, we haven't seen them for years," Andy exclaimed. "We knew each other in Antigua in the '60s and '70s. How did you find out they knew us?"

"We heard them talking ashore and as their accents sounded just like yours, we asked them!" This was just too bizarre!

The positive side of forced delays is catching up on chores. We focussed on the list of 'to do' jobs when back in civilization. Including work on the boat and business back home they grew at an alarming rate. It's amazing how easy it is to put life on hold while offshore but unfortunately its responsibilities still go on.

Also it was easy to enjoy life ashore, and a walk down the Pelican Path around the Old Town, where traditional conch houses are adorned with brightly painted shutters, railings and gables, and a ride on the Conch Tour Train gave us an insight into this town's colorful history.

The Conchs (pronounced Konks) were the original settlers that came from the Bahamas in the late 18th century. Key West became part of the

Old Key West

State of Florida in 1822 when a settler bought it for $2000 in a Cuban bar. Fortunes were made from plundering shipwrecks and a display of treasure can be seen at the Mel Fisher Museum, a large part, over 85,000 artifacts, made up from the Spanish galleons Nuestra Señora de Atocha and Santa Margarita. At one point Conchs had the highest per capita income in the country. Later, a cigar factory was set up by Cuban immigrants and a United States naval station was also established. Now tourism is the main source of revenue. With its attractive buildings, fascinating history, famous past residents, numerous bars and restaurants, lively music and subtropical climate it is not hard to understand why.

There was a long line-up at the Customs office on Tuesday morning. Those who had arrived from Mexico also had to wait. Three hours later Andy returned to the boat alone.

"Aren't they coming on board to inspect?" I asked.

"No," replied Andy. "And they were an hour late arriving at their office. At least we had a good time here, but let's get going!"

Some weeks later we were incensed to receive a bill from Customs for overtime!

It was a turbulent overnight ride to Fort Lauderdale, a fast passage as we were still in the Gulf Stream, but *Bagheera* was pounding into wind. The log reads 'very bumpy, getting soaked, ships everywhere, lightning all around, wind up to 26 knots, 16-mile electrical storm'. But we also caught more mackerel and dolphin fish and in due course could ease sheets for a final romp to Port Everglades.

After following a large freighter through the entrance channel we peeled off to starboard to enter Fort Lauderdale. Fortuitously the 17th Street bridge opened almost immediately so we rushed through. Ahead a marker with a green square lay mid-channel.

"Can you look at the chart to see what that means?" I asked Andy who was busily looking around at the many vessels through the binoculars.

"I think that's *Eileen*," he was saying excitedly, about a vessel that looked like the old Fife-designed yawl on which we had first crossed the Atlantic in 1973.

I throttled back and said, "O.K. I'll leave it to port." The mantra *red right returning* coursing trance-like through my well-programmed brain.

Wrong! In no time we were nudging the mud. It is important to be aware of the Waterway's system of aids to navigation before making a transit! The Waterway is delineated by day markers, usually about 15 feet high, with green squares to starboard and red triangles to port when headed north. Once you know this, it is easy to follow—until the waterway coincides with a shipping channel marked by conventional buoys of the opposite colors! At this point one must look for yellow reflective stripes, triangles and squares that are on all the ICW aids whether buoys or markers.

With boat maintenance to do we docked at the brand-new Las Olas City Marina, and as a series of storms marched through we never regretted the expense. The largest center for boating in the southeast with its many waterways, Fort Lauderdale offers every facility imaginable. Getting around, however, can be difficult, though we were fortunate enough to have friends lend us their cars. It's horrifying how quickly the cash disappears when you're exposed to the temptations and facilities of civilization once again. But it was good to get equipment repaired, exchange our dinghy for a new one (an Avon this time), get photos developed, visit Costco to restock on bulk supplies and easily connect with our family and businesses back home.

Before continuing north we studied our options. The Intracoastal Waterway was one obvious choice. Officially the waterway runs from Texas to Massachusetts, but most people focus on the section that stretches from Miami, Florida to Norfolk, Virginia—precisely the part that interested us. The fixed bridges all have at least 64' clearance (except for the Julia Tuttle Bridge in Miami, which is 56'). This suited us, but the distance is over 1,095 miles, and as it is not advisable to travel at night, the trip in its entirety would have taken too long for our schedule. We decided to pass on the southern section, which tends to be more built up and has many more bridges (55 of the 92 opening bridges are in the southern 285 miles), and take the offshore route to Charleston.

Ever since being struck by lightning off the South African coast we have been rather sensitive about—and keen to avoid—electrical storms. During the boisterous week spent at the Fort Lauderdale dock we had been watching the weather carefully. An old sailing friend was also monitoring weather with far more resources available.

I first met Peter Bowker in France in 1971, when he was campaigning *American Eagle* for Ted Turner. I had become friends with his crew and they persuaded Peter to let me hitch a ride back to England on board, after we had all finished the ocean racing circuit. I had called Andy in England before departing, "I think you might like to join me on this 70-foot racing machine," I teased him tantalizingly. "You can join us in the Channel Islands; we're planning a stop in Guernsey."

I had recently met Andy in Venezuela at the Sunfish World Championships. He was already envious that I was off ocean racing, but sailing aboard this twelve-meter yacht was a real coup! The sleighride sail back to Cowes in England is one we will never forget. We subsequently joined Peter on other passages and were delighted when he married Jo, another old friend from Antigua during the '60s. They had been wonderful over the last week, rounding up many 'old salts' from the pioneering days of Caribbean chartering.

Finally, the weather forecast was ideal for Peter to start off across the Atlantic and for us to head for Charleston. After the first day of calm, (but with a favorable current with us of 4.5 knots), we spent the rest of the 400-mile voyage dodging storm cells! Although we were able to avoid the worst by using radar, winds still fluctuated between 10 and 25 knots and lightning flashed all around us. We reefed and unreefed continuously, it seemed. What a relief to have our Profurl in-boom mainsail furling system so that the off-watch person did not have to be disturbed.

Charming Charleston, founded in 1670, struggled over the years through fires, earthquakes, hurricanes and economically difficult times, so many of the houses were patched and jacked up instead of being torn down and rebuilt, as with some of their more well-heeled neighbors. The result is a downtown core full of character with many lovely old dwellings and a busy central market square. Arriving on Sunday, we decided to become tourists for the day and took the horse and carriage tour. It was very sedate until the horse, spooked by noisy motor bikes, reared up out of the carriage shafts and took off at a gallop. After a quick glance at each other we leapt to the ground—give us a storm at sea any day over being stranded in a carriage half attached to a runaway horse!

We were welcomed by the Beneteau U.S.A. crew at their head office and gladly took an offer of a car to explore nearby plantations whose mansions and grounds give an insight into the southern lifestyle of days long past. We also accepted an invitation to join a Beneteau owners' rendezvous on the Chesapeake ten days later. Getting there required long, high-mileage days on the Intracoastal Waterway as far as Norfolk, but this turned out to be a thoroughly enjoyable experience. Known by a variety of names such as the Inland Waterway, the Intercoastal Waterway, the Ditch, I.C.W. and Inside, this route weaves through wetlands with beautiful mansions, along rivers and canals, crosses lakes and passes through inlets from the ocean.

We had been concerned about our draft and were not surprised when we went aground soon after entering the Waterway at Charleston, but this turned out to be one of just two groundings we suffered during the entire inland trip to Norfolk. It is critical, however, to stay in the channel and keep an eye on the depth sounder, and to use the outside of a bend where depths are greater. At times the markers are far apart and it was essential to have binoculars at hand, and also use the GPS and radar when visibility was poor. To our surprise there are only a few places where the Waterway is a narrow 'ditch' where space is critical when meeting an oncoming barge, but by monitoring VHF channels 13 and 16 it is easy to know their movements.

"I've found a great spot to sit with the new remote autopilot control," I announced to Andy as he came up on deck after a nap. I was perched on cushions in the companionway, and with the panels in the dodger raised I had great visibility.

This Autohelm hand control gives most of the information displayed by all our systems including depth. It plugs into a socket on the coach roof next to the radar. It made life easy to push plus 10°, minus 20°, whatever was required.

"It would be absolutely perfect if we had a seat with a back-rest that fits in the companionway." I continued. A week later we won one at the rendezvous!

"These strip charts work well," I continued. "And I'm finding this movable arrow (made from electrical tape) really useful to mark our position, as some of the markers have altered position and numbering has changed."

There are several cruising guides for the waterway that provide the necessary information regarding bridge openings, anchorages and marinas, but they do need to be the latest issue.

'Let's plan tomorrow's run now," Andy suggested after anchoring for the night. We'd had a frustrating day waiting for bridges to open as many are now time restricted. In addition there had been a long stretch

Advance planning around bridge opening times paid off

with anchorages few and far between, so we had to stop well before nightfall.

We also hadn't anticipated the lack of facilities, having expected more towns en route.

"Any milk?" we inquired yet again at one of the many convenience stores by the fuel docks.

Along with a fear of running out of toilet paper, early morning tea is a top priority for Andy! There was no problem finding beer, pop, chips, chocolate bars, fish bait and ice—but no luck in locating a carton of milk or a loaf of bread, let alone fresh produce. In the end we stayed one night at a marina that had a courtesy car, and juggled times with other cruisers so we could drive ten miles to the nearest store.

"We've been surprised how little traffic there is on the Waterway," Andy commented while we were filling with fuel.

"It's the time of year," the attendant replied. "By June most boats have already gone north. It was really busy earlier in the year and will be again in the fall."

It was much busier, of course, at weekends.

"I've been using Mark's strategy," Andy told me on Saturday afternoon.

Mark Reuther runs Profurl U.S.A. and while in Fort Lauderdale he told us about his waterway adventures. "I was invited to help deliver a powerboat, and soon realized why powerboaters get frustrated with us sailboaters."

"How so?"

"Either you have to keep behind a sailboat and do their speed which is frustrating or it takes forever to pass them when they are doing six knots, without causing a huge wake."

"So what's the answer?"

"If the sailboat slows down briefly and lets the powerboat through there is far less grief for everyone."

On a busy Saturday it worked like a charm, well worth the small delay for a far more comfortable ride, and everyone waved their appreciation. We found that generally other boaters were courteous and only the occasional rogue barreled past at high speed regardless of wake.

The changing vistas and wildlife were absorbing. From Florida to Virginia one passes from the sub tropics to a temperate climate. Vegetation varies from the palms trees and mangroves of Florida, to gracious forests of magnolia, cypress, gum and oaks draped with Spanish moss in Georgia and the Carolinas. We loved the vast stretches of wetlands, bright green and a birdwatcher's paradise. Water-life is a fascinating mix of fresh and saltwater species with visits even from dolphins.

Also intriguing is the history along the Waterway and the wonderful museums that have sprung up. Since the earliest settlers sailed through the sounds of North Carolina, fortunes have been made and lost, great battles fought during the Revolutionary War and the Civil War began when Fort Sumter was fired upon in Charleston's harbor.

A memorable stop was Georgetown, South Carolina's third oldest city after Charleston and Beaufort—although with a Spanish outpost established in 1526 some historians claim this is where American/European history began. Georgetown also played a part in history during the American Revolution by sending both Thomas Lynch Senior and Junior to sign the Declaration of Independence.

Following the Revolution rice became the staple crop. The lowlands surrounding the six local rivers were ideal for its cultivation so Georgetown prospered and in 1832 it became an official Port of Entry. By the 1840's the area produced almost half the rice grown in the United States and the local variety, 'Carolina Gold', was in demand worldwide. The accumulated wealth from the large production of both rice and indigo (dyestuff) is shown by the elegant homes that still adorn the oak-canopied streets, and the people reflect its multinational heritage of Native Indian, Spanish, English, French, Scots and Africans. Production declined during Reconstruction (1865-1876) due to labor unrest, poor weather and lack of capital, and never recovered. With the industrial revolution the area turned to lumber, then developed a paper industry that still thrives today.

This history is portrayed in the Rice Museum that is housed in the grand Old Market Building, its tower adorned with a distinctive town clock that has faces on every side. It seemed sad that I was the only visitor but lucky, as the elderly attendant showed me around, tirelessly explaining the maps and artifacts, and pointing out features on the dioramas that made the whole area come alive.

We had been looking forward to reaching Beaufort, North Carolina. Pronounced Bo-fort, it shares the Beaufort Inlet with Moorehead City just below Cape Lookout at the southern extremity of North Carolina's notorious Outer Banks. Not only had we heard a great deal about this 1709 town that hums with yachting activity, in Fort Lauderdale Jo had given us the phone number of Mike Beal, who had been the skipper of *Eileen* when we had crossed the Atlantic right after our wedding.

Next morning we walked down a street of stately old homes to join Mike and Mitty for breakfast. Although we hadn't seen each other for nearly 25 years, it seemed like yesterday that we had crossed the Atlantic from Antigua to the Azores, where we indulged in the thick red wine siphoned from barrels and painted our picture among many others on the sea wall.

"Then I was delayed in Gibraltar after you left to tour Europe because *Eileen* was seized! The owner had been involved in the Watergate scandal," said Mike, reminding us of the insecurity of being a professional yacht captain.

"We passed an empty bottle of gin every afternoon and tons of Portuguese Men of War (jellyfish), and we still have the glass fishing float covered in goose barnacles that we picked up," I added. "And I remember laboring over celestial navigation and that us novices, (the rest of the crew other than Mike and Andy!) initially positioned *Eileen* all over the Atlantic!"

"Where are you headed now?" Mike asked. "If you're going up the east coast I've got lots of charts and guide books."

"You have? Wonderful!"

We had some chart books but these are sometimes awkward to use and lack large-scale detail. To have the real thing was a bonus indeed. While Andy and Mike went off to sort them, Mitty and I became acquainted. Like Andy and I, she and Mike had run charter boats together for a while in the Caribbean, but that lifestyle appeals to most women for only a limited time. After a successful visit to Beaufort they had decided to make it their home.

After recent hot weather it suddenly turned cold, with a front bringing icy northerly winds. As we now had to cross the open Pamlico and Albemarle Sounds to reach Norfolk we needed a reliable engine. Although ours still ran, with over 10,000 hours it was losing its zip and struggling in the choppy head seas.

"We are soon going to need a new one or have it reconditioned," warned Andy. Either seemed an expensive proposition. We would put up with motoring at only four knots and smaller boats shooting past a while longer!

The last day before reaching Norfolk was a busy one with three road bridges, a railway bridge and a lock in rapid succession and as one bridge opened late it was a push to reach the next. As we relaxed in the lock we chatted with a family that had just spent six months in the Virgin Islands. After the gates opened the mother said to the children, "Now back to school." I laughed to myself, it sounded so familiar. I remember well how many diversions there were when we were cruising, that were always so much more interesting to the boys than set lessons!

We also talked to an Ocean Cruising Club boat. This is a British organization and we were pleased to run into another member, not thinking the chances high on this side of the Atlantic. How wrong we were. While anchoring off turbulent Hospital Point a launch came roaring up also flying an OCC burgee.

"Hi *Falcon Quest* and *Bagheera*, welcome. I'm Gary, the Norfolk OCC Port Officer and I've got free moorage for both of you ashore."

"Fantastic, lead the way!"

Not only was it convenient to explore the Hampton Roads Naval Museum in Norfolk, with its displays of two centuries of local naval activity, it also gave a great excuse to party the night away!

Before leaving the next morning, Ted and Jo from *Falcon Quest* brought back our visitor's book. It was a great entry.

Who is that waving, just behind
It looks as if they know us.
We can't stop now, we'll miss the bridge,
To talk will only slow us.
Oh! Look they've got a flying fish.
They're in the club as well.
In that case talk on the VHF
The bridge can go to hell.
In Norfolk, hanging on the hook,
Things will soon get better.
Who is that coming out this way?
It must be Gary and Greta.
A lively evening enjoyed by all,
Too soon we all must part.
Tomorrow's journey means that they
Will be away at sparrow fart.

Several warships were arriving as we departed Norfolk at dawn. It was an impressive sight with crews smartly lining the decks. Hampton Roads, across from Norfolk, is the site of the famous 1862 naval battle between the *Monitor* and *Merrimac* during the Civil War. Now these waters teem with commercial traffic.

North of this busy metropolis, the land is a rural delight. After a pleasant daysail we arrived at Deltaville, Virginia, in good time with an hour before the welcoming party for the Beneteau Rendezvous, only to go hard aground at the harbor entrance. Being towed in on our side through the shallow channel was hardly the entry we were planning as 'the experienced cruisers'! Despite the inauspicious arrival it was a great weekend, the beginning of what was to become a much longer association with the area.

Stretching 200 miles from Norfolk to the C & D Canal and 20 miles at its widest point, Chesapeake Bay has almost 4000 miles of coastline. With both its eastern and western shores indented by innumerable rivers and inlets it is a cruisers' paradise, but depths do have to be monitored closely as passages often silt up and charted depths are not reliable. In addition, there are hundreds of commercial craft on the bay that must be watched carefully. The shipping lanes are narrow but busy with freighters, ore carriers, tugs hauling barges, and tankers. There are also menhaden fishing boats, oyster and clam 'drudge' boats, and numerous crab traps, not to mention the many recreational boats that are active, particularly on weekends.

Despite all the traffic, away from the main channels and marinas the Chesapeake has given us some of our most peaceful coastal cruising. Wending one's way up the rivers, the calm waters give marvelous reflections of the shoreside foliage and the small towns have delightful histories, beautifully restored old buildings and welcoming residents. As the rates were so favorable at the Deltaville Yacht Yard we decided that we would return to this area to leave the boat for the winter. On subsequent visits we have come to love the Piankatank and Rappahannock Rivers and enjoyable events such as the Urbanna oyster festival, also communities like Onancock, on the less developed southern part of the eastern shore.

St. Michaels

One can cruise north to Annapolis in a couple of days, but far better to dawdle with a visit up to Washington, D.C. along the beautiful Potomac River, a worthwhile expedition in itself. Up St. Mary's River, at the mouth of the Potomac, is a replica of the *Dove* which brought the first settlers to Maryland and the reconstruction of St. Mary's City makes an interesting visit ashore.

Solomons is a popular destination when transiting the west side of the Bay, as is the charming town of Oxford, and St Michaels with its fascinating Maritime Museum on the Eastern Shore

"Where do you want to anchor?" Andy asked, with Annapolis in sight.

"Let's go into Back Creek and anchor close to Steve's boat," I replied.

Those who have read **Still Cruising** may remember our tour of U.S.S. Willamette in New Orleans with Steve Womack, then the Captain. Now stationed in Washington D.C., he keeps his cruising boat here in one of the many marinas.

"We can easily get together with him and if we leave the dinghy on the Eastport side it is only a ten minute walk to downtown."

The boating mecca of Annapolis with its 18th century central core and large Naval Academy is always a great place to visit. This town made history when the Treaty of Paris, which officially ended the American Revolution, was signed there in 1784 at the time when Annapolis had a one-year stint as temporary capital of the United States.

"Wow, it looks so different without wall-to-wall boats," I exclaimed as we reached the City Dock. Generally we are here during the Annapolis Boat Show when hundreds of visiting boats fill the inner harbor, marinas and anchorages.

It was a good opportunity to explore and friends gave us a tour around the attractive old streets, pointing out St. John's College, chartered in 1784, with the 400-year-old 'liberty' tree under which a peace treaty was signed between settlers and Indians in 1654. We stopped to wander around the 1779 State House, the oldest in the country in continuous legislative use, and visited the impressive Naval Academy Museum with its intricate models of old sailing ships.

With the appearance of several old friends, and the resulting lively parties on board, it was hard to tear ourselves away.

"Now, what day did you say Colin is arriving in New York?" Andy asked about our son's visit.

"In a week's time—we had better get going!"

It was hot as we headed north and there was very little breeze. We decided not to stop. The upper eastern shore is popular due to its proximity to urban centers, including Baltimore, that lie on the western shore.

There are dramatic changes at certain points up the U.S. coast and the contrast between the Chesapeake and the New Jersey coast is one. From the pretty undulating countryside, charming dwellings and gardens trailing to the water, one enters the 12-mile Chesapeake and Delaware Canal, then a broad and rather boring Delaware Bay and the flat, built-up New Jersey coast.

The C & D Canal forms a vital link in the ICW system. It is easy to transit with no locks or toll, is 145' wide and has a controlling depth of 35 feet. It is busy with freighters and commercial craft and one should listen to the dispatcher on VHF Channel 13. The canal mark system is based on entering from the Delaware so red lights are on the north side of the canal with green lights to the south, making it easy to transit at night. It is preferable to time a transit to take advantage of the current as it can run up to two knots.

"The tide usually floods for five hours and ebbs for seven," said Andy studying the current charts of the Delaware in *Reed's Nautical Almanac.* "There's a convenient anchorage close to the eastern end of the canal where we can wait until the current is favorable."

"It's 50 miles between the C & D Canal and Cape May, at the northern entrance to the Bay. Although there are some cruising stops on the Delaware, they don't seem particularly interesting," I added, after reading the cruising guide, "So we might as well do the bay in a day and head out into the Atlantic along the New Jersey coast."

Studded with sandbars and shallow waters the Delaware River and Bay have to be piloted with care. We followed the shipping channel, for the most part staying just outside this busy routeway, then decided to stop at the harbor at Cape May, New Jersey. Proclaimed a historic landmark, this Victorian seaside resort dates back to the 18th Century.

Only boats with a draft less than three feet can realistically travel the ICW up the New Jersey coast, so most sailboats complete the 120-mile passage from Cape May to Sandy Hook offshore. This long sandy shoreline, covered with high-rise hotels and neon signs, has few harbors with all-weather entrances so it is important to keep a close check on the often turbulent Atlantic Ocean and its variable weather. On this passage north in early July, from a calm we suddenly had 28 knots from the west. At the time this gave welcome relief from the intense heat.

"What's happening?" I asked, peering up the companionway. We were motoring in a calm stretch and I had been woken by frequent unidentifiable thuds in the cockpit.

What met my eyes made me howl with laughter. Donned in pajamas, that I can only recall him wearing in my parent's house before we were married, and odd socks, Andy was crazily swatting at the boat and himself like a mad thing. That he was shredding an unread yachting magazine seemed inconsequential; he was a man possessed!

"Killed four that time, " he acknowledged victoriously, as more black flies fell through the cockpit grating. "They have vicious bites," he explained. "I can't understand why they're out here, we're more than three miles offshore."

"Have you tried insect repellant?" I asked.

Whap! "It doesn't seem to work." Whap, whap!

"What about the extra strong DEET that Caroline and Wilson brought down to Panama?"

"Where is it?" Whap!

I fetched the powerful repellent that drives away mosquitoes instantly and Andy gratefully anointed himself, but he had hardly finished when he was dancing frenetically and swirling the magazine again. The flies were now swarming him in delight. I am never bitten as much as Andy, so I suggested he go below and put up the mosquito netting. As the flies particularly attacked ankles and feet, I took the precaution of donning socks. Far more effective, however, was keeping my feet in the air, but then I had the challenge of how I could still keep watch!

We took three days to reach New York. Having previously only visited Atlantic City to work at boat shows, it was fascinating to see the skyline from the ocean before anchoring in the harbor for the night. Our next stop was Shark River where we gorged on soft-shelled crabs at a waterside restaurant. Like many of the inlets, Shark River has a bridge right at its entrance, which isn't opened until the last minute when a boat is just a few lengths away. Tricky for the sailor who has a following wind and a flood tide!

It is an 8-mile run due north from Sandy Hook to The Narrows at the entrance of New York Harbor. In strong southeast or easterly winds the passage can be rough and it is then worth considering the route to the west of Staten Island, but it was calm for our passage. Although busy, New York Harbor is straightforward to negotiate and on our entry there were more sailboats around than commercial traffic.

The Verrazano Narrows Bridge crosses the Narrows from Staten Island to Brooklyn and is an impressive landmark, one of the world's largest suspension bridges. After passing Staten Island a magnificent panorama of New York unfolded.

I was again e-mailing at the single sideband radio below, when Andy called out jubilantly "I can see the Statue of Liberty. It's huge."

When told by Mark Scott, a Manhattan architect who we first met in Antigua just after we had both just completed our circumnavigations, that it was possible to anchor under the Statue of Liberty, it had seemed a magical way to spend one's first night in New York City. We dropped the hook between the 300-foot statue on Liberty Island and Ellis Island, distinctive with its Moorish architecture, where 15 million Europeans immigrants were processed into the United States. Uncomfortable at first from the wash of tourist boats, we questioned our wisdom, but at dusk the last one departed. We were absorbed in watching a sail boat race off downtown Manhattan when the skyline started to change, gradually morphing from brilliant sunlight, through a golden dusk, to a mass of twinkling lights as night descended. It was indeed an enchanting setting and set the tone for our visit.

We took several photos of the Statue of Liberty the following morning from the dinghy.

"It would be really neat to get some pictures of *Bagheera* sailing by the Statue," I enthused to Andy. "We can get everything organized and one of us go off in the dinghy with the camera."

"Wouldn't it be easier to wait for Colin?"

"It would, but this is just such a perfect day." I had learnt the hard way not to delay taking the perfect shot. Even the wind co-operated with enough to fill the sails but not too much to pass by too quickly.

There have been many articles recently extolling the virtues of New York, its new cleanliness and safety, the friendly people, as well as the sights and shows. We couldn't agree more. The second night we went into the expensive Newport Marina, but we could do laundry, shop for supplies and had a stunning view of downtown Manhattan for our son Colin's arrival from British Columbia that evening.

The next morning we moved up to the West 79th Street Boat Basin on the Hudson River. As the current rips past at 4 knots with four changes in direction daily these mooring buoys at $10.00 a night are the best bargain around! They are next to a park, dinghies can be left safely at the dock and two blocks up on Broadway there are the most wonderful, inexpensive food emporiums in the country.

"We should eat a meal before going ashore, to curtail our purchases!" Andy insisted.

"There wouldn't be a problem if I could keep you out of Zabar's!" This delicatessen with its stunning cheeses was our particular downfall.

A memorable day was spent with Margaret Grace and husband Rod who toured us around the smaller art galleries including the one where Margaret had her current exhibition. Colin's style is very similar and I obviously grew in his estimation.

"Amazing," he'd commented, "that you actually have a friend who really knows how to paint!"

My first meeting with Margaret was a far cry from the art world, as it was at the Atlantic City Boat Show where she was working as a yacht broker. For several years we shared hotel accommodation at the show, and while friends on expense accounts were finely wined and dined, we had become fast friends over many a bottle of wine in our room.

"And I'll never forget those 'two for one' breakfasts," Margaret reminded me.

"They were so good, anything you wanted from an incredible buffet, in fact they were our lunch too," I explained to the others. "The down-side was we had to be there at dawn and watch the same grotesque scene from Ben Hur's chariot race as we ate!"

It is easy to get around New York by subway from West 79th Street and we did all the tourists' favorites in town. These included the formal art galleries for Colin, a Broadway show, taking photos and analyzing our route into the harbor from the top of the Empire State Building, as well as great walks and refreshing $10.00 back massages in Central Park.

We were secured to the buoy next to the dock and many cruisers stopped to chat. Several had either come from Lake Ontario through the Erie Canal or from the St. Lawrence River through the Richelieu River, Chambly Canal and Lake Champlain. One vessel was on a 'great loop' cruise that took them across four of the Great Lakes and down the Illinois and Mississippi Rivers to New Orleans. All food for thought!

"I've never liked New York before," Andy commented as we headed down the Hudson in the afternoon, to time our arrival for a favorable passage with the current through Hell's Gate that would take us into Long Island Sound.

"But after this visit I can't wait to get back in the Fall—especially to shop at Zabar's!"

15. Long Island Sound to Maine

Unfortunately we had only two months to explore this phenomenal cruising region with so many destinations demanding a visit. The contrasts found within just a few hundred miles offer 'something for everyone' whether sailing in protected waters, coast-hopping or offshore passage-making. There is a plethora of marinas and historic towns, also deserted anchorages, abundant wildlife and exquisite seafood.

After leaving New York harbor, busy with shipping, we entered Long Island Sound that was teeming with yachts. Cape Cod, at the sound's northeastern end, marks another transition on the U.S. coast. To the north, summer temperatures are cooler, cruising in the open Atlantic Ocean more demanding, and the coast becomes increasingly more rugged. From the Cape Cod Canal it was just a day's sail to rocky Cape Ann, Boston and Marblehead then an overnight run 'down east' to the dramatic coast of Maine.

After motoring down the Hudson River and past the terminal of the bright-yellow Staten Island ferries, we turned into the East River. While Manhattan's tall buildings soared above, there were fleeting glimpses of areas we'd visited with Rod and Margaret—The New York Stock Exchange on Wall Street, the South Street Sea Port with its historic sailing ships, and the glistening Art Deco Chrysler building, the world's tallest building when completed in 1929, a short-lived glory as it was topped by the Empire State Building just a year later.

Bagheera *sailing past the Statue of Liberty*

Keeping a firm hand on the helm as *Bagheera* skewered around in the swirling eddies we surged through Hell's Gate and were catapulted into Long Island Sound.

We anchored in Manhasset Bay in good time for a brilliant red sunset, a great backcloth to the numerous sailboats at anchor. Being a yacht broker, Andy tends to notice this number of masts!

"Think of the boat business here," he commented. "How come you took me to western Canada, not to the east?"

"Because there aren't many boats in Nova Scotia, and I love Vancouver!"

Long Island Sound stretches nearly one hundred miles from northeast to southwest and is up to twenty miles across at its widest point. Not only a great area to cruise it is also a major commercial artery, and a great fishing and lobstering ground. The two rims of the Sound are quite different.

While the southern shore (north shore of Long Island) has large, natural harbors with room to anchor, the north shore bordering on New York State and Connecticut has many rocky outcroppings, islands, small harbors, inlets and river mouths. Often crowded by development, whether suburban, industrial, summer resort or year-round small towns, the area is also generously supplied with boating facilities.

Despite the congestion we enjoyed gunkholing this coast, and were made most welcome at yacht clubs after producing verification of our club affiliations. We even found several attractive deserted anchorages. Although moorage is expensive for a long-term cruiser (often $30.00 per night on a mooring buoy) it is convenient and safe to leave the boat for shoreside expeditions. Often we found the only space to anchor was at the entrance of a harbor in crowded conditions. All was not lost, however, as there we usually found ourselves among other cruising yachts, also on their own hook. Great camaraderie sprung up between us with many a good party into the night.

Memorable visits were first to Greenwich with its good shopping and immaculate mansions, although both Andy and Colin had a few words to say about them.

"Too much overt affluence," commented Colin.

"And although the gardens are neatly groomed, they're soulless. Why don't they have any flowers?" questioned Andy, an avid gardener. Having grown up in England and now living in an area where gardening is almost a spiritual ritual, this lack of color was an unexpected cultural difference.

"It's all right," I consoled them. "This area is far beyond our budget!"

Stamford, settled in 1640, and Norwalk's historic 'SoNo' area also made pleasant stops. We had been fascinated by the many lighthouses up the coast and the Green Ledge Light off the Norwalk, that resembles a large spark plug, was another that caught our attention.

While dining in the cockpit at the beginning of an overnight passage to Stonington, Andy commented, "I wouldn't like to be flying tonight, it's such a hazy sky and there's absolutely no horizon."

A former fighter pilot in the Royal Navy, Andy takes a great interest in aircraft, particularly those in military service, but I can't recall him ever making a spontaneous comment about flying conditions.

The next morning there was constant traffic on the VHF radio with security instructions; a search was obviously in progress. Later it was announced that the Kennedy plane had gone down. We were close to Martha's Vineyard and to be in the vicinity gave the tragedy full impact.

We found the harbor crammed at the delightful old village of Stonington, Connecticut's most eastern seaport that lies close to Mystic.

But *Bagheera* was safe on a mooring buoy in this protected harbor for Alan and Marilyn, friends from numerous boatshows, to indulge us in a stay at their Hartford home, especially well-timed on a heat-wave weekend. Driving along the Connecticut River, we could see that it would be worth a side trip to cruise 45 miles up to Hartford, Connecticut's capital, with a stop in Essex, another attractive 'sailing' town.

Avid cruisers themselves, they insisted we come with our laundry and a list of chores that they could help us complete, as well as having planned that we see the local sights. We strolled gracious gardens and viewed Hartford's ornate old buildings. Foxwoods Casino would not have been our usual choice, but it is attractively designed and had a stunning display of golden orchids. Its development was an amazing success story for the local Indian band and their Mashantucket Pequot Indian Museum was especially impressive. No expense was spared for this display of their heritage, with life-sized replicas and a large self-touring section of a traditional village.

Mystic Seaport made another delightful visit back in time. Its bustling 19th Century village is filled with historic trade shops, homes and an impressive collection of wooden vessels including the barque *Charles W. Morgan* and schooner *L.A. Dunton*. It has a shipyard area where visitors can witness first hand the re-creation of the freedom schooner *Amistad* and a gallery alive with artifacts of the nation's past with fascinating models and a collection of figureheads. We spent some time in the art gallery devoted to marine works and of course checked out the bookstore!

"All the way up the coast we've found the history of America is so well displayed," I said to Alan and Marilyn as they drove us back to the boat.

"Next time you should come into the Seaport dock," Alan suggested. "But you have to book well ahead." As we unloaded groceries and gifts from the car I couldn't believe the number of bags; they had been so generous.

Thirty-five miles to the east at the entrance to Narragansett Bay the vibrant, historic yachting center of Newport, Rhode Island, was bursting with boats. We toured the harbor fascinated, as we had known several of the yachts when Caribbean chartering and offshore racing.

"Is that *Ticonderoga*?" I queried, pointing out a vessel on the far side of the harbor.

"It certainly looks like her," Andy agreed, but as he looked through the binoculars he added, disappointedly, "No, it isn't, but the design is very similar."

We were married aboard the 72-foot *Ticonderoga* in 1973, sailing across the bay in Martinique. Designed by Herreshoff and launched in 1936, '*Big*

American Eagle

Ty' set a blazing pace never to be repeated. At one time she held thirty elapsed time records including the Transpac, TransAtlantic Race and all events in the Southern Ocean Racing Circuit, many of which still stand today. We last saw this graceful yacht in Antigua in 1991 after arriving from South Africa. It was our 18th wedding anniversary and we were thrilled to be invited on board to celebrate—with French champagne of course!

Weaving our way through the boats we saw a line-up of old 12-meter yachts. In their midst was *American Eagle*. Painted her original cardinal red, she looked immaculate.

We moored *Bagheera* to a Cruising Club of America buoy by 'mansion row', summer homes of society's elite, then went off to visit several boats that were flying Ocean Cruising Club burgees and soon became part of another great cruising community.

Founded in 1639 by settlers seeking religious freedom, with its protected harbor Newport soon became a major seaport. Newport rum, made from West Indian sugar, became famous as did the pineapple as a symbol of hospitality. A pineapple placed in the doorway of a Captain's home indicated his return from a voyage and was an open invitation for visitors. With British occupation in 1776, Newport's era as a seaport ended and after the Revolutionary War it became a favorite destination for writers and artists. Because of its cooling summer breezes it also attracted the nation's wealthy and the mansions sprung up as their 'summer cottages'. Today the town reflects all aspects of its past and hums with tourists. "Make your visit to Newport another first," read a pamphlet at the Visitor's Bureau.

"Newport has an impressive list of 'firsts' itself," I commented to Andy as I glanced through the list. "It was the first of the thirteen colonies to declare its independence from England (1776), had the first passenger airline, ferry service, gas illuminated street lights, automobile arrest (for going over 15 miles an hour!) and the White Horse Tavern, built in 1657, is the oldest pub in continuous use in the United States."

"Great," said Andy, "It's so hot we had better go there FIRST and check out its beer!"

In contrast to the heat and bustle of the coast, the sandy islands of the Sound offer a complete contrast in ambience and cooler temperatures than the mainland shore. Blustery, pork-chop shaped Block Island, named after Adriaen Block who arrived in the early 1600s, stands alone amidst Atlantic swells. The passage there can be tricky through the frequent cotton-wool fog and current that swirls out of the Race, causing piloting nightmares before the days of GPS.

Great Salt Pond in the island's center was overflowing with boats. Ashore we rambled across moors and shingle beaches filled with tourists, reminiscent of the south coast of England and the Isle of Wight, summer destinations of our youth. In contrast, when returning this way in the Fall, there were few visitors and it was the birds that crowded the island, which hosts over 150 migratory species.

At the entrance of Buzzards Bay, formed by the long southwest arm of Cape Cod, Cuttyhunk Island gave a similarly pleasant visit, as did several of the many inlets with popular summer communities. We had great sails between them with a southwest wind ever blowing. Notable stops were at picturesque, clapboard Mattapoisett and quaint Padanaram (South Dartmouth). The white-sand bay of Victorian Onset was a pretty and convenient overnight anchorage at the entrance to the Cape Cod Canal.

Cutting across the neck of Cape Cod, since 1914 the canal has saved an arduous passage around the Cape and through the Nantucket Shoals. The seven-mile land cut is frequently clear of fog when areas to the north and south are 'socked-in' and transit through the well-marked 10-mile canal between Cedar Point, on Great Neck, and Cape Cod Bay is straightforward, with a few considerations.

"We must enter the dredged channel early to avoid the shallows and calculate a passage to go with the tide, as it can run up to 4 knots," Andy commented. "The current floods north, and gets quite powerful due to the five-foot difference in height between the waters to the north and south."

The canal authorities use VHF Channel 13 and although a yacht does not have to check in, we found it useful to monitor this channel to learn about other shipping in transit. Vessels moving with the current have the right of way, except that boats under 65' must always keep clear of larger vessels. We furled the sails as none are allowed, and with a fair wind and positive tide had an easy passage, passing the railway bridge at dead slack.

The Mayflower

When heading southwest on our return in the Fall, however, despite a fair current the southwest wind caused a steep chop that greatly slowed our passage.

Above the Cape, *Bagheera* entered a whole new world of cruising in the cool waters of the open Atlantic Ocean. There was a definite northern gray to the sky but twenty-five knots of wind from astern and calm seas gave us a great sail to Plymouth. Winding our way down the channel it was a thrill see the monument over Plymouth Rock and the Mayflower II, a replica of the ship that brought the Pilgrim Fathers from England in 1620.

"It is certainly far removed from modern sailing vessel designs," Andy commented.

"Yes," I agreed. "It so high and narrow and looks incredibly unstable. What an uncomfortable crossing it must have been. I wonder what they took for seasickness then!"

Plymouth Rock, the boulder where the Pilgrims are said to have landed in the New World (although others claim the first steps ashore were taken at Provincetown, which was rejected due to poor soil), is now located in an inshore arcade. Although moved several times it has played a significant role, particularly as a symbol of liberty during the American Revolution.

The Pilgrims' arrival marks the beginning of a vital maritime history along these shores. The great clipper ships such as *Flying Cloud* and *Sovereign of the Seas* sailed out of the nearby ports and Gloucester schooners made their fortunes fishing for cod on the Grand Banks. The towns and villages reflect this period. Many buildings are beautifully maintained and it is rewarding to visit ashore, although getting to a supermarket that is several miles away on the highway can be a challenge for car-less cruisers.

The downtown Freedom Trail is a splendid introduction to Boston's history, but when approaching by water Boston's skyline is modern in every way. We have visited this delightful city on many occasions, but it is our visit when southbound in *Bagheera*, that will always stand out in our memories, as we had to hole up for a hurricane!

There had been a pleasant 12-knot northwesterly breeze as we departed from Lunenburg, Nova Scotia for Marblehead, Massachusetts. Floyd was still to the west of the Bahamas but it was growing into a category four hurricane and three times larger in area than Andrew, which had devastated the Florida coast in 1992. Our concern grew as we heard of preparations for massive evacuations up the U.S. east coast. Predictions were that Floyd would turn north and east and that the entire coast from Florida to Nova Scotia was under threat.

We arrived in Marblehead after an easy sixty-hour passage and quickly explored this yachting center with its attractive 18th and 19th century houses lining the winding streets while waiting to clear customs. The harbor was crammed with yachts on moorings, with no room to anchor and exposed to the northeast. By this time Floyd was punishing the northern Bahamas with winds of 135 knots, gusting 165 knots, with seas of 36 feet.

We asked around for a good hurricane hole. "Don't worry," we were assured. "We never get hurricanes here." As Floyd was now devastating North Carolina we were not convinced. We also noticed fishermen pouring into the harbor, their boats piled high with traps that they unloaded onto the dock—including a boat called *Bollocks*, a name that definitely indicated defiance rather than caution!

There were two days left to find a haven and we headed for Boston Harbor. Our confidence that there would be ample room for a visitor was soon put to the test. Marinas were trying to clear boats out and every travelift was working overtime. We moored downtown and rushed to the *SAIL* Magazine office.

"A hurricane hole in Boston?" exclaimed Patience Wales, the Editor. "That is not a usual request!" Instantly rising to the situation she called Webb Chiles, four times circumnavigator and liveaboard at the Constitution Marina. He went to bat for us at the marina office and with some reluctance they allowed us in.

Floyd was continuing to create havoc up the U.S. coast. There was some speculation that it might turn out to sea at Cape Cod but if it continued on its present course it would hit Boston the following night.

Boat owners and marina staff went into a frenzy of activity. *Bagheera* was on the end of the dock and we set two large anchors, a Bruce and CQR, from the bow to the north and east, the most exposed directions. Being in a double slip with no neighbor, we were able to weave a web of nylon lines, keeping us sprung from the docks all round. It was reassuring to be told that these docks were secured by heavy chains and anchors rather than piles, so there was plenty of 'give' to the swell and no danger of the floats being lifted off piles by the expected storm surge. We well remember the damage in Bundaberg, Australia, where a cyclone had created such a surge (over twelve feet) that the docks complete with boats had floated off the piles and been driven ashore.

It took all morning to remove sails, lines, cockpit cushions, and loose gear and stow them below. Halyards were wrapped around shrouds, flags struck, bimini removed, bilge pumps checked and steering gear locked.

The local TV station was by now broadcasting full-time information on Floyd's destructive progress and it seemed that the eye would pass right over Boston at about two in the morning. The barometer plunged during the afternoon and the atmosphere in the marina became tense as the teeming rain caused instant floods in the parking lot and surrounding roads. The winds continued to rise and it became increasingly difficult to walk safely down the dock.

Expecting to have a sleepless night Andy catnapped for much of the afternoon. I phoned Steve in Annapolis. Winds were at 50 knots but all was well in the marina in Back Creek. After a final check on the boat we went to bed after sunset. Minimum winds were at 25 knots, with strong 'bullets' that whipped through at 40.

We are very sensitive to changes in conditions and were not concerned that we would be caught asleep if the wind increased to dangerous levels. It was with some surprise that we woke at two o'clock in the morning to find that although the wind was now blowing a full gale, few gusts exceeded fifty knots and there was no wave action. The next time we woke it was dawn and the storm had passed! What had happened?

It appeared that our haven was in a great spot. The eye did indeed pass right over Boston, (and Marblehead!) and the steep drop in pressure that is recorded on our barograph was followed by an equally steep rise, displaying an impressive 33-millibar spread. Areas close to us, particularly at the nearby airport, had experienced storm-force winds. We were lucky, our marina was directly downwind of downtown Boston and we were sheltered by its high buildings as the hurricane approached, and by the industrial and residential buildings to the north of the marina when the wind switched around behind the eye. This, coupled with being at the bottom of a nine-foot tide at the windiest time, gave us complete shelter from damaging wind forces.

The following morning was spent recovering anchors and replacing the gear. Our plan was to find an anchorage for the night some miles away at the entrance to the bay in readiness for a dawn departure for Cape Cod. We knew that there was still some strength in the wind, but were surprised by its vigor when we cleared the shelter of the inner harbor and found ourselves surfing under bare poles from gusts exceeding fifty knots. It was a relief to tuck in behind an island at dusk and to find good holding. It was obvious that most boat owners had taken Floyd seriously. Everywhere we found boats hauled or stripped of gear as a precaution, although we did see several sunken dinghies and many furling genoas in tatters.

We opted for an overnight passage from Boston to Maine, making our landfall at pretty, protected Boothbay Harbor, a bustling old seaport and popular tourist destination where the Vikings are reputed to have been the first European visitors. Although we had enjoyed a variety of seafood up the coast here it is displayed in its full glory.

"Just arrived?" we were asked while perusing the menu outside a restaurant. We explained we had just sailed up from Boston. "Then you must be hungry and we have the best lobster in Maine right here off the Sheepscot River!"

"Well," said Andy, needing no more encouragement. "We had better try some!" We had an amazing lobster feast and did so frequently over the next few weeks along with gorging on local oysters, mussels, clams and salmon!

The down-side of lobstering for the boater is the constant hazard from the thousands of traps, particularly in shallower waters. Tricky to avoid when visibility is good, they are a nightmare when the inevitable fog descends or at night. We had already snagged one on the passage north when the line between its two buoys had caught around the keel, in 230 feet of water. It was impossible to untangle in the dark, stormy conditions and the poor lobsters must have felt quite seasick when we were finally able to free the trap at dawn. We felt badly for the owner, however, as we had dragged it some miles.

It had been an eventful trip. Not only were there frequent flashes of lightning astern, at midnight a large fishing boat put out a distress call. When they gave their position to the Coastguard we calculated they were just 18 miles away, so we offered to give assistance. Another vessel called in who was closer and faster, but when they arrived there was no sign. The men were finally picked up from their liferaft; all were well but shocked by the speed with which their vessel had sunk.

The incident made Maine feel remote. Maybe it was due to a lingering memory from our Caribbean chartering days when the small number of yachts heading up this way gave it great mystique, or the typical comment as we cruised north, "You're going ALL the way to Maine? Very few cruisers go THAT far."

Once past Cape Elizabeth there is a radical change to the coast. We started heading east instead of north, and passed long rocky peninsulas studded with deep bays, inlets and islands that were typically wooded and uninhabited. Although the Maine coast is only some 250 miles long in a straight line, indentations and over 3000 islands give 3,500 miles of coastline for cruising that is such a maze one wonders at the patience of those who charted these shores. Although topographically less dramatic than British Columbia, we found Maine very attractive, with its comparatively time-worn glacial features, a richness to the vegetation due to the fertile topsoil and attractive old communities.

Although some historians believed that Monhegan Island was visited by the Irish monk, St. Brendan in 560 AD, others claim the first visitors were the Norsemen around 1000 AD. Documented European history of the coast of Maine dates back to the early 1500s with the Florentine explorer Giovanni da Verrazzano entering these waters after sailing up the American east coast from present day North Carolina, and the Portuguese Estevan Gomez, in the employ of Spain, who approached from the opposite direction. With Cartier's inroads into the Gulf of St. Lawrence in 1534, France's activity in the Americas increased. After Champlain founded a settlement in the St. Croix River, he explored the coast of Maine as far as Penobscot Bay. He was surprised to find that European fishermen had used the islands for centuries, as were the several British explorers who were soon to follow.

In 1607 George Popham and Raleigh Gilbert founded the Popham Colony on the banks of the Kennebec River, competing with Jamestown, Virginia as being the first permanent settlement in the New World, but due to a harsh winter it did not survive. It was the enthusiasm of the governor of Virginia, Captain John Smith, after his 1614 visit to New England that inspired many courageous adventurers to head out to the new colonies to make their fortunes. He was also the person who recognised that Maine's treasure was the abundance of cod.

July 1st to Labor Day is the typical cruising season. Being mid-July our timing was perfect. It is also the season for the ubiquitous fog, but it was brilliantly sunny for our arrival. We were welcomed by the local Ocean Cruising Club Port Officer, Phil Brooks. That evening we met several of his neighbors, including an interesting pastor whose parish was the outer islands.

"Amazingly few of the islands are inhabited," he told us. "Under twenty have year-round communities and most of those are south of Mount Desert and in Casco and Penobscot Bays. Weather conditions can be harsh in winter and even in summer, with the typical fog, piloting can be treacherous."

"But you have picked the right year to visit," several chorused. "There has been no fog at all."

Famous last words. The next morning we awoke to pea-soup fog, which never entirely went away until just before we left for Canada!

The Calders had kindly invited us for a day of inland touring and to visit their home. As we had agreed to meet Nigel at Round Pond, about fifteen miles away in Muscongus Bay, we turned on the radar, took deep foggy breaths, slipped the line off the courtesy mooring and headed out.

Although we have frequently cruised in fog, this was unbelievably dense and it was tiring to peer through the gloom, trying to pick a way through the lobster traps. My mind kept 'telling' me that I had forgotten to put on my glasses! It was also spooky hearing an engine closeby or seeing a marker, surf or rocks jump out of the gloom, even though they were 'visible' by radar. We kept our horn close at hand.

"One long blast for a vessel under power, a long and two short for a sailing vessel," Andy reminded me, taking a deep breath and blowing for practice. We had to use our antique brass foghorn, as the air horn had died after one valiant squeak.

Although quite crowded with lobster boats and pleasure craft on moorings, Round Pond was tranquil, unlike Joshua Slocum's visit in 1895 when 'the wind rattled among the pine-trees on shore'. Andy checked out lobster prices at the fisherman's co-op ashore before Nigel whisked us away by car. Immediately we were struck by the pretty countryside which, except for its size is like England with its mixture of smaller conifer and deciduous trees, lush open grassland and abundant wild flowers.

There had been an era of great prosperity for the first settlers in this area due to the great quantities of fish and almost limitless lumber. The Caribbean trade brought early wealth and when shipbuilding began in earnest in the mid-1700s fortunes were made with European trade. This golden age came to an abrupt end with the Napoleonic Wars, but houses from these affluent years, now over 200 years old, are abundant. In addition to being the homes of those who made their fortunes from the land and sea locally, many were the dwellings of sea captains who, back from passages around The Horn, spent time here to oversee the building of their new ships.

Nigel and Terrie showed us around their own and some neighbors' attractive homes. We learnt that many of the houses were built to a standard pattern and 'erecting' parties were held to raise the walls, with pins inserted to keep them in place. Interiors were beautifully paneled and originally brightly painted, with moldings that are like the designs of those so popular with decorators today. Subsequently a barn was often added to the side, giving homes a distinctive two-tiered façade.

Unlike our experiences further south, here gardens bloomed profusely, with white daisies, pink lilies and purple, pink and white petunias flourishing in this season. Vegetable gardens appeared the norm, one of the enticements for the many struggling artists who are attracted to the area.

Lunch was primarily from Terrie's garden and then it was time for the Summer Meeting of the historic Head Tide Church. This gathering was to prove continuing interest in the old clapboard, almost-square church with its high spire, and a way to fund raise for its preservation. We were delighted to attend this community gathering that attracted both old and young, and listen to their singing and prayers. The lively band was led by a Baptist preacher, who told us he had been baptizing in the Sheepscot River that morning. Music ranged from a Country and Western singa-long, to gospel themes, with the kids, including the Calder's children Pippin and Paul, doing a great job with songs from Samson.

Wandering back through the village Nigel pointed out an old wooden dam and mill by the river and The Old Head Tide Store. The day wound up with a potluck dinner with friends. The conversation was lively and diverse, from making mead to environmental issues, to techniques for grow-ing produce and home schooling. Not only had it been delightful to see the Calder family again, it was enlightening to get a flavor of this rural lifestyle in a state whose coast would otherwise have dominated our memories.

And so began two weeks of cruising magical Maine in Muscongus and Phenobscot Bays, along the Fox Islands and Deer Island Thorofares and Casco Passage, to Mount Desert Island and ending in Bar Harbor. We wound our way through rocky channels and around treed headlands, in fog that varied from misty swirls to cotton-wool, interspersed with sudden patches of brilliant sun. It was amazing how quickly visibility changed with the banks of fog rolling in and out.

Some of our anchorages were deserted, others had just a few boats, while the towns of Rockland, Camden and Bar Harbor were busy with boating traffic. The distinctive lobster fishing boats were ever present, roaring past *Bagheera* then suddenly stopping for traps to be checked. Using a hydraulic hoist, fishermen bring the traps on board, take out the catch, then throw back the unwanted seaweed, crabs and lobsters that are undersized. The trap is then re-baited and put back over the side, with hundreds of traps lifted in a day. This is serious business and we learnt to give these boats a wide berth, as their paths are unpredictable. Lobstermen have their own float colors, and we found colors showed up differently in the varying visibility, some being easily picked out while oth-ers blended into the ocean. Whatever the color, buoys are frequently close together, and again our Autopilot remote control was invaluable, allowing us to stand by the dodger and weave *Bagheera* between them.

Rambles ashore were a delight. We hiked across fascinating rock for-mations with striations of upturned sandstone, granite and slate. The wide intertidal zone was crammed with shells—winkles, mussels, clams and oys-ters, and rounded boulders were draped with deep green carpets of sea-weed and golden ribbons of kelp. Above the beach wild roses made beds of contrasting color to the bright green grass, and wild raspberries bushes gave excellent pickings.

"Look at the butterflies," Andy pointed out. The beautiful red mon-archs newly emerged, posed conveniently for a photo.

"They have an incredible life cycle," Andy informed me, "as they go all the way to Mexico to hibernate for the winter."

Birds also kept us entertained. As usual the seagulls were the scavengers, with several varieties here. We watched bald eagles as they soared above, rows of cormorants on rocks drying their wings, gliding sooty shearwaters, rafts of razorbills and had a fleeting glimpse of an Atlantic puffin. Ospreys were everywhere, often perched in massive nests atop rocks, and young birds would pop up and cheekily peer at us, then suddenly duck back down as we passed.

We were in luck for our visit to Rockland as it co-incided with a gathering of Friendship sloops. Neatly lining the dock these boats were immaculate, with wooden masts gleaming, and sails and gaffs neatly stowed. Friendship, in Muscongus Bay, was the birthplace of these graceful sloops over a century ago and although originally workboats, their lovely lines, topmasts and long bowsprit make them outstanding performers under sail. The next morning we were treated to a parade of the gathered fleet, with many of the vessels flying five sails, three forward of the mast with a mainsail and topsail aft.

The bay was full of boats. As usual we were anchored at the outer fringe along with other cruisers. Some belonged to the same cruising clubs,

Old Friendship sloop

including the Seven Seas Cruising Association and Cruising Club of America as well as the Ocean Cruising Club. Others we had heard on the radio, mainly on the 'Crewtimers' Net, and again it was fun to chat in person with the 'voice'.

We also enjoyed the town with its attractive brick High Street. Although once industrial, its fishing businesses have closed down, and it is morphing into a pleasant destination with several attractions ashore, including a farmer's market. The Owls Head Transportation Museum was recommended and we spent an enjoyable afternoon looking at exhibits that showed the development of planes since the Wright brothers, with several old planes still flown on weekends. The displays of engines and cars were equally well done.

"Look," Andy said to me delighted. "There's a look-alike vintage Rolls-Royce, just like the one I once owned when I was in the Royal Navy."

"And there's a Mustang, just like my first car," I added. "Oh no!" I con tinued.

"What's the matter?"

"Both cars are called 'antiques'. I don't think I'm ready for something I once owned new being in that category!"

Just ten miles to the north lies Camden. Anchoring in the outer harbor was the only option, and the fog became so dense while motoring ashore in the dinghy we almost got lost! No chance of seeing the impressive backcloth of the Camden Hills so frequently referred to in our cruising guides. Touristy, but very attractive, it was here that we found the best deal on lobster! The harbor also has one of the best collections of classic wooden boats.

We were treated to a fine parade of 'windjammer' schooners a few evenings later as several were gathered for the traditional Friday night gathering in Pulpit Harbor, across the bay on North Haven Island. It was impressive watching these 80-100 foot vessels negotiate their way through the channel in the fluky winds, and douse their sails smartly as they anchored in the confined area. There are many of these windjammers in the charter business; some are original workboats that carried lumber, granite or lime, while others are relatively new.

Another 'oldie' in the harbor immediately caught our attention. Lying peacefully at anchor at the far side of the bay, the immaculate yacht *Suzannah* sat in a picture-perfect reflection. Long, narrow and graceful, we recognized her as a Laurent Giles design, very similar to the 1938 12-meter *Flica II* that we had run as a charter boat in the Caribbean. That she was so well maintained impressed us; having run *Flica* for a living we knew just how much work was involved.

Approaching her while exploring the bay in our dinghy, Andy recognized a Royal Naval Sailing Association burgee flying at the spreader. This warranted a visit and after a short exchange Andy realized he had served with the father of the member, a guest on board. The owner graciously invited us for sundowner drinks and it was lovely to see just how much she loved this vessel and cruising these waters with friends every summer.

The fog began to lift as we entered Southwest Harbor on Mount Desert Island, named L'Isle de Monts Desert when Samuel de Champlain visited in 1604. For a while just the tip of the trees tantalized us as the shore remained completely blanked out, then on entering the bay the fog suddenly cleared to reveal the a large fleet of boats that were obviously racing.

"I can't believe it!" exclaimed Andy after staring through the binoculars. "Those are IODs (International One Design boats). I used to race them at Cowes in the 50s."

"There's so much that's like England here," I replied. "It even has the same Atlantic salty smell, quite different to the smell on the Pacific coast!"

We poked our noses into Somes Sound, Maine's only fjord. It was lovely, but we are spoilt by the fjords in British Columbia so decided not to linger. Instead we headed straight up to Bar Harbor and the sun had completely dispersed all traces of fog as its large mansions came into sight. We couldn't have asked for a clearer final day to sightsee this attractive, colorful town. The top of the park gives a panoramic view of the bay, and it was a perfect place to watch the four-masted red-sailed schooner head out across the bright blue sea for its run of the day.

It was time for us to 'run' up to Nova Scotia as Duncan was soon due to visit.

On a last trip ashore for final shopping and phone calls, I happened to glance at a tourist board and it read:

Sightings on 12:30pm trip

8 Finback whales up to 80'

50 pilot whales

2 humpbacks

1 minke

1 basking shark.

I rushed back to Andy, excited. As much as we were reluctant to leave Maine we couldn't wait to head out on the ocean for similar wildlife sightings. We also looked forward to cruising Nova Scotia with Duncan and an inland trip by car to Kingston on Lake Ontario, where Jamie was racing in the Laser>> World Championships.

PACIFIC PANAMA

Typical Cuna Indian dress

San Blas Islands

Portobelo

GUATEMALA

Lake Atitlán

Chichicastenango Market

Mayan Tikál

The outer barrier reef

Belize City

Izamal

Old Havana, Plaza de la Catedral

Taxis outside the Capitolio Nacional

Marina Hemingway (one of four channels)

Smithonian Institution

Williamsburg

Fall in the Chesapeake

Bagheera *sailing past the Statue of Liberty*

Helming Bagheera *down the East River*

Mashantucket Pequot Indian Museum

Bar Harbor, Maine

View from Bar Harbor

Peggy's Cove

One of many lobster feasts

Lunenburg

Eastern Canada

16. Nova Scotia including the Bras d'Or Lakes

Although heading to Canadian New Brunswick into the turbulent tide-driven waters of the Bay of Fundy is becoming more common, just a few adventurous cruisers cross over Nova Scotia, and only the intrepid venture further offshore to Newfoundland, where icebergs hover year-round. With sails unfurled after leaving Bar Harbor, Maine, *Bagheera* eagerly rode the ocean swells, driven by the fresh 16-knot north-northwesterly wind, the autopilot set for Cape Sable on Nova Scotia's southern tip.

We had decided to head straight for Halifax, Nova Scotia's capital, to be in good time for Duncan's arrival. When touring by car, we had seen that east of Mount Desert the coast of Maine becomes more austere and challenging, and when continuing east to Canada the giant tides in the Bay of Fundy and frequent fogs are additional hazards.

In contrast, the pretty, benign St. John River in New Brunswick is a rewarding cruising destination despite the grind to sail there in bad weather and the challenge of passing through the Reversing Falls, that lie just above the busy commercial Saint John Harbour. Twice each day close to 30 feet of tide surges up this inlet, compressing the river's normal flow into a narrow gorge. At low water the level in the gorge can be as much as fifteen feet above the harbor. At high water the falls are reversed and the harbor can be ten feet higher than the river. There is less than twenty minutes of slack when the falls are passable. At all other times there are lethal currents, swirling whirlpools and a mass of debris—particularly impressive to watch from the shore!

Once through the falls a new world lies ahead. The warm, fresh water is pleasant for swimming; the weather is generally fine and clear, however foggy it is on the ocean; and the sailing most enjoyable, past verdant farmlands with steep-roofed farmhouses backed by forests and mountains.

After leaving Bar Harbor we actively looked for whales. Our expectations were high with the tourist boats having so many sightings, but although on the alert and scanning the horizon through the binoculars, the wide expanse of ocean appeared devoid of wildlife. The wind died with dusk and as we soaked in the last warmth from the sun's rays there were finally ripples approaching us, easily visible on the glowing, glassy sea. For a moment we thought they might pass us by, then all at once an explosion of white water and dancing dolphins enveloped the boat. They leapt, spun and dove, then glided out of the water glistening, ready to jump and spin again. We are often befriended by dolphins, but only rarely see such exuberance. Previous special memories include a welcoming party at dawn in Chagos, a remote atoll in the Indian Ocean, and being led by pods from Ceuta in North Africa to Gibraltar and also into Nosy Be in Madagascar.

"Look Liza," Andy pointed excitedly. "There's a basking shark."

"It's huge," I exclaimed. "At least 25-feet long." I later read they grow even larger, up to a massive 40 feet.

"And look at the whales blowing," I pointed behind us. Four humpbacks spouted in turn close-by and there were several more in the distance framed against a crimson sunset over Mount Desert Island, now thirty-five miles astern.

There was considerable fish boat and shipping traffic, including the distinctive black high-speed catamaran that runs from Bar Harbor to Nova Scotia, an efficient means of transportation but of environmental concern in an area so full of sea life.

It was a pleasant two-day, 310-mile passage to Halifax; Andy did record a few complaints in the log, however. 'It's too dammed cold! And getting colder. And colder!' At noon, this wasn't promising, but the mainsail was blocking the sun. By 2:00pm I note 'Sun now shining into the cockpit and down to shirt sleeves', but also 'the sea temperature is only 42° F!'

"Definitely time to get the duvet out from under the mattress," I commented that evening as it was chilling down. "It needs an airing anyway as it hasn't been used since the Baja."

We were so far north that the eastern horizon was tinged with pink by 4:00am and by 05:00 the sky was a brilliant orange, both picturesque and energizing, as this meant that there was only one completely dark night watch. On the second morning Andy had a special treat. He saw three green flashes as the boat rose and fell on the waves.

"Two firsts," he declared jubilantly. "I've never seen a green flash at dawn before, or three simultaneously."

After rounding Cape Sable *Bagheera* headed along Nova Scotia's indented southern shore where countless fishing villages, sheltered harbors and coves begged a visit on our return journey. Shelburne, Canada's reputed lobster capital, came particularly recommended. Also known as the 'Birthplace of Yachts', it was home to *Svaap*, a 32' foot ketch built in 1925, that was sailed around the world by William Robinson and made famous in his book '10,000 Leagues Over the Sea', and *Malay*, a yacht designed by W.J. Roue who was also the designer of the famous *Bluenose* schooner.

Unlike most of the communities along this coast that were bases for fishermen, pirates and privateers (pirates employed by the government!), Shelburne was originally founded by Loyalists, New Englanders loyal to the British Crown who fled from revolutionary America in 1783. Being farmers, they turned to the land for a livelihood and with a population of over 10,000 it was the largest community in British North America. Today the tree-lined streets are still full of beautiful old buildings and historic sites.

This shore is part of the peninsula of Nova Scotia that is connected to the North American continent by an isthmus just 30 miles wide. The province also includes Cape Breton Island that lies to the northeast, joined to the peninsula by a mile long causeway across the Strait of Canso. This second smallest province (after Prince Edward Island) is just over 21,000 square miles in area, and one is never more than 35 miles from its 4,625 miles of coastline. As the land is also dotted with lakes and rivers, water plays a part in most people's lives.

When Europeans first arrived the land was inhabited by the Mi'kmaq Indians. The Loyalists and immigrants from across Europe followed. Thousands of Scots came to the familiar scenery of Cape Breton, and the French Acadians have a special, but also tragic, connection as we learnt on our later travels. The current population of Nova Scotia is under one million.

We arrived at the entrance of grand Halifax harbor at dawn. Not only a large, deep natural harbor, it is protected from the prevailing westerly winds (SW in summer, NW in winter) and, significant commercially, is ice free.

"There's a sailing ship coming towards us," I pointed to Andy as he came up on deck. "I wonder if it's the replica of the *Bluenose*?"

"It's certainly a traditional schooner," Andy agreed, "but I thought the *Bluenose* was based in Lunenburg."

It was her and she passed close by. One hundred and six feet overall, she was a magnificent sight under sail and we could see her name prominently on the bow. The first *Bluenose* fishing schooner was built in 1921. Besides being a workboat on the Grand Banks she was designed as a fast sailing ship to capture the International Fisherman's Trophy back from New England. She won many of the classic regattas along the U.S. East Coast; she also brought this trophy home at the end of her first fishing season and in an 18-year racing career never lost it. In 1937 she was honored with a special place in Canada's history and her imprint has graced the Canadian dime ever since. She retired a champion in 1938. The Second World War saw an end to this great era of the sailing schooners, as they were then replaced by steel trawlers. In 1942, despite considerable effort to keep her in Nova Scotia, *Bluenose* was sold to carry freight in the West Indies and in 1946 this 'Queen of the North Atlantic' was wrecked on a Haitian reef.

Built by the same yard, Smith and Rhuland, *Bluenose II* was constructed from original plans and launched in July, 1963. She is owned by the government of Nova Scotia and has a crew of 18 to handle the largest working mainsail in the world measuring 4,150 square feet. It certainly looked vast as she headed out to sea for her regular run to Lunenburg.

We made our landfall at the Royal Nova Scotia Yacht Squadron whose beginnings in 1837 make it the oldest established yacht club in North America. It has a designated dock to clear in with Canada Customs. Procedures were completed over the telephone and were straightforward, although we were dismayed that we were only allowed to bring in six bottles of wine; it is so much cheaper in the United States! Generally the officials inspect the boat and check personal and boat documentation, but they didn't come down this visit. It is wise to arrive during working hours to avoid overtime changes.

It was a race night at the club and during the post-race barbecue we met several members including the Commodore, who graciously offered us his own berth for *Bagheera* while we traveled inland to Ontario to watch our youngest son, Jamie, racing. His cruising boat, like many others, was in Mahone Bay for the summer.

We were keen to go to Bedford, at the head of the bay. Jamie had participated in several summer sailing events here and had so much fun that on returning to Vancouver he tried to convince us that Bedford was where we should live!

We were instantly impressed. Before even arriving at the yacht club the manager had sent out the launch with an offer of a free mooring buoy. It was the beginning of a most hospitable stay, although we were quite late for the first event having forgotten to change our watches. Nova Scotia time is just three hours behind Greenwich Mean Time in summer, not four like the rest of the eastern seaboard!

Two shopping malls are conveniently located, and we frequently visited the extensive produce store, enjoying the wide variety of inexpensive fresh fruit and vegetables. It was also a convenient location for the airport, and Duncan and girlfriend Heather were quite impressed that I arrived to pick them up in the early hours in a borrowed Volkswagon Jetta.

We headed back through Bedford Basin in *Bagheera* that afternoon to explore the busy waterfront of Halifax, and found a visitor's dock where we could tie *Bagheera* alongside. Although Samuel de Champlain had passed through in 1605, Halifax's permanent colonization came in 1749. This made the year of our visit Halifax's 250th anniversary year and in June there had been a re-enactment of the landing of the founder, Colonel Edward Cornwallis.

The settlement's original purpose was to counter the threat of the French fortress in Louisbourg on Cape Breton Island's east shore (now impressively restored) and several of the fortifications were completed by Prince Edward, Queen Victoria's father, who arrived as Commander in chief in 1794. In 1803 he presented the city with a four-sided domed clocktower, a city landmark, to ensure there was no excuse for soldiers' or sailors' tardiness. The prominent star-shaped citadel that lies atop the hill was started in 1828 and gives a panoramic view of the city, Halifax Harbour and Dartmouth beyond.

With a history longer than that of any other Canadian city, Halifax has gone through tremendous changes, with many a fortune made and lost. A British naval base during the 1775-83 American Revolution and the War of 1812, it was a distribution center in both World Wars for supply ships going to Europe. In 1917 devastation occurred when a Belgian relief ship collided with a French munitions ship in the harbor. Its cargo of TNT made the biggest man-made explosion before the nuclear age, flattening much of the city and killing over 2000 people.

We found this hilly city, that lies on a rugged, boot-shaped peninsula, pleasant to visit with its parks, a mix of old and new buildings, and leisurely pace. Care has been taken with the substantial renovations and we enjoyed visiting the 'Historic Properties', wood and stone buildings dating from 1800-1905 that represent the town's military and seafaring past.

While Duncan and Heather hiked up to the Citadel, Andy and I enjoyed the atmosphere along the waterfront. Vibrant with Celtic music, the attractive shops and restaurants were buzzing with activity. Many visitors enjoyed the opportunity to board old ships such as the *CSS Acadia*, a hydrographic vessel that was a pioneer in charting much of the North

Atlantic, and the corvette *HMCS Sackville* that was used in World War II. The large Maritime Museum of the Atlantic was impressive with well-documented historical information, models of regional vessels and a decorative array of ship's figureheads.

The museum also has a fascinating display on the *Titanic*. We were interested to read that the people of Halifax played a significant role in the rescue of passengers off the 'unsinkable' ship that was on its maiden voyage from England to New York when it hit an iceberg and sunk off the coast of Newfoundland in 1912.

Clouds were gathering during our walk. "It doesn't look like great weather for a passage to Cape Breton Island tomorrow," Andy commented. "The last weatherfax showed a front coming through in a few hours."

"Maybe we should rent a car and go sightseeing," I suggested, "particularly as Heather hasn't done much sailing."

"Good idea. Didn't we see a tourist office somewhere?"

Located by the water and close to *Bagheera*, its staff couldn't have been more helpful. A rental car was soon arranged, ideal tours for a one-day trip discussed and we had been given a bag full of maps and literature.

It didn't take long to realize that Nova Scotia is a jewel. The province is beautifully kept, the houses freshly painted often in bright colors and the gardens overflow with flowers. It was a blustery day but with patches of blue sky and sunshine the beauty of the southerly 'lighthouse' route showed to perfection. First stop was at the picturesque fishing village of Peggy's Cove with its clapboard houses, weathered sheds and painted fishing boats. While we visited the Post Office in the graceful lighthouse, Duncan and Heather leapt between the huge wave-worn granite boulders that line this shore.

Continuing westward, we entered enchanting Mahone Bay, acclaimed as the finest cruising area on Nova Scotia's coast.

We certainly enjoyed many of its anchorages, including those of St. Margarets and Lunenburg Bays, and the LaHave Islands, when returning later in *Bagheera*. Meanwhile, our fleeting glimpse of the stately frame homes at Chester, that was settled in 1760, and a curbside lunch overlooking the three spires of the waterfront churches in the town of Mahone Bay, showed us its great cruising potential.

If one could visit only one place in Nova Scotia it would have to be Lunenburg, its most famous fishing town. Viewed from the water or from the green slopes on the south side of the bay, it is like a film-set with red and blue buildings lining the shore, sailing ships at the wharves and ornate old mansions peeking through the trees on the slopes behind.

Little wonder that UNESCO declared it a World Heritage Site.

Mahone Bay

Founded by German and Swiss settlers in 1753, the town still has a European atmosphere and we enjoyed exploring the back streets as well as the waterfront. Both *Bluenose* schooners were built here and it is home to the Fisheries Museum of the Atlantic (one of 25 branches of the Nova Scotia Museum). This one focuses on the history of fishing, whaling, and boat building which also includes the lucrative rum-running business that thrived during the U.S. Prohibition days in the 1920s.

"Do we have time to go to the Bay of Fundy?" asked Duncan. "It sounds awesome with the incredible rise and fall in tides."

We poured over the map to see how long it would take us to get to Nova Scotia's north coast.

"I wonder what time low tide is over there," Andy commented. "There's no point in driving all that way if its high tide."

"I think it will be about mid-tide," I said. "I looked it up yesterday but the table wasn't for the inner end of the Bay."

It was a 1 1/2-hour drive to Halls Harbour and we were in luck. It was just before a spring low water and fishing boats were impressively high and dry, over twenty feet down in the small harbor, with the tide even further out down the beach.

What caught Andy's attention was a huge tank of live lobsters for sale. We all gazed in, trying to decide which to buy.

"I think we should get that one," Andy declared finally. He pointed to a large lobster whose shell was laden with barnacles. "It obviously hasn't

Low tide in the Bay of Fundy

changed its shell for a while." In Maine we had learnt that the lobsters that had just changed their shells had much less meat inside.

It weighed four pounds. "Do you think one is enough?" queried Duncan with a grin, ever the refrigerator vacuum cleaner.

"We have two more small ones in the freezer," I reassured him. "We bought them for you in Maine as we weren't sure if lobster was in season here." In fact there is a revolving season in Nova Scotia in summer for conservation purposes but lobster is generally always available from the area that is open.

Some other tourists suggested we go to Grand Pré for an even more dramatic view of low water in the Minas Basin, which holds the world's record for the highest tide of 54'. We were stunned by the distance from the high water mark to the water's edge. In no time Heather took off running, her words to Duncan of, "Beat you there," trailing behind her.

It was a great sight watching the two lithe figures becoming smaller by the minute as they raced across the rich red sand out to the cerulean sea. Finally they stopped and waved from on top of a rock. It was a deceptive distance and one must be careful going to the water's edge as the bay fills extremely fast when the tide turns.

Meanwhile, Andy and I walked along the shore. Abundant minerals can be found in the Bay of Fundy, produced by volcanic activity over 200 million years ago that triggered the separation of the ancient continent Pangaea. We were rewarded with zeolite crystals and agate but no amethyst, however! We needed Colin, who has an amazing 'nose' for rocks and fossils and an impressive collection.

Next morning there was a sloppy sea but the winds were the ideal, being southwesterly at 15 knots, giving a comfortable motion with the wind on our quarter as we sailed along this demanding red-cliffed shore. Heather did well, sleeping initially to get her sea legs, then joining Duncan on his watch. It was relaxing having another watchkeeper on board, after I had deprogrammed myself not to wake up after three hours!

The wind eased and veered in the early hours and we jibed when changing watch at 1:30am. Sunrise was at 04:59 and at 05:20 Duncan and Heather enjoyed watching an eclipse of the sun. The 178-mile passage took exactly 26 hours and at noon we were pulling into St. Peter's Canal at the entrance of the Bras d'Or Lakes, that consist of the upper Great Bras d'Or and lower Bras d'Or. The relaxed staff immediately took our lines and we were quickly through the half-mile man-made canal, tidal locks compensating for the difference in water levels between the lake and the ocean.

Almost cutting Cape Breton Island in two, the lakes provide another idyllic area of mostly fog-free cruising and benign winds, with minimal tides and warm salt water for swimming. The lakes, channels and bays are dotted with inlets and islets and the rolling shores are picture-perfect with deep green spruce, bright meadows and immaculate homes.

Ambling along under spinnaker we made our way north, lazing on deck and soaking up the sun. Duncan was in his element and Heather commented to us, "You two have got it figured out!"

We gorged on the lobster that evening—seven pounds of succulent lobster thermidor with garlic roast potatoes, mixed salad and a freshly-baked, nutty brown cottage loaf made a grand cockpit feast. To avoid the advancing mosquitoes we retired below to play our favorite card game, 'Oh Hell'. Duncan explained the rules to Heather. "I think I've played it before," she commented and soundly defeated us all!

The busiest anchorage, except for Baddeck, had only four other vessels. They were gathered in peaceful Maskells Harbour where a local farmer was the Cruising Club of America and Ocean Cruising Club Port Officer. It turned out that he wasn't home but it gave us an excuse for a hike along the grassy path to the square white lighthouse on Gillis Point, sampling the sweet wild raspberries and blackberries along the way.

The wind increased as we approached Baddeck and Heather was given an exciting moment when *Bagheera* rounded up in a broach before Duncan doused the spinnaker. Steeped in yachting tradition since the early 19th century, protected Baddeck is the center for yachting in the Bras d'Or Lakes and a Port of Entry into Canada.

Lying in the center of Cape Breton Island, this attractive small town, in its pastoral setting, is often the starting point for the Cabot Trail. This 186-mile route that encircles the northern part of the island is known for its dramatic coastline, mountains and a plateau of forests, lakes and tundra. The trail was named after the navigator and explorer John Cabot who first sighted Cape Breton Island on 23rd June, 1497.

Another famous name connected to the area is Alexander Graham Bell, whose enthusiasm for the region is shown by his words, "I have travelled the globe. I have seen the Canadian and American Rockies, the Andes and Alps and the Highlands of Scotland; but for simple beauty, Cape Breton outrivals them all." He did much of his work during summers spent at his estate Beinn Bhreagh on the banks of the Bras d'Or Lake. The Alexander Graham Bell National Historic Site is well worth a visit as it provides an excellent insight into this inventor's passions, from the telephone, to man-carrying kites, to hydrofoil speedboats. It also shows how his wife, Mabel Hubbard Bell, helped shape the development of Baddeck.

"There's a dance on tonight," I told Duncan and Heather. "There are notices everywhere. Maybe there will be some Gaelic music and dancing." Gaelic folklore is famous in Cape Breton Island, and when visiting previously I'd been to lively Ceilidh gatherings.

They returned laughing. "There were just a few young people and we tried to get them dancing to their favorite songs on the jukebox, but they were too shy. In the end we just gave them our own performance!"

So much for bagpipes, fiddles and Celtic dancing! It reminded me of the country Ceilidhs I'd gone to when at university in Ireland, where the boys sat at one end of the room and the girls at the other. We English stood in the middle in couples, talking to each other when a song ended, until we realized from the frowns of the chaperones that this was not the thing to do!

Time was running out for Duncan and Heather and they decided to get the bus back to Halifax to be able to enjoy a Saturday night on the town. It was a smart move as it was a bouncy trip to windward returning by boat!

Andy and I had an interesting evening, however, rafted along the wall of the Canal for the night where we chatted to a few other cruisers. We were sorry not to have had time to visit Newfoundland and were delighted to find that one couple had just circumnavigated this most easterly part of Canada.

"We were overwhelmed by the friendly welcome," they reported of Britain's first colonial outpost, "and loved the cruising. But it's rugged with deep anchorages, a lot of kelp and dramatic, unpopulated, barren shores. We wouldn't want to be there without a reliable engine and anchor windlass, or a heater."

They had found just one marina, in Lewisporte, but most towns have government docks that are either free or have a minimal charge. They suggested circumnavigating Newfoundland in a clockwise direction to see the distinctively different regions and recommended the fjorded south coast and the island-studded northeast coast for the best cruising. They particularly enjoyed the sea life but water temperatures had been chilly in June, consistently in the low 40° F. By August, however, they were in shorts and t-shirts and the sea temperatures were in the 60s. Similar to our experience in Alaska, after the initial awe of remoteness and icebergs, they felt a longing to return to cruising in the warmth of the tropics!

On a whim, while standing on the Royal Nova Scotia Yacht Squadron dock waiting for car arrangements to be made to go back to Ontario, I called some old Caribbean friends who had bought a property on Nova Scotia's northern shore.

"I can't believe your timing," said Linda. "We're having a Caribbean gathering this weekend, you must come and join us." It was a great co-incidence, particularly as one of the guests was Ken McKenzie, who was the owner and captain of *Ticonderoga* when we were married on board, another person we hadn't seen for twenty-five years!

Our friends, Ken and Linda Argent, had bought a home on the Bay of Fundy, north of the Annapolis Basin between Digby and Annapolis Royal.

Annapolis Royal

After years of running charter and brokerage businesses in hot climates they were attracted by this region's benign temperate climate. It was great to catch up on the intervening years while we dug for clams, chatted with neighbors and toured the attractive town of Annapolis Royal, with its gracious Victorian homes and wide tree-lined streets. Known as Canada's oldest settlement, it has over 150 heritage buildings, including the oldest wooden house in Canada that was built in 1708. This area is soon to celebrate its four hundred-year anniversary from the founding of Port Royal by French explorers in 1604. Just a few miles away lies a replica of de Champlain's fur-trading post.

It was here that we learnt about the Acadians. When the French first settled this region, in particular developing the fertile land south of the Minas Basin with dykes typical of those in northwest France, they called the land Acadia and soon thought of themselves as the Acadians. The British, however, always considered them French and the rivalry of these two nations in the New World was to spell disaster for them. The land changed from French to English and back, but in 1703 at the Treaty of Utrecht Acadia became English Nova Scotia (New Scotland). The Acadians, however, refused to take an Oath of Allegiance to Britain and in 1755, with France and England again locked in conflict, the Lieutenant Governor decided that the Acadians must sign or go. Over 14,000 Acadians were forced to leave, most by boat, and their properties burned.

Many went south to Louisiana and New Orleans, where they have become known as 'Cajuns'. Others went inland and most of the French Canadians in the Atlantic Provinces are their descendents, while some went to Martinique in the Caribbean or back to Europe. A few stayed and we noticed both here and when traveling through New Brunswick that there is now an upsurge in Acadian pride.

As we organized *Bagheera* at the Royal Nova Scotia Yacht Squadron dock for a three-week trip inland by car, it almost felt like the end of our cruise. We had now completed our original plan of cruising around North and Central America, from British Columbia to Nova Scotia through the Panama Canal, in a year. We would be moving fast as we sailed back down to the Chesapeake, to arrive in time for the Annapolis Boat Show, then lay *Bagheera* up for the winter.

Thoughts of seeing Jamie and his friends perked us up. Our conversation moved to the drive that would take us through New Brunswick, Quebec and on to Ontario. It would provide a great opportunity to explore the cruising possibilities of the St. Lawrence River and the Great Lakes.

Epilogue

The distances involved in traveling across Canada reminded us that it is the largest country in the world, after Russia. It took fifteen hours to drive from Halifax to Kingston, Ontario. When Jamie, a friend and I drove boats from Vancouver to Kingston another year it took a straight 54 hours, all on fast highways, which puts the east/west border in perspective. As Thunder Bay on Lake Superior is almost half way across the country, there are vast inland cruising opportunities.

The completion of the St. Lawrence Seaway in 1959, with its locks, canals and channels dredged around the rapids, opened up a shipping route from the Atlantic Ocean to the Great Lakes, but although busy with ocean-going commercial vessels, it is still an arduous journey for a cruiser heading upstream. Stretching 800 miles, and ninety miles wide at its mouth, the river's descent of 224' and large drainage area produce an average outflow of 500,200 cu ft (14,165 cu m) per second.

Instead, most boaters reach the Great Lakes via New York and the Hudson River. North of Albany at Troy (where you can have your mast unstepped) there are two choices. You can continue north through spectacular Lake Champlain, Rivière Richelieu and the Chambly Canal (controlling depth 6-6.5') to Sorel on the St Lawrence River (400 miles north of New York). Alternatively you can take the Erie Canal and detour on the Oswego Canal to Lake Ontario or go on to Buffalo on Lake Erie (just over

500 miles from New York). Interestingly, the distance of taking the triangle route from New York up the Hudson River, east on the Erie Canal to Oswego, across Lake Ontario, up the St. Lawrence River to Sorel and down through Lake Champlain and the Hudson to New York is about 900 miles. This is similar in distance to a voyage from New York to Maine and back and it is mostly in protected waters, but one needs an efficient engine.

Those who wish to see historic walled Quebec City, originally settled by French explorer Samuel de Champlain in 1608, can go 100 miles downstream on the St. Lawrence from Sorel, making use of the many marinas to await favorable winds and tides. You will find it hard to resist the fine French cuisine ashore. Although James Wolfe's British troops defeated Montcalm's French forces in the famous battle on the Plains of Abraham in 1759, wiping out New France, patriotism is as strong as ever, and many Québecois only speak French. Beside its majestic Chateau Frontenac, high on the cliff's edge, we gazed down on the might of the St. Lawrence River, witnessing its infamous tides and strong currents at this point where the river narrows.

Forty miles upstream from Sorel lies the island city of Montreal. With its French culture, art and flair for fashions, large student population, cosmopolitan restaurants and active nightlife, it has an unforgetable vibrancy and should not be missed.

From Montreal one can take the Ottawa River to Ottawa then the

Viewing the St. Lawrence River from Quebec City

Rideau Canal to Lake Ontario or travel up the St. Lawrence through several locks to the Thousand Islands, the river's best cruising ground. From its beginning at Lake Ontario over 1800 islands stretch 50 miles, tapering from 15 to 5 miles across. These attractive tips of former mountain peaks give relaxed gunkholing in both Canadian and U.S. waters, which are particularly accessible with a shallow draft.

We turned off the 401 freeway for Brockville to take a route close to the river. This was the easterly end of my territory when I worked out of Kingston as a Vocational Rehabilitation Counselor in the late sixties, my first job after emigrating to Canada. I wanted to show Andy this old historic city that was founded by United Empire Loyalists in 1784, as well as the pretty Thousand Islands themselves. I had visited many of the islands by dinghy and camped ashore while working and when a student at Queens University in Kingston. It was a long time ago but although busier now with tourism, the island vistas still begged a visit.

It seemed like returning home to drive into the old city of Kingston passing Royal Military College on the point, the old downtown core and familiar campus. We continued to Kingston's small airport and it was a heartwarming sight to see Jamie and his friends climb out of the plane.

As usual, he was staying with the Davies family whom we met sailing across the South Pacific in their Yacht *Archangel* when he was four years old. Now, *Archangel* is owned by New Zealand's Sir Peter Blake, and Michael has Archangel the helicopter, which he uses to commute to his farm. On a previous visit he had taken me up to watch Jamie racing from the air. It was an amazing sight to see so many dinghies below, all taking part in CORK regatta, and view the surrounding mainland, islands and waterways. It was also poignant to find, sitting close to his craft at the airport, a Cessner 150 that looked remarkably like the one in which I had soloed in 1968.

Andy and I were staying with John and Virginia Gordon. We had greatly enjoyed Virginia's company on board a charter boat in the Virgin Islands four years before, when we were guiding a Canadian group. Now they generously lent us their small motorboat. For ten days we were the happy 'nanny' boat, surrounded by dinghies between races, handing out juice, fruit and bagels to the Laser >> fleet, while ashore in the evenings Andy was kept busy with not a few fiberglass repairs!

We also had time to talk to local and transient boaters about local cruising areas. Ontario has four canals that radiate from its shores and I could remember an interesting trip on the Trent. It came highly recommended. Meandering across Ontario for 240 miles the Trent-Severn Waterway provides a route between Lake Ontario and Lake Huron's premier cruising area, Georgian Bay. In 1827 work began to link the many lakes and rivers that had been used by both First Nations peoples and European traders. Although not viable commercially when completed, it has become an incredible recreation success that is now operated by the Parks Board and open from mid-May to mid-October. Vistas are pleasant with farms, villages, rolling hills, a couple of towns for supplies and lakes dotted with islands. There are 43 locks to keep one from being totally idle and one must take the mast up/down either at Belleville or Trenton at the southern end, and at Midland or Penetanguishene in the north. Unfortunately the controlling depth is around 5', no good for *Bagheera*. Instead we would have to go the long way round, through the St. Lawrence Seaway's Welland Canal which lifts boats up to Lake Erie, by Niagara, then on to Lake Huron to reach Georgian Bay and its adjoining North Channel. A magnificent area for cruising with its many islands, the rugged landscape of the region also inspired Canada's celebrated Group of Seven painters.

We met no one who had continued to Lake Michigan and south. I was, however, interested to see in a guidebook that there are two routes south to the Gulf of Mexico. We've often heard about riding the Mississippi down to New Orleans, but also popular is diverting at Cairo to join the Tennessee-Tombigbee Waterway to Mobile.

Jamie joined us for the car ride back to *Bagheera* in Halifax and had a week of relaxing on board before returning to Vancouver to enter his grade 12, and final year, at school. We then quickly headed south, with a brief visit to Lunenburg to wait out head winds and a few days in Boston to wait out Hurricane Mitch.

Bagheera spent her last cruising weekend in the Chesapeake at an Ocean Cruising Club rally in serene Wilton Creek off the Piankatank River. Surrounded by reflections of Fall foliage, now brilliant with reds and golds, the yachts made a pretty picture. It was a wonderfully relaxing setting with visits between boats and special evenings at Bill and Alice Caldwell's beautiful Williamsburg-style home that they built themselves. Both in their late 70s, always so welcoming and still cruising, this enthusiastic couple is an inspiration to us all.

On Sunday we all headed out in our dinghies to lay extra anchors, but felt little wind as a tropical storm passed overhead that night. Within a few hours the Creek was empty of OCC yachts. They were headed in every direction, with future destinations around the globe. After a final evening with Bill and Alice, we sailed around the headland to Deltaville to lay up *Bagheera* for the winter.

On our way down through the Chesapeake we had stopped to work the Annapolis Boatshow, which had been as pleasurable as always. One memorable conversation was with another older couple.

While looking at the pictures in *Just Cruising* Cornelia commented, "These people look familiar. Were you in the Pacific in '87?"

We soon realized that we were both in Raratonga, in the Cook Islands, together and had celebrated Halloween in Fiji.

"You know I've always felt badly," she confided. "I promised to send this young boy some special art supplies and I never did."

"It's all right," I reassured her smiling, "he's 21 now!" Although the numbers were correct, she was shocked, as so many people are, that time has passed so quickly!

Interestingly, many of the people that I mention in *Just Cruising* that we cruised with in '87, after having had a period ashore, are cruising again. The Sellers on *Nimbus*, for example, from Vancouver, are currently sailing in Australia. Bob and Betsy Baillie from Bermuda, who had *Belair*, now have a New Zealand-built boat in the South Pacific. Chris and Boo on *Onskan* , their Beneteau First 38, now have three children and are soon to cross the Atlantic. Tim and Leisa, who ran *Mustang*, have headed north from Sydney with their two young sons. Gary and Karen on *Coolchange* are cruising the Caribbean; Steve and Andrea, who had *Severance*, have just cruised around North and Central America west-about with their two children; and recently in Europe we had dinner with Dennis and Jo, who had *Sweet Salera*, now at the start of a circumnavigation.

What draws people to cruising? In so many ways, it is not an easy lifestyle—the sea is unforgiving, boats demand attention and there is always something to repair. Passage-making can be uncomfortable and life hard work, with few 'mod cons' of the 'real' world. When you tell your friends of your plans, many will retort that you have taken leave of your senses!

For dreamers, cruising represents an attractive escape from the routines of regular life, the means of setting their own pace and guiding their own destiny. They look forward to exchanging the stress of commuting, telephones and business demands for the calm and freedom of an empty horizon. For others, the lure of the life is the stimulation of new destinations and intimate visits with nature. Those who live their dreams successfully also explore the practicalities of cruising and the skills required, and all crew members work together to achieve their goal. Most find that the planning skills and self-sufficiency acquired are bonuses in themselves.

Some cruisers cross oceans; others choose to coastal hop, initially maybe not very far. After leaving the United States, many west coast-cruisers laze around the Sea of Cortez for the first year or two, catching their breath. As their friends move on and they acclimatize to the lifestyle they are enticed further afield. Some head down the coast, as we did, to

Costa Rica and Panama; others sail to the South Pacific, as Mexico is a great stepping stone. Increasing numbers continue west-about and circumnavigate the world. The east coast of the United States offers a variety of wonderful cruising opportunities in its own right, but then so do the Bahamas and the Caribbean! Many cruisers then continue to the Mediterranean, where they spend several years immersing themselves in its many cultures.

There is no doubt that the camaraderie of those out cruising is an important part of the enjoyment of the lifestyle. Cruisers are unique people and bonding comes quickly. To be a long-term cruiser you have to have made the break from your traditional lifestyle and have left your dock. As everyone who has done it knows, it is never easy to get away, but we've all had the strength of our conviction and succeeded. There is an instant rapport, special pleasure from sharing new destinations together; satisfaction, too, from being able to help with equipment problems on board. Cruisers become fast friends and, as with those mentioned above, there is the continuing enjoyment of keeping in touch.

Cruising full-time, however, is not for everyone. Most long-term cruisers build into their budget a regular trip home. Many spend all summer living ashore, enjoying being back in the familiar world of friends and facilities, and luxuriating in the extra space. With the winter rains they happily head down south to their boat for winter wanders in tropical waters. Like myself, they find both lifestyles compatible and the change of venues invigorating.

Others, my husband being one, would happily sail into the sunset . . . and this is what we have just done for the last three months, although, as we were sailing east, we were chasing the sunrise! Instead of heading north to the Great Lakes, Andy felt he would like to have a change of pace and go back to Europe. When we received a phone call from my nephew, announcing that he and his Spanish girlfriend were getting married in the Balearic Island, Menorca, it seemed meant to be!

Of course we then had a deadline for crossing the Atlantic, which is never wise, and, as the Azores High had yet to consolidate, the frequent low pressure systems gave a rough ride! But it was wonderful to have Duncan with us, a tower of strength, and to finally see Bermuda and enjoy several of the Azores Islands before revisiting Gibraltar. After finishing their exams at university, Colin and Jamie joined us in Alicante, on the Spanish mainland coast. At the same time the bride entrusted us with her wedding dress—so we had to arrive in Menorca in time!

Three days early we sailed into Mahon harbor, where we had wintered in 1985/6, and memories were flying around in the cockpit.

An unexpected, "Oh no!" came from below. Jamie was in the starboard aft cabin, arms stretched, holding up the engine instrument cover at its aft end.

This box had fallen down just once before, also when we were in these waters. At that time Jamie was just two years old. As the coiled wires descended he had been terrified, calling out anxiously, "Autohelm fall down, autohelm fall down." Although the box actually hides the engine electrics, he was convinced they were associated with the noise he knew was the self-steering. It took a period ashore for him to get over the fear of this cabin, despite my attempt to disguise the box with teddy bear fabric.

"I can't believe it," he now gasped between laughs, "I don't think I've slept in this berth since the last time it happened!"

My sister died of cancer at the time of our circumnavigation. Though we've lived in different countries, my nephews and I have remained close and they have all cruised with us at some stage. The wedding celebration was a week long, during which there was a perfect day to take all of the gathered family, with spouses and children, for a sail. With our black cat spinnaker flying we headed along the coast for lunch.

I wish I could pack the atmosphere of that day into a ship's bottle, to be inhaled and savored over and over again—the excitement and enthusiasm, the contentment that everyone felt. It was the very best of cruising. The sky was a cloudless brilliant blue and as *Bagheera* glided effortlessly through the azure ocean, wavelets chuckling around her hull, our skin was caressed by the warm wind that billowed her sails.

★　　★　　★

APPENDIX A
Route Planning and Weather Considerations

The coasts of North and Central America not only allow coastal cruising, they also provide a huge variety in their cruising grounds. With the additional cultural diversity, stunning physical and historical sights, abundant underwater and wildlife and the opportunity for exploration we find them a match for any cruising area in the world.

As weather conditions are an integral part of route planning both are discussed for each area. Although much of this information appears within the narrative, I thought it useful to have the facts in one place for reference.

The West Coasts of North the Central America

There are four distinct weather regions along this coast—the Pacific Northwest to northern California, southern California to northern Mexico, the hurricane belt of Mexico, Guatemala, El Salvador, Honduras, Nicaragua and northern Costa Rica, and the inter-tropical convergence zone of southern Costa Rica and Panama. Our logged distance from Vancouver to the Panama Canal was 4,761 nautical miles.

The Pacific Northwest to Northern California
Weather
The preferred months for the 700-mile passage from the Pacific Northwest to San Francisco are June to mid-September. At this time there are typically long periods of fine sailing weather, gales are uncommon, usually moderate and short-lived. Departure later in the season should only be considered with a favorable long-range forecast and with experienced crew. Winter passages are not recommended.

Prevailing winds in this region are northwest and usually stronger well offshore. The cold California Current also flows towards the southeast, and is strongest close to the coast. Fog is common, particularly in summer and often extends forty to sixty miles offshore, sometimes further. Air temperatures are cool due to the low sea temperature. Winds ahead of frontal systems have a southerly component that is welcomed by vessels heading north, but these winds are usually brief and with the passage of the front veer back to northwest.

Route Planning

The Inside Passage of the Pacific Northwest is one of the most dramatic areas in the world to cruise. In contrast, after leaving the Strait of Juan de Fuca the rugged Pacific coasts of Washington, Oregon and northern California have few protected harbors, with the entry to most of these inhospitable in severe weather.

Three alternative routes for this first leg may be chosen after departing the Strait of Juan de Fuca, depending on the type of craft, time available and crew experience. The coastal route is favored in settled weather by power boats and shallow draft sailboats who wish to take the time to harbor-hop, where fuel and shelter are available and overnight sailing is usually unnecessary. A close eye must be kept on the weather to avoid being caught on a lee shore in deteriorating conditions. Bars at the entrances of most of the harbors quickly become dangerous in strong winds. Popular all-weather ports are Newport in Yaquina Bay, and Coos Bay. *Charlie's Charts of the U.S. Pacific Coast* is a valuable source of harbour information. Up-to-date bar reports can generally be obtained from the coastguard.

A course paralleling the coast fifteen to thirty miles offshore is the most popular summer sailing route and this is the one we chose for our passage. Here one is a reasonable distance from the lee shore, has full co-operation from the prevailing wind and current and is outside the coastal fishing fleet. However, bigger fishing vessels and freighters are common and fog will still be encountered. Abundant wildlife on this route keeps everyone entertained with whales on their migratory routes and numerous dolphins .

An alternative offshore passage, sixty to one hundred miles offshore, is the final option but will add many miles to the trip and there will often be higher winds and seas, though it does have the advantage of less shipping and fog. This is the choice for vessels without radar and for those that are not at their best to windward in a blow and need considerable sea room. It is also the best route for passages made at times other than the summer months.

After passing under the famous Golden Gate Bridge there are many options for transient cruisers in the large, attractive Bay area. Yacht clubs such as Sausalito, Oakland and Encinal are extremely welcoming, and generous with moorings or dock space available. Boating and sightseeing opportunities abound (a wine-tasting visit to the Napa Valley is a must) and the clearing-in procedure (for non-U.S. boats) in downtown San Francisco quick and efficient. Those contemplating stopping on their way down the Washington/Oregon coast, however, should clear into the United States before leaving the Juan de Fuca Strait, for example at Port Angeles, south of Victoria.

San Francisco to the Mexican border

Weather

Prevailing winds offshore are still northwest, though calms are common until warming of the land induces a westerly sea breeze. The favorable current starts to diminish and in summer may even flow north between Point Conception and the Mexican border. Fogs may persist in summer all along this coast. Passages can be made at any time of year based on a good weather forecast. Winds ahead of fronts are still briefly from the south.

Point Conception, known as the 'Cape Horn of the Pacific', has a reputation for violent winds and seas as the sea breeze accelerates around the point and is constricted by the Channel Islands. Except in calm weather this point should be passed a few miles offshore to avoid a wet and rough experience. Fresh winds may persist from the Point into the Santa Barbara Channel, between the islands and the mainland south of the point. Weather is likely to be calm in the early morning, with wind and seas building during the day, often reaching gale force.

A local weather phenomenon is the Santa Ana. This is a hot wind that periodically blows out from the dry interior between Point Conception and Newport, most commonly during the winter months. Within minutes a calm can change to a full gale. Local forecasts give warning of conditions favorable for these winds to occur.

Route Planning

Cruising south along the Californian coast, temperatures are on the rise and welcoming harbors are numerous should bad weather threaten. South of Point Conception to San Diego there are innumerable harbors and marinas to explore, as well as the Channel Islands and Catalina Island. San Diego is the final port for those heading on south to Mexico and many hospitable yacht clubs offer visitors three days of free moorage.

Cruisers typically go into a buying frenzy here. After Ensenada there are few facilities until Cabo San Lucas, or better La Paz, so one should stock up on food for the trip. (See Appendix B for other items worth buying in advance.)

Mexican visas and fishing licenses must be obtained and reciprocal HAM licences purchased in Tijuana. It is also the last chance to pick up equipment for the boat and West Marine, Boat US and repair facilities are conveniently located. Downwind Marine is especially accommodating (see their website **http://www.downwindmarine.com**). First-time voyagers can cruise in company to Cabo San Lucas by joining the 'Baja Ha-Ha' rally.

The hurricane belt: Mexico to Costa Rica
Weather
Departure from San Diego is usually not until November. The hurricane season in the south lasts from June to November, when tropical storms and strong SE winds may occur and rains are frequent.

The weather is generally clear and pleasant during the 750-mile leg down to the southern tip of Baja with prevailing northwesterly winds for eight months of the year. From November to February winds from the SE to SW are frequent with occasional moderate gales accompanied by rain. There may also be strong N/NE winds in December and January and fierce Chubasco winds in Fall at the southern end of the peninsular. At several prominent capes the winds accelerate, causing rough seas. Fog and haze are also experienced.

With a favorable wind and current of 1/2 to 1 knot, and working the weather systems, the trip south is generally a downwind run. In contrast the trip north, commonly known as the Baja Bash, can be an uncomfortable and demanding passage and insurance companies may limit cruising on the southern Pacific Baja coast between June and September.

Just north of Cabo San Lucas there is an abrupt change in weather and rise in temperature. Winds between November and May are usually light northwesterlies, from this point south. Calms are frequent, although a seabreeze may fill in. Currents are unpredictable.

The Gulf of Tehuantepec is notorious for its unpredictable currents and strong winds that frequently reach 60 knots and effect vessels up to 70 miles offshore. At Huatulco there are updated weather forecasts at the Port Captain's office. We found the most accurate information came from the fishermen who work this area.

The Bay of Fonseca, bordered by El Salvador, Honduras and Nicaragua, is known for its strong winds, currents and shallows, and must be entered with caution. This is also the northern limit of another local strong wind, the Papagayo, which plagues sailors down the Costa Rican coast as far as the Panama border during the dry season. This north wind frequently blows at up to 40 knots for days at a time.

Route Planning

The long peninsula of Baja California is dry, desert-like and sparsely populated, but it has numerous overnight anchorages which can be day-sailed, except for the 150 miles between Magdalena Bay and Cabo. There are numerous anchorages and marinas in the Sea of Cortez and many cruisers spend years here. Except for the southern section most of the west coast of Mexico can be day sailed until the Gulf of Tehuantepec which has a formidable reputation with a yearly average of Force 6 winds. particularly in the north, and strong currents. The usual strategy is to hug the coast for calmer conditions. Yachts are discouraged from stopping at the port of Salina Cruz. Be sure to clear out of Mexico at Puerto Madero.

The west coast of Guatemala has just one port, Puerto Quetzal where cruisers can leave their boats to tour inland to visit Mayan temples, colorful highland markets and the old Spanish town of Antigua. La Union (Cutuco), in the Bay of Fonseca, was the most sheltered anchorage in El Salvador, although Barillas Marina at Bahia de Jiquilisco now makes a convenient stop. The large Bay of Fonseca is an interesting and remote area to cruise with many dramatic volcanic islands.

The short coast and islands of Honduras offer limited anchorages. Nicaragua has anchorages at San Juan del Sur and Puerto Sandino (Samoza) and a marina, Marina Del Sol, north of Port of Corinto. Costa Rica has many good stops although unfortunately, many of the anchorages are open to the ocean and very rolly. Playas del Coco is the first Port of Entry where a cruising permit must be obtained. We particularly enjoyed Ballena Bay, Quepos and Manuel Antonio Park, as well as many smaller anchorages.

Southern Costa Rica to the Panama Canal

Weather

Except for the Caribbean trade-wind driven Papagayo, the winds are mainly light sea breezes created by the heat of the day ashore. The Intertropical Convergence Zone now influences the weather and thunder squalls can be expected even in the dry season. In the May to November wet season, heavy rains, lightning and squally winds are a daily occurrence. Hurricanes in southern Costa Rica and Panama are extremely rare. Currents are variable and can be quite strong, particularly in the Gulf of Panama.

Route Planning

We enjoyed Bahía Drake in southern Costa Rica and found good supplies (also a 'Free Zone') in Golfito to stock the boat for cruising northern Panama.

Panama offers some of the best cruising of the entire Pacific coast south of Juan de Fuca Strait. Islands, bays and rivers abound, offering varied, deserted, cruising opportunities with good anchorages. Marina facilities and fuel docks, however, are scarce. A visit to the Las Perlas Islands in the Bay of Panama is rewarding as is Taboga, close to the entrance of the Panama Canal.

Cruising the Caribbean Coasts of Central America

Panama to Florida

We were enchanted with this region, feeling we had been transported back to our days in the eastern Caribbean in the 1960s. It is a perfect finale for those circling the Caribbean, or cruising up from the Canal like ourselves, or for a season's visit from the United States.

Weather

Cruising is best enjoyed during the dry season, from late November to May. At this time the weather is generally clear and fine, with the exception of 'norther' frontal systems.

Winds

The easterly trade winds provide perfect sailing, generally keeping the temperatures in the comfortable low 80s, dying off to a gentle breeze at night. Winds tend to be more northeast in the early part of the winter, southeast in late spring or summer.

The onset of the wet season in early June brings humidity, frequent thunderstorms and the possibility of hurricanes, most likely in August, September and October. The Rio Dulce in Guatemala is the only reliable hurricane hole in the entire region. Most cruisers will either make for the Rio or vacate the area, north or south, before the middle of June.

Unlike the eastern Caribbean where weather is generally settled during the winter months, the western Caribbean is affected by 'Northers' that often reach gale force in strength. These winds are associated with cold fronts that move down from Canada and the U.S., and they march through from October through April, with the greatest frequency in December and January.

Currents

Caribbean currents are strong, a result of the North and South Equatorial currents converging as they enter the eastern Caribbean. After sweeping along the north coast of South America the current is deflected along the Central American coast. The flow becomes even swifter as it squeezes through the narrow Yucatan Channel between Mexico and western Cuba. It then turns east and north around Florida to form the Gulf Stream that carries the warm tropical waters up the eastern seaboard and across the North Atlantic to Europe.

For 200 miles north of Panama, cruisers can carry the current on the beam. After San Andrés they can ride it all the way to Florida, although wind against current north of Cuba can make a very uncomfortable passage. For those sailing south to the Yucatan from the States, the areas of the strongest currents are well charted and counter currents can be used to advantage. Sailors heading for Panama from Florida normally follow the Bahamian chain southeast, then go round the eastern end of Cuba and make a stop in Port Antonio or Port Royal (Kingston) Jamaica, before broad reaching the 550 nautical miles SSE across the current to the Canal.

Route Planning

Panama to Honduras

Any transit of the Panama Canal is a memorable experience. The 2010 canal fee for a yacht under 50' is $500 with an additional deposit ($1000) most of which is a breakdown security deposit which is returned promptly if not used. The fee can be paid by VISA. Unless 8 knots can be maintained most boats may take 2 days. Five people are required on board (4 line handlers and a helmsperson) and four lines of 125'. Boats may go through singly or in pairs in center chamber, or alongside a tug who is against the sidewall.

For those who are prepared to beat east from the canal against strong trades and currents, a visit to the ancient Spanish port of Portobelo with its fort-lined harbor is rewarding, and the 370 Panamanian San Blas islands have an irresistible charm.

Along the Caribbean coast to the west of the Canal, Laguna de Chiriqui offers wildlife and plenty of deserted island anchorages although from here it is a beat to windward to go north.

Although both inshore or offshore passages are possible when heading north most head offshore, as most of the coasts of Costa Rica, Nicaragua (with its famed Mosquito Coast) and eastern Honduras do not offer good cruising due to shallows and hot humid climate. A countercurrent along the coastline can be used to advantage by those heading south.

Offshore Colombian Islands of San Andrés (200 miles north of the canal) and close-by Providencia are popular stops as are several reefs such as Quita Sueño, Serrana and Serranilla Banks, particularly for those heading straight north to Swan Island off Honduras.

The Gulf of Honduras

One passes around the shoulder of Central America on the passage to the Honduran Bay Islands There are no aids to navigation and diligent piloting is required. The Vivario Cays are a popular anchorage en route.

The three islands of Guanaja, Roatán and Utila, along with several small cays, comprise the Bay Islands. Lying midway along the Honduran coast, 20 to 30 miles offshore, they are a cruising paradise and full of 'old-world' charm.

There are few harbors along the north cost of Honduras and most cruisers head overnight from here to Guatemala's Rio Dulce, Guatemala. Because of the sand bar at the mouth of the river, boats drawing over 6' 6" may plow through the bar occasionally or have to be heeled over to reduce their draft. The mid-channel marker (when in place) is supposidly at latitude 15° 50.18'N and longitude 88° 43.80'W. It is recommended that the crossing be made just before an afternoon high tide when a foot can be gained by the trades pushing the sea against the outpouring river.

The Rio Dulce has a magical jungle gorge that twists and turns for over six miles, then opens out into a series of lakes. Several marinas can be found close to the town of Fronteras where many leave their vessels safely and inexpensively whether for colorful visits inland or the hurricane season.

The Caribbean coast of Guatemala is only 50 miles long and it is possible to clear out of Livingston and make Belize's Punta Gorda in a day. Then you enter the magnificent cruising playground of the Belize barrier reef, second only in size to the Australian Barrier Reef, with three huge atolls offshore.

After hugging the mainland shore in Mexico, the reef diverges about 25 miles from the coast in southern Belize. The dozens of island cays, protected turquoise seas and brisk trade winds give wonderful cruising but care is required with drafts greater than six feet – especially between the outer reef, where there are often only day anchorages, and the inner, mangrove-covered stretch. Here anchoring is mostly in thick sea grass. The waters are even more brilliant and diving superb on the atolls, but one must watch weather closely as the anchorages are poor in northerly winds and there are only a few passes to re-enter through the barrier reef to find shelter.

Although the coastal regions of Belize are mainly swampy and uninviting, the settlements of Dangriga, Placencia and Punta Gorda are interesting to visit and offer adequate facilities for provisioning. A small marina on Moho Cay just north of Belize City is convenient for leaving the boat to explore inland, complete a major shop, top up with fuel and water, and do laundry.

North of Belize City, the channel becomes shallow and most keelboats sail north outside the reef, clearing out of Belize at Ambergris Cay, and clearing into Mexico at Xcalak, a few miles farther north (no charges here or mention of a fishing license). The fourth Caribbean atoll, Banco Chinchorro, is only 15 miles off the south Yucatan coast

The Mexican Caribbean coast of the Yucatan stretches 200 miles. Much of it is low-lying and featureless, but there are a few good anchorages and clear waters. Boats gather in the protected anchorage of Isla Mujeres, off Cancun, to await good weather for the 2/3 day trip to Florida. The boat can also be left in a marina to tour the Mayan temples at Chichen Itza, Uxmal and Palenque.

It is 333 miles from the Yucatan to Key West. Wind and current play an important part when planning the passage. Those heading north back to the States should head towards Cuba (staying outside the 12-mile limit) to ride the current, which runs at up to four knots. Coming from the States heading southwest, it is best to hug the Florida coast, Keys and Dry Tortugas before continuing down to the Yucatan, all the while keeping note of your position as there are strong and unpredictable eddies. November offers the least chance of southerly winds. For those heading north, April, May and June are preferred, as there is less chance of having to beat into a northeasterly. To be avoided is any passage during a 'Norther'. The strong north winds against the Yucatan current produce dangerous seas.

Another option is a visit to Cuba. The first port of entry, after leaving Mexico, is Maria La Gorda, a 130-mile sail to the northeast. With its 4000 cays and 3,000-mile coastline, and a similar number of offshore keys, Cuba is enjoyed by internationals from around the world and a new cruising destination to explore for Americans in the future. For those cruising Cuba extensively, especially with a draft over 6', it is worth purchasing the GeoCuba chartbooks that are GPS corrected. Cruising guides are also extremely helpful as well as travel books for a background into the complex history and changing culture. Although generally very pleasant be prepared to be boarded by officials frequently.

The Dry Tortugas, located 70 miles to the west of Key West, the site of the Fort Jefferson National Monument, make a pleasant layover but are best approached in daylight. The overnight sail east to Key West, the first U.S. Port of Entry, is generally on the wind and uncomfortable, as is short-tacking up the Keys. A draft of less than 4 1/2' is required to cruise up inside the Florida Keys.

The U.S. and Canadian East Coasts

The North American east coast offers incredible cruising diversity. It is nearly 2,500 nautical miles from Key West, along 14 American States, to Canada.

Fort Lauderdale to New York
Weather
Winds

On the passage from Florida to the Atlantic coastline of Canada you pass from trade-wind dominated weather in the south, through an area of variable offshore winds in the horse latitudes (around 30° N.), then into the westerlies of the North Atlantic. Subject to favorable forecasts, passages may be made at any time of year south of Cape Hatteras, North Carolina. North of the Cape, the summer months are preferred and the farther north and east one goes, the shorter the summer season becomes.

In the extreme south, the winter trade winds predominate offshore, with fine sailing conditions. During the winter Florida also experiences the cyclic 'norther' in which moderate to strong northwest winds clock around through northeast to east and on to south, when they diminish in strength. This veering continues through southwest to west, when the wind increases in strength, peaking again from the northwest. The cycle takes three or four days and occasionally produces winds of over 40 knots.

The June-November wet season in the tropics that lasts from June to November bringing squalls, thunderstorms and rain, together with uncomfortable heat and humidity. At this time of year hurricanes originating in the tropics can affect the east coast as far north as Cape Cod, Massachusetts, and occasionally all the way up to Nova Scotia.

Heading north during these months, the prevailing winds become southwesterly, the result of the Azores High that dominates summer weather in the North Atlantic. Near the coast, the heating of the landmass by day induces a sea breeze, while calms are frequent at night. Summer frontal systems can bring rain and strong winds, even gales, but these are usually of short duration.

The inland waterways have their own idiosyncrasies. While weather in the Chesapeake is generally hospitable, except during the cold winter months, conditions can change rapidly on any given day. Being shallow an ugly chop builds quickly when the breeze is over 15 knots and this can make progress to windward slow and uncomfortable. In spring and early summer, winds are generally southerly, often calm in the morning then frequently pick up in the afternoon. During the hot and humid months of July and August, there is generally little breeze. Frequent intense thunderstorms in the afternoons, however, are a familiar Chesapeake Bay trait with greatest incidence in September. They are generally short-lived, and half an hour after one's appearance the sky can be clear and bright. We particularly enjoyed Fall in the Chesapeake, with temperatures comfortable into November, breezes steady and anchorages deserted, though one does have to watch out for the 'northers' and their cycles, as previously described. There are several good hurricane holes in the Bay.

Spring and Fall are the best time to travel the Waterway, with the desirable combination of warm days and cool nights. The bi-seasonal window is convenient for heading north to avoid summer in the south, and back again when winter encroaches. However, the warming and cooling can produce fog, which descends quickly at any time of day. Although winds are light most of the year, except near ocean inlets, from Mid-December to mid-February they can be strong, reaching 40-60 knots with a typical 'norther', which complicates if not impedes an ICW passage while they last.

Tides and currents

The Gulf Stream flows like a warm river in the sea around the southern tip of Florida and up the coast. Cruisers heading north offshore can take advantage of this current when winds are favorable, but when 'northers' descend, daunting conditions with wind against current can arise. Hurricanes leaving the Caribbean draw renewed energy from the heat of the Stream, and can devastate coastal areas with wind and floods a long way north of their tropical origins.

Currents in the ICW are tide driven and in places they can be strong, particularly in the Carolinas and in Georgia. In Georgia tides have a range of eight or nine feet. With the resulting swift currents, particular care must be taken while anchoring, docking and approaching bridge openings, and boaters should always have an anchor and tackle at the ready. Currents can be difficult to calculate, and they are particularly strong around ocean inlets, producing a combination of positive and negative flow as one passes these portals. In areas such as the Cape Fear River, where currents can run at up to three knots, they are more predictable, which means that time and fuel can be saved with advanced planning. Tides and currents also play an important role in route planning when transiting the C&D Canal and when optimizing a passage through Delaware Bay.

Route Planning

Florida to Virginia
There are various options for heading north. The ICW is a popular choice rather than making an ocean passage. Know the buoyage system and your accurate mast height! (Both are described in the text.) Planning your timing for the next day's run saves delays with bridge openings and be aware that 'healthy' food may not be readily available. To compensate many of the marinas provide courtesy cars to replenish supplies.

Chesapeake Bay
Stretching 200 miles from Norfolk to the Chesapeake and Delaware Canal and 20 miles across at its widest point, the Chesapeake enjoys almost 4,000 miles of coastline, although much is very shallow. With both its eastern and western shores indented by innumerable rivers and inlets, it is a cruiser's paradise, but depths do have to be monitored closely as passages often silt up and charted depths are not reliable. The hundreds of commercial craft on the bay require diligent attention. Solomons, Oxford, St. Michaels and Annapolis are popular destinations, as is a cruise up the Potomac River to Washington D.C.

The Chesapeake and Delaware Canal
The 12-mile C&D Canal forms a vital link in the ICW system, connecting the upper reaches of Chesapeake Bay to the Delaware River and Delaware Bay. It is easy to transit at night and movements of commercial craft can be monitored on VHF Channel 13. Preferably time a transit to take advantage of the tidal current, that can run at up to two knots.

The passage down Delaware Bay between the C&D Canal and Cape May, New Jersey is about 50 miles. The tide usually floods for five hours and ebbs for seven so working the current pays off.

The New Jersey Offshore Route
Only boats with a draft less than three feet can travel the ICW up the New Jersey coast, so most cruisers complete the 120-mile passage from Cape May to Sandy Hook, New Jersey, offshore. This long sandy shoreline has

just a few anchorages for deep-keeled vessels, so it is important to keep a close check on the often-turbulent Atlantic Ocean and its locally unpredictable weather. The coastline can be particularly treacherous for those heading south in the Fall.

It is an eight-mile run due north from Sandy Hook to the Narrows at the entrance of New York Harbor. In strong southeast or easterly winds the passage can be rough and it is worth considering the route to the west of Staten Island. Although busy, New York Harbor is straightforward. At $25 a night the West 79th Street Boat Basin on the Hudson River is a bargain, perfectly placed for visits to the famous delicatessen Zabar's, museums and to access Manhattan's sights. Consult the tide before heading north through Hell Gate on the East River.

New England and Canada

This region offers tremendous variety for cruisers from sailing in protected waters, to coast-hopping and offshore passages. Cape Cod marks another transition on the U.S. coast. While Long Island Sound teems with yachts, to the north of the canal summer temperatures are cooler, cruising in the open Atlantic Ocean more demanding and the coast becomes increasingly rugged. From Cape Cod it is just a day's sail to Boston and Marblehead or an overnight run 'down east' to Maine. Just a few adventurous cruisers continue to Canada, both to St. John River, New Brunswick, or across to Nova Scotia and the Bras d'Or Lakes. Even fewer continue to Newfoundland, where even in summer icebergs are common.

Weather

This region is known for its rapidly changing and variable nature, particularly as one goes further north and east.

Winds

Throughout the whole of this coastal area the prevailing summer wind is south or southwest, due to the effect of the Atlantic Azores High. Winter winds are generally from the west or northwest caused by the dominance of North American continental high and the Icelandic low during this period. Contrasts in surface temperatures between the cool polar air and warm Gulf Stream cause rapid low-pressure systems to move eastwards, bringing periodic storms to the region. These are often heralded by a murky afternoon, showers the following day then crystal clear conditions as the northerly wind fills in. In late Spring and early Fall a shift in the jet stream causes these lows to track down the St. Lawrence Valley generating gales from the southeast. They may also move out to sea from Cape Cod when they produce northeasterly gales that are dreaded for their cold, moist arctic temperatures and high winds, avoided by prudent cruisers.

Also to be watched is hurricane development in the Atlantic and Caribbean from June to November, with the greatest incidence of tropical storms in September. These bring squalls, thunder and huge quantities of rain. On occasion hurricanes affect the East Coast as far as Nova Scotia; we had to find a hurricane hole in Boston for Hurricane Floyd. There is generally ample warning although the exact path of the hurricane can be unpredictable.

Overlaid on this pattern is a daily occurrence of land and sea breezes that give ideal conditions for the summer cruiser. With the heating of the land the sea breeze generally fills in around 10:00am in the early June, sometimes not until 1:00pm by August, and usually there is a fine 10-20 knot sailing breeze for the rest of the day. After a calm sunset a light land breeze may spring up lasting for much of the night, although by morning generally all is flat calm.

Temperatures

While Long Island Sound endures hot, humid conditions during the summer months the temperatures of Maine and Nova Scotia (averaging in the high 60s) give comfortable, if occasionally cool, cruising. Ice conditions in the Gulf of St. Lawrence and Northumberland Strait keep spring temperatures lower in Nova Scotia and Newfoundland, and the cool summer seas also help suppress storm development. The warm Gulf Stream water delays the onset of Fall, making it one of the most pleasant seasons to cruise in Nova Scotia.

Fog

The most common type of fog is advection sea fog. Warm, moist air spawned over the Gulf Stream is blown onshore across the cooler Labrador current and condenses into dense fog. Visibility can be lost in minutes at any time of the year, but annoyingly for the average cruiser, most frequently in July and August. Fog becomes a significant hazard north of Cape Cod and is a reality of cruising both in Maine and Nova Scotia. Although it can be a little nerve-racking to sail in dense fog, for the most part it need not inhibit cruising. Radar is invaluable; particularly a sensitive unit able to pick up the lobster trap floats, of which there are thousands.

The mouth of bays, rivers and inlets is sometimes free of fog as well as the north side of inlets. For the most part, although not always, winds are light when there is dense fog, as a strong wind will often disperse it.

Navigating in fog

Much of the time fog is light or patchy and it can be quite exhilarating piloting from buoy to buoy and seeing a headland appear out of the gloom. On occasion we 'leapt' out of the fog in little more than a boat length. What a revelation it is to suddenly be able to view the stunning rocky, treed inlet- and island-ridden shore. A good lookout must always be kept with frequent changes in watch, as the job is quite tiring. Most stationary hazards are well-marked by whistle, gong or bell buoys and you should have your own horn or whistle handy to blow regularly – one long blast for a vessel under power, a long and two short for a sailing vessel. Mobile hazards are another matter. The fishing boats are active during the summer months, and as they rarely hold a straight predictable course should be given a wide berth.

It is important to calculate currents and keep a careful DR, as it is easy to become disoriented. Although radar and GPS take away much of the fear of piloting in dense fog, the thousands of lobster trap floats present in shallower waters are a constant hazard.

If you awake to find the sky dark and deck ringing wet, and find it hard to see the mast in the swirling gray, it is prudent to plan a day at anchor. Enjoy relaxing on the boat, walking ashore picking blackberries or visiting one of the charming towns. It may also be possible to organize cruising plans around the fog, heading for areas that tend to be fog free, such as on the lee side of a high island and up the rivers.

Tides and Currents

The flood flows north and east, the ebb south and west. Tides increase in height and vigor up the coast. Bay of Fundy, in particular experiences mammoth tides with the Minas Basin, at the head of the bay, holding the word's record for the highest tide at 54'. In Maine and Nova Scotia the large ranges and strong tidal currents require cautious anchoring with the charts studied carefully. Allowance must be made for swinging with tidal change and enough rode let out to hold at high tide but not to drift ashore on the low. A Bruce, CQR, Delta or Spade type anchor is recommended with enough rode to allow a scope of 7:1 in the area of intended cruising. For example Penobscot Bay has 11' and Passamaquoddy Bay has 20-foot tides. Canadians and Europeans who are used to chart tide datums based on extreme tidal ranges must get used to American charts where negative tides have to be allowed for, and vise versa for Americans who buy Canadian charts.

Route Planning

Long Island Sound and Cape Cod Canal

Long Island Sound stretches nearly one hundred miles from northeast to southwest and is up to twenty miles across at its widest point. Almost an inland sea, it is a great body of water for both racers and cruisers. As mentioned there is usually a pleasant afternoon breeze in summer but plan to make windward miles early as an uncomfortable chop can develop later in the day. Although summer weather is generally hospitable occasional fog and a few thunderstorms can occur and a northeaster can bring high winds, torrents of rain, low temperatures and steep waves.

The two shores of the Sound are quite different. While the southern shore has large, natural harbors the north shore has frequent rocky outcroppings, islands, small harbors, inlets and river mouths. Crowded by development there are hundreds marinas, yacht clubs and mooring buoys. Although these facilities are convenient they are expensive for the long-term cruiser and anchorages were often at the entrance of the harbor in not ideal conditions. Book well in advance for moorage in Mystic Seaport

The sandy islands of the Sound offer a complete contrast in ambience, and cooler temperatures. Buzzards Bay also offers pleasant stops before entering the Cape Cod Canal, which saves the passage around the Cape through Nantucket Shoals.

Transit through the 10-mile canal is straightforward but go with the tide (floods north) as the current can run up to 4 knots. The Canal authorities use Channel 13 for monitoring shipping traffic. Vessels entering the Canal from the Sound with a fair wind and positive tide should have an easy passage. When heading west on a fair current, however, a typical southwest wind up Buzzards Bay may cause a steep chop that greatly slows down a passage. After passing buoy 10A one can head southward on starboard tack across the calmer flats—but watch your depth!

Massachusetts and Maine

Above the Cape is a different world of cruising in the cool waters of the open Atlantic Ocean. The replica of the *Mayflower* sets the tone of European arrival and there are many attractive communities to explore.

Although the Maine coast is only some 250 miles long in a straight line, indentations and over 3000 islands give 3,500 miles of coastline. July 1st to Labor Day is the typical cruising season, although this is also the time for fog. There are 'endless' anchorages along this dramatic coast although fog may dictate progress and route. We particularly enjoyed cruising the waters of Muscongus and Penobscot Bays and Boothbay Harbor, Rockland, Camden and Bar Harbor along with deserted anchorages, and loved the numbers of traditional wooden craft.

Canada—New Brunswick, Nova Scotia and Newfoundland

East of Mount Desert the coast becomes austere and challenging. However, although it can be a grind to sail to the St. John River in New Brunswick, and cope with the huge tides of the Bay of Fundy, the valley gives pleasant fog-free cruising in warm fresh water. Just above the busy commercial Saint John Harbour boats enter the river valley by passing over Reversing Falls at slack water.

The South coast of Nova Scotia has many attractive anchorages, with Mahone, St. Margarets and Lunenburg Bays particularly attractive cruising grounds, and the large Halifax harbor has many welcoming yacht Clubs. There are fewer anchorages along the demanding shore northeast of Halifax and many make the 178-mile run to the St. Peters Canal on Cape Breton Island direct. The picturesque Bras d'Or Lakes give serene, generally fog-free cruising and a variety of anchorages.

The cruising in Newfoundland is rugged, anchorages are deep and the vegetation sparse on the rocky shore. There is just one marina, in Lewisporte, but most towns have government wharves, that are either free or have a minimal charge. Circumnavigating Newfoundland in a clockwise direction is preferred and winter woolies are definitely in order! All the cruisers we've met were impressed by the friendly reception.

There are many opportunities to continue exploring this region of Canada, such as heading up the St. Lawrence River to the Great Lakes or taking the preferable shorter route via the Hudson River and Lake Champlain or the Erie Canal. The Thousand Islands region of the St. Lawrence River off Lake Ontario offers great gunkholing opportunities. Those with a draft less than 5' can take the attractive Trent-Severn Waterway to the scenic cruising area of Georgian Bay and the North Channel in Lake Huron. (Those with a deeper draft can go the long way round, across Lake Ontario and Lake Erie.) Many continue to Lake Michigan and complete a grand U.S. circle by going down the Mississippi or the Tennessee Tombigbee Waterway to the Gulf of Mexico.

Wherever you go—HAPPY CRUISING!

APPENDIX B

Resources

WEATHER
Accessing Weather Forecasts
VHF-FM
There is a continuous VHF service along the U.S. and Canadian coasts of weather forecasts, warnings and radar reports. Reception can vary but is usually up to 30 miles line-of-sight. Weather channels (WX) 1-7 are commonly used. (Note for example: WX-1 is on 162.55MHz WX-2 162.4MHz WX-3 162.475MHz) for which an American programed VHF radio is required. The U.S. and Canadian Coast Guards also broadcast weather warnings, check Channel 16 and 22a in the U.S., 21b in Canada. There are no similar services in Central American countries.

SSB/HAM/HF Receiver/computer/weather software
After leaving U.S. waters an SSB or Ham radio, or HF receiver with SSB capability is invaluable for obtaining weather information, including weatherfax pictures and grib files with appropriate demodulators and software. See **www.nws.noaa.gov/om/marine** for U.S. National Weather Service schedules.

Reeds Nautical Almanacs—North American West Coast, Caribbean and North America East Coast also provide excellent radio resources.

Navtex text forecasts are available on 518kHz up to 200 miles offshore, with stations giving coverage to most of the U.S. and Canadian waters.

The Internet
There are any number of sites with weather information on the internet that can be checked in local public libraries, Internet Cafés or through onboard systems.
For example: **http://www.nws.noaa.gov**
http:/www.weather.org/marine_weather.htm

Satellite telephones Can be used to download weather forecasts and grib files as well as access shore stations.

Port Captains/marinas in Central America

Many have information available and some give VHF forecasts, though a knowledge of Spanish may be necessary. Weatherfax charts are sometimes on display in their offices.

Local Resources

Radio, TV, airports, commercial fishermen and ships (call on channel 16 for initial contact). Ham and single sideband nets. Note phone numbers of local weather resources en route.

Alaska to Panama

High Seas Forecasts - Check before leaving for changes

Voice

NOJ   (USCG Kodiak, Alaska)
USB 6501 kHz
Start Broadcast at 0203z, 1645Z

VAE   (Tofino Coastguard Radio, British Columbia)
USB 2054 (repeated 2182) kHz
Start Broadcast 0250, 0850, 1450, 2045Z (Prince Rupert 20 minutes later)

NMO   (USCG Honolulu, Hawaii)
USB 6501, 8764, 13089 kHz
Start Broadcast   6/8 kHz at 0600, 1200Z
                       8/13 kHz at 0005, 1800Z

NMC   (USCG, Point Reyes, CA)
USB 4426, 8764, 13089, 17314 kHz
Start Broadcast   4/8/13kHz at 0430Z, 1030Z),
                       8/13/17kHz at 1630Z and 2230Z

NMG   (USCG New Orleans, L.A.)
USB 4316, 8502, 12788 kHz
Start Broadcast 0330Z, 0500Z, 0930Z, 1130Z, 1600Z, 1730Z, 2200Z, 2330Z
(0500, 1130, 1730 and 2330Z may be pre-empted by radiofax broadcast.)

Weatherfax

Select a frequency 1.9 kHz below when using a single sideband radio

NOJ (USCG Kodiak, Alaska)
USB 2054 (10Z,18Z), 4298, 8459, 12412.5 (4Z, 22Z) kHz
Start Broadcast 0400, 1000, 1800, 2200Z
Broadcast Schedule 1830Z

KVM70 (DOD Honolulu, Hawaii)
USB 9982.5 (11Z), 11090 (except 23Z), 16135 (except11Z),
23331.5 (23Z) kHz
Start Broadcast 0533, 1150, 1733, 2350Z
Broadcast schedule 0533, 1150, 1733, 2350Z

NMC (USCG Point Reyes, CA)
USB 4346 (except 19z,23Z), 8682, 12786, 17151.2,
22527 (19Z, 23Z) kHz
Start broadcast 0245, 0800, 1100, 1430, 1930, 2300Z
Broadcast Schedules at 1104Z and 2324Z

Ham and SSB Nets

In northern Mexico the airways are alive with nets (refer to Downwind Marine's Cruising Guide on **http://www.downwindmarine.com**.) The quality of weather information is dependent on current participants. Nets generally include weather, check-in, general traffic and information.
For weather forecasts try:
The Baja Ham Net at 1600Z on LSB 7238.5 kHz and *The Chubasco Ham Net* at 1530Z (1415Z during DST) on LSB 7192.0 kHz.
The Papagayo SSB Net operates between Panama and Nicaragua at 0430Z between USB 4024-4030 kHz. *The Central American Breakfast Club Ham Net* operates around Central America between 20° N & 20°S at 1300Z on LSB7083 (80-85) kHz. It has several shore based participants.

VHF Nets

These are common in major ports—Cabo, Puerto Vallarta, Zihuatanejo, La Paz, Mazatlan etc. Check for channels. Besides weather their wealth of social plans, goods to trade and local events often make it hard to leave!

Carribean Central America
High Seas Forecasts
Voice
NMC (USCG, Point Reyes, CA) and **NMG** (USCG New Orleans, L.A.)—see Alaska to Panama section

NMN (USCG, Portsmouth, VA or Cheasapeake)
USB 4426, 6501, 8764, 13089, 17314 kHz
Start Broadcast   4/6/8 kHz at 0330, 0500, 0930Z
6/8/13kHz at 1130, 1600, 2200, 2330Z
8/13/17 at 1730Z

Broadcasts include forecasts for a large area, for example NMN has a synopsis for New England, the west and central North Atlantic, the southwest North Atlantic (including the Bahamas), the Gulf of Mexico and the Caribbean. The above times are the beginning of the broadcast cycle; as area forecasts are repeated on a regular basis it is worth noting relevant times to avoid future delays. Always check schedules before leaving.

Weatherfax
Select a frequency 1.9 kHz below when using a single sideband radio.
NMC (USCG Point Reyes, CA)—see Alaska to Panama section)

NMG (USCG New Orleans)
USB 4317.9, 8503.9, 12789.9 kHz
Start Broadcast at 0000, 0600, 1200, 1800Z
Broadcast Schedules at 0630, 1830

NMF (USCG, Boston, MA)
USB 4235kHz (02Z, 08Z), 6340.5, 9110, 12750 (14Z) kHz
Start Broadcast at 0230, 0745, 1400, 1720, 1900Z
Broadcast Schedules at 0243, 1405Z

Local Resources
Research country resources. Belize, for example, has the Belize Weather Bureau - **www.hydromet.gov.bz.**

Ham and SSB Nets
The Central American Breakfast Club Ham Net operates around Central America between 20° N & S at 1300Z on LSB 7083 (80-85) kHz. It has several shore-based participants.

USB

Chris Parker Weather SSB 1230Z (07.30) on USB 8104 kHz
South West Caribbean Net 1315Z (0815) on USB 6209kHz
Panama Connection Net 1330Z (08:30) on USB8107 kHz
Pan Pacific Net 1400Z (0900) USB 8143kHz
The Northwest Caribbean Ham Net 1400Z (0900) on USB 6209 kHz.
Herb Hilgenberg - Southbound 11 VAX498 USB 12359 kHz daily at 2000Z.
Herb is an amateur weather forecaster who operates an invaluable SSB
weather net for cruisers in the Atlantic from his home in Ontario. His call
sign is VAX 498 but he commonly uses Southbound II. He moves in a
geographic pattern around the Caribbean and Atlantic and likes cruisers
to check-in before the net starts. For further information and his protocol
check   **http://www3.sympatico.ca/hehilgen/vax498.htm**. You must
have a ship's radio license to transmit.

Florida to Nova Scotia

VHF
Unless going offshore most cruisers will use the weather channels on VHF

High Seas Forecasts
Voice and weatherfax
NMN, NMF and Herb Hilgenberg—see Caribbean Central America
CFH   (Halifax, Nova Scotia)
            USB 122.5, 4271, 6496.4, 10536, 13510 kHz
            Continuous fax broadcast (1.9 kHz below on SSB radio)

Automated Marine Weather Information
There are many telephone weather recordings, some examples are:
Charleston SC (843) 744-3207
Annapolis MD (410) 936-1212
Nova Scotia, New Brunswick and Prince Edward Island (902) 426-9600
Newfoundland Northeast and East coast (709) 256-6868,
            Grand Banks, East Coast and South Coast (709) 772-5534
            Corner Brook, Northeast Gulf and Gulf Port au Port
            (709) 637-4570

Environment Canada
http://weatheroffice.ec.gc.ca

THE BEAUFORT SCALE

Force	Winds	Terms	Sea/Land Conditions	Wave Height
	kts			ft
<1	calm	calm	calm , smoke rises vertically	calm
1	1-3	light air	ripples, smoke drifts	ripples
2	4-6	light breeze	small wavelets, leaves rustle, flags wave slightly	less than 1
3	7-10	gentle breeze	large wavelets, small crests, small flags extended, leaves in constant motion	1-3
4	11-16	moderate breeze	small waves, some whitecaps, small branches sway, flags flap	3.5-5
5	17-21	fresh breeze	moderate waves, many whitecaps, small trees sway	6-8
6	22-27	strong breeze	larger waves, whitecaps, large branches sway, flags beat, umbrellas used with difficulty	9-13
7	28-33	near gale	heaped seas, foam from breaking waves, whole trees sway, difficult to walk	13.5-19
8	34-40	gale	moderate high waves of greater length, foam blown in well marked streaks, twigs break off trees	18-25
9	41-47	strong gale	High seas, seas roll, dense streaks of foam, spray may reduce visibility, branches break off trees, tiles blown from roofs	23-32
10	48-55	storm	very high waves hiding ships from view, overhanging crests, white seas, some trees blown down, damage to buildings	29-41
11	56-63	violent storm	exceptionally high waves, seas covered with white foam patches, visibility more reduced, widespread damage to trees and buildings	37-52
12	63 kts +	hurricane	air filled with foam, sea completely white with driving spray, visibility greatly reduced, severe and extensive damage	over 45

The Beaufort Scale was developed by Sir Francis Beaufort in 1806 as a simple scale to relate state of the sea and reactions of ships, particularly fully rigged man-of-war sailing vessels, to the strength wind. It was officially adopted in 1838 and is still used internationally today, in an expanded and modified form. Criteria used by the World Meterorological Organization is also included in the chart.

Note: 1 nautical mile = 1.85 kilometers = 1.15 statute miles

1 knot = 1 nm/hr

Cruising Information, Guides and Charts

General Resources

US Government Sailing Directions (Enroute) specific volumes for the United States and Canada, West Coast of Mexico and Central America

REED'S Nautical Almanacs—North American West Coast, Caribbean and North American East Coast (pilot, lights, currents, communication and weather resources, ephemeris, also includes tides) a comprehensive source of information that is updated annually.

World Cruising Routes Jimmy Cornell

www.noonsite.com is an invaluable, frequently updated resource for cruisers with worldwide coverage. Started by Jimmy Cornell it is now run by *World Cruising Club*, the organizers of the Atlantic Rally for Cruisers.

Charts

Increasingly cruisers are using chart plotters and computer charts, but in case of failure, paper charts should always be carried, particularly as in much of this region electronic repair facilities are rarely available. (Significant for all information stored on a laptop.) As charts are expensive we compromise when possible by having small scale paper charts and printing out large-scale chartlets of harbors from a computer chart programme ahead of time.

Caution—charts are frequently inaccurate in Mexico and Central America and not GPS corrected.

Note: The metric system of measurement is now standard on U.S. Government nautical charts 1 meter = 3.28 feet   1.829m = 1 fathom 1.852km = I nautical mile 1.609km = 1 Statute mile.

Increasingly soundings for low water are being based on lower low water (i.e. the lowest depth of the day) rather than mean low water. This should not be confused with British and Canadian charts that use the lowest low water recorded under normal atmospheric conditions.

Chartbooks

These are handy and avoid bulky portfolios. There are several available this region, check carefully for coverage before using as a sole paper resource.

Cruising Guides

Cruising guides are available for all areas covered, although they vary in coverage and quality of information. With frequent changes in regulations and facilities, particularly due to the increase in numbers of cruisers, it is important to have recent editions.

Cruising guides can never be a substituted for charts. They do, however, give invaluable information regarding anchorages, marinas, shoreside facilities and give handy chartlets. They can be particularly useful in areas where both British Admiralty and U.S. Defense Mapping Agency Charts have inaccuracies due to old surveys as in much of Central America.

Check marine book suppliers for availability such as:

U.S.	**www.bluewaterweb.com**
Canada	**www.nauticalmind.com**
U.K.	**www.bookharbour.com** (Kelvin Hughes)

www.Amazon.com also lists most guides. It is easy to search and often has the useful feature of being able to 'look inside the book'.

Travel and Cruising Tips

Reference books on local fauna, flora and travel opportunities ashore (we use *Lonely Planet*, *Moon Publications* and the *Rough Guides*, oriented to adventure travel and the Audubon series for nature when available) will greatly enhance your cruising experiences, as will learning some Spanish. If possible buy books ahead of time to study to make the most of sightings at sea and ashore.

Officialdom

Check ahead of time regarding visas, remembering that guests of different nationalities may have different requirements. Make many copies of crew lists, also copies of boat documents and passport information pages, one copy to be kept on file as a record. Be prepared to be patient with officials! For visits to a country that are longer than 6 months temporary import permits for the boat may be required. A fishing license must be purchased to cruise Mexican waters if there is any fishing gear on board. There are increasing numbers of conservation areas, do respect them.

Except for the United States and Canada it is always necessary to clear out of a country to be accepted into the next. Do not stop in a country before clearing into a Port of Entry or after clearing out. Find out procedures for the particular port ahead of time or call on channel 16 (maybe 12) before entering. Usually only the captain goes ashore to visit Customs, Immigration and Port Captain but you may be required to go alongside a particular dock or anchor out and officials will come to you. Have the boat and yourselves looking immaculate. Try to get passports stamped (except Cuba). Procedures and costs may vary from one boat and port to the next.

Procedures for Entering Canada

As in all countries immediate clearance is required. Call CANPASS (1-888-CAN-PASS) or Customs at 1-888-265-5633. Many marinas have local numbers. Landfall must always be at an approved Port of Entry such as Yarmouth, Shelburne, Liverpool, Lunenburg, Cape Breton in Nova Scotia, Campobello Island, Deer Island, Grand Manan, St. Andrews in New Brunswick and on the West coast, Victoria, Sidney, Bedwell Harbour (Gulf Islands) and Vancouver, but CANPASS will inform of other official docks for check-in, sometimes at the local yacht club. Customs and Immigration must be contacted by phone on arrival; officials may or may not come to the vessel. There is no fee to enter Canada. Visits longer than

45 days have some requirements. Over six months are allowable but must be justified – such as for specific yard work on the boat. In line with most countries, all firearms must be declared on arrival, most types have to be given up and can be collected from the Port of Entry on departure. Some produce and meats products are also not allowed and will be confiscated. The vessel must have State Registration or Federal Documentation. All national except U.S. citizens must have passports. Americans may have government identity and photo ID or Nexus card. There must be letters of permission from an absentee owner and from both parents of minors who are traveling on board alone (giving consent and reason for the visit). All dogs must have had a rabies inoculation within the last 3 years (or a certificate of good health from a Veterinarian if the animal is too young). See Canadian Border Agency **www.cbsa-asfc.gc.ca.**

Entering the United States

Security will require anyone entering the U.S.A. by land or sea, including American citizens, to carry one of the following identification documents: passport, NEXUS card, Free and Secure Trade card (FAST), enhanced drivers licence (EDL) an enhanced identification card (EIC), or a Secure Certificate of Indian Status that is U.S. approved, including boat identification, letters of authority for children and rabies shot for dogs. A cruising permit is issued with a 12-month stay allowed for a fee of $25.00 for boats over 30 feet. Official Ports of Entry in Maine include Eastport, Lubec, Cutler, Belfast, Portland and Bar Harbor on the east coast: Roche or Friday Harbor (San Juan Island), Anacortes, Port Angeles on the West coast. Most cruisers arriving from the Caribbean will make their landfall in Key West or Fort Lauderdale. It is best to check in between 8am-4.30pm Mon-Friday to avoid an overtime fee. Produce may also be restricted-particularly citrus and potatoes.

Non-U.S. cruisers (except Canadians) must purchase a visitor's visa in advance when arriving by pleasure boat. These are expensive, so request the maximum time allowed. Foreign cruisers must keep Customs informed of the vessel's whereabouts while cruising U.S. waters or may incur a fine. A check-in phone number will be given with the cruising permit.

Telephones and E-mail
Internet cafes and free wireless connections in coffee shops and restaurants are widely available. Many only use Skype for phoning overseas, downloading the program free of charge. Skype is free calling

computer to computer with the advantage of being able to use a webcam. The charges are small computer to landline but you must pre-pay into your account. Use a headset with microphone for the best reception.

When using a landline find out the country access codes for AT&T, Canada Direct etc: These services are much cheaper than calling direct or collect. Local phone cards are often extraordinarily inexpensive although have multiple numbers to dial. Some have a connection fee so you get better value from long calls.

There is often a surcharge when credit cards are used.

Making overseas calls is sometimes not possible outside tourist areas and there may be special phones for overseas calls. Use phones marked Ladatel for international calls when in Mexico, for example, using their easily purchased cards.

Check cellphone plans to extend coverage if offered.

Note: The international standard for cellphones (known as mobiles) is the GSM system. Be sure to have a tri-band phone that is unlocked for international usage with different sim cards. Sim cards can be purchased in the country on arrival or on the internet with some covering several countries. When calling a mobile GSM phone be aware that the caller pays all the charges, there are only charges for receiving when outside the sim card coverage area.

Send e-mail from the boat via onboard systems, satellite phone, or laptop, SSB radio and TNC (terminal node controller) usually a Pactor 111. Those with the required Ham license send e-mail free (no business allowed). Others use a company such as SAILMAIL, currently $250 a year per vessel. The U.K. MailASail is popular, offering communication management including weather information and a web diary.

Money Management

ATM machines are found throughout the area, but carry a variety of cards using different international systems, e.g. Plus and Cirrus, and make sure that your card is activated correctly for overseas travel before leaving.

If a bank machine states it is out of cash, or that you have insufficient funds, make a note of the date and bank so you can check with your bank statement later to make sure no amount was debited. Many suggest it is safer and more reliable in Mexico and some of Central America to go into the bank to make a withdrawal. Some U.S. cash on board is useful but find out the official exchange rate in advance. Check all pockets before leaving a country as it may be hard to exchange the currency elsewhere.

World News and Current Affairs: Listening to local radio is informative and we find the BBC World Service an enjoyable way of keeping up on world news. See **www.bbc.co.uk/worldservice/** for schedules. We also listen to Voice of America and Radio Canada International.

Clothing

Although for the most part casual attire is appropriate ashore, people in Central America tend to be conservative in dress and often we felt it more appropriate to wear long pants or a skirt. Those who suffer from mosquito attacks should always take repellent and cover up at dusk. Although hot on the coast in Central America it can be quite cool inland in the hills, requiring a sweater or jacket.

For those used to the hot summer temperatures in the southern United States it is also easy to go 'down East' to Maine and Canada poorly prepared. Nights tend to be cool, even in the middle of summer, and days can be damp and chilly. Plenty of warm and waterproof clothes are needed, including gloves and hats. In the early and late season, and sometimes mid-summer, a cabin heater is a boon.

Photography

Whether camera or camcorder never hesitate to use it. This record will stimulate wonderful memories for a lifetime. Some cultures are sensitive about being photographed, however, so always ask permission. I find showing local people a picture of ourselves in the viewing window of the digital camera a huge barrier breaker with others wanting their photos taken. A printed picture makes a treasured gift. As there is frequently surf on the west coast of Central America dinghy landings can be wet, we recommend a water-resistant camera or bag. As camera theft is rampant around the world having a small pocket-sized camera to take ashore can have its merits.

As digital photos require considerable space to store on a computer and large computers are power hungry on a boat's electrical system, an external storage unit is recommended.

Supplies

We find eating like the locals and visiting their markets part of the adventure of cruising. However, buying in bulk before leaving the United States for Mexico and Central America is easy and economical for brand name items—but don't overload the boat to the gunwales! Also stock up on favorite items—I frequently hear peanut butter and chocolate chips discussed as expensive further south, although for us it is Hellmann's mayonnaise (often used in dips), Earl Grey tea and 2-ply toilet paper! Once supplies are used up be prepared to find few familiar brand names on the shelves.

Those who are cruising slowly to Cabo will need all their supplies for that period, as they will find few stores en route. It is also wise to purchase some pesos in advance, also carry enough fuel.

Other items worth purchasing in the United States are heavy duty, air-tight plastic containers for storing dry goods—in hope of avoiding the inevitable weevils; an ample supplies of Ziplock bags; cockroach hotels, cleaning materials, insect repellent, meat tenderizer and white vinegar (for jellyfish stings) and sun block.

Buying lube oil, biocide and diesel, oil, fuel and water filters will ensure you have them when needed and are of your preferred brand. Remember that once out of the United States metric measurements are the norm. Stock up on fasteners, hoses etc. As there are few docks in Central America self-charging electrical tools are handy with an inverter, also nec-essary for your laptop. Although much of Central America is 110 volts and 60 cycles like the United States, if going further afield note that most of the world uses 220 volt 50 cycle AC power.

Those heading for Canada will find all the supplies they are used to, and more, often at cheaper prices than in the United States.

Entertainment

Books, cards and other games will all be put to good use. Book and video swaps with other cruisers and in internet cafes, are common. Remember to have boat cards made and maybe a visitor's book (plain pages inspire creativity), and find a visible place for it on board, so you don't forget to give it to your guests!

If you have a television on board, an active antenna is a necessity. *Note:* Although Canada, the United States, most of Central America and the Caribbean uses the NTSC television system, the rest of the English speaking world uses PAL which is not compatible with your NTSC DVDs and swaps with European, Australian, New Zealand etc: boats will not work.

Medical

Visit your local travel clinic well in advance for the immunizations required for your route. You can also check **www.tripprep.com.** We had vaccinations for Hepatitis A&B, typhoid and tetanus for Central America. In some areas malaria prophylactics are necessary. Although medical sup-plies are available in Mexico and Central America one should always have a well-stocked medical chest (airtight plastic containers serve well), with at least one course of antibiotics, and antihistamine. Those on specific medication should have supplies for the duration. In Mexico seasickness sufferers can buy Stugeron (cinnarizine), the accepted medication by boaters around the world. It is wise to be covered by travel medical insurance. Those away for shorter periods will find it inexpensive through travel agents and automobile associations.

Keeping Comfortable

Fans below are a necessity in the tropics, particularly over each berth and in the galley. We have found the German Hella fans quiet, efficient and long lasting. Wind scoops are also efficient in bringing air below. We put extra opening hatches at the end of our aft cabins to increase the airflow, also over the galley. Mosquito barriers are essential. Most modern boats come with fitted screens for the hatches, but extra netting for the companionway is also useful.

Sun is your greatest danger while cruising. Be sure to have a bimini to give shade in the cockpit. Opening panels in the front of the dodger are important for a cooling airflow when at anchor. An awning over the boom can be used for additional shade while at the dock or at anchor. Comfortable cockpit cushions are a must as this is your living area in the tropics.

Security

We had no concerns when cruising any of the countries in this book but regular wise tourist practises should always be followed. Find out about the area and adhere to local customs. On arrival talk to officials after clearance procedures are completed and get to know the people. Avoid areas with poor reputations. Only carry necessities ashore and hold onto bags and cameras tightly. Be cautious ashore at night. In large cities it is wise to use a secure marina. Stow items away from the deck and always lock the boat, and dinghy and outboard to the boat or dock ashore. Have grids for companionway and hatches to facilitate security with airflow below. Follow the local laws, in most countries it is illegal to carry a gun and fines are large. Research local fauna and flora. The most dangerous tree in the Caribbean is the poisonous manchineel, found on most of the beaches and easily recognized from its bright green leaves.

For an extensive discussion of these issues (including tools and spares to buy in advance), and every other aspect of the cruising lifestyle from boats to equipment, life on board and travel ashore, see our how-to text *Cruising for Cowards*.

APPENDIX C
Our Boat and Equipment

BAGHEERA after 116,000 miles

We purchased *Bagheera*, a Beneteau First 38s, from the factory in France in 1985. Our criteria for a cruising boat included sound construction, good performance on all points of sail, and sufficient accommodation and storage to provide a long-term home for a family of five. Budget was a major consideration. We planned to cruise for two years in the Mediterranean and Caribbean, then sell the boat in Florida. We never dreamed that six years later we would have completed a circumnavigation. To date, we have cruised over 116,000 miles aboard *Bagheera* and visited 114 countries.

The Beneteau First 38s is a Jean Berret-designed sloop was introduced into the European market in 1979 with both medium- and deep-draft versions available. A tall double-spreader "S" rig, keel-stepped as opposed to the standard deck-stepped single-spreader rig, was available also. In 1985, the tooling was updated to become the First 405 using the same hull and keel but with a modified deck and interior. At this time, Beneteau considered the Beneteau First series a line of performance cruisers, with the Iylle their traditional cruisers and the First Class models representing the racers. More recently, Beneteau oriented their Oceanis line toward bluewater cruising and the First series has become more race-oriented.

About our dream
Our love affair with the Beneteau First 38 started in 1983. Andy was a partner in a yacht dealership in Vancouver representing Swan, C & C, Whitby and Yamaha. The French boats exhibited at the London Boat Show that year were noteworthy, and a few weeks later both of us toured the five major French manufacturers. The Beneteau company's approach to the building of high-quality, affordable cruisers was impressive, as was their willingness to adapt their production to suit the North American buyer. Andy returned to Canada as their dealer, and that summer we took delivery of our own personal First 38, a boat that subsequently we sold to order the new boat in Europe.

Some may question whether a production-built boat has the structural

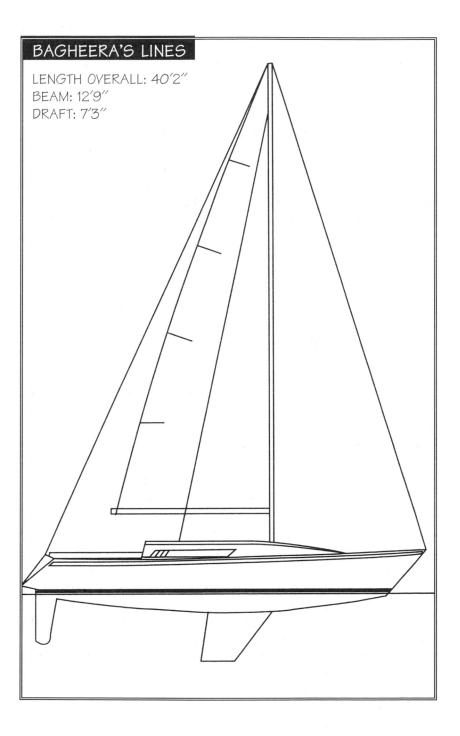

BAGHEERA'S LINES

LENGTH OVERALL: 40'2"
BEAM: 12'9"
DRAFT: 7'3"

integrity to undertake a prolonged offshore cruise. The French government has long imposed strict requirements on their builders, who must specify the standard to which each boat is constructed. The First 38 has a Category 1 certificate, built for unrestricted offshore use. Others may question the modern hull and keel and the moderate displacement that contrast with the traditionalist's view of the ideal passagemaker, but we had no doubts on the matter.

Dozens of offshore passages were being made each year by the better production boats, and in Andy's dealership they had encountered no structural problems with Beneteaus. As to design philosophy, we both had sailed offshore extensively—as amateurs and as professionals—in a variety of boats ranging from ultralight racers to the heavy and traditional. Over the years we had grown to favor boats that are somewhere in the middle—quick, well mannered, not too heavy, and a joy to sail. For us, the most desirable characteristic from the perspectives of safety and comfort in an offshore cruiser is sailing efficiency; the ability to make fast passages and to sail out of trouble upwind and down.

Had money not been a consideration, we might have chosen a boat such as a Swan, similar in design concept and beautifully built. But being on a budget we felt that the First 38 offered us the most "bang for the buck." It's a decision we have never regretted. In fact, we know of several First 38s besides ours that also have circumnavigated.

Bagheera, named after the black panther in Rudyard Kipling's Jungle Book, is a standard deep-keel Beneteau First 38s, the tall-rigged version with American specs. Besides its performance, workable deck design and comfortable cockpit, we were attracted to the layout below. For our family of five, the accommodation works well: two aft double cabins, convenient galley, large chart table with abundant space for electronics, long settee/sea berths, full-sized table in the main cabin, and spacious forward cabin.

The boat came with two heads, but before long we'd turned the small aft head into storage. To give each of our three children his own sleeping area, Andy added an upper berth in the port aft cabin. We had the berth cushions divided lengthwise and fitted with leecloths — both in the interest of sea berths and to provide extra storage on long passages. To protect the upholstery, we had light slipcovers made, comfortable and easy to launder.

The interior has good stowage, including four hanging lockers and a wet-locker. We modified the galley to include extra drawers, and Andy fitted bookshelves and lockers outboard of the settees, soon filled with school supplies and books. Whether fiction or reference, reading was a major source of recreation for the whole family; at one time we had over 600 books on board.

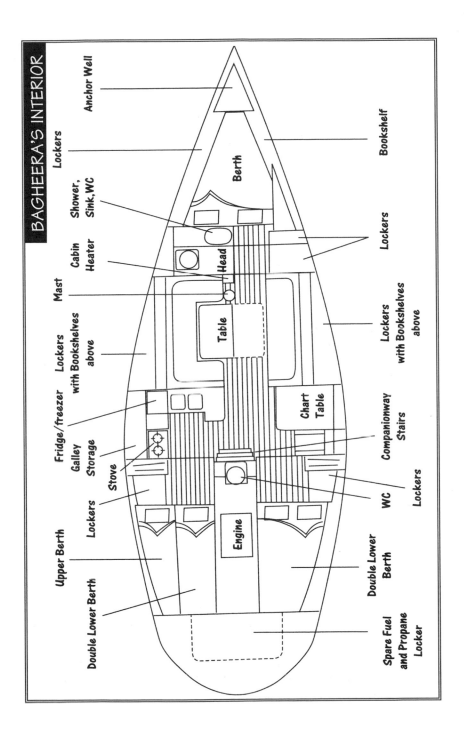

BAGHEERA'S INTERIOR

Anchor Well

Lockers

Bookshelf

Shower, Sink, WC

Berth

Cabin Heater

Head

Mast

Table

Lockers

Fridge/freezer

Lockers with Bookshelves above

Lockers with Bookshelves above

Galley Storage

Chart Table

Stove

Companionway Stairs

Upper Berth

Lockers

WC

Lockers

Double Lower Berth

Engine

Double Lower Berth

Spare Fuel and Propane Locker

Initially, *Bagheera* enjoyed basic electronics. These included a log, wind, depth, VHF radio, Transit satnav and Autohelm 6000 pilot. Three furling headsails, a storm jib, a conventionally battened mainsail with three very deep reefs, and a racing spinnaker completed our sail inventory. Two changes included a) going up one millimeter in wire diameter for all standing rigging, and b) fiberglassing in a 5/8-inch marine-ply horizontal bulkhead at the waterline under the V-berth forward to improve impact resistance should we encounter a hard floating object. Below decks, the stove, batteries, floorboards, drawers and lockers were all made secure in the event of a knockdown.

About our voyages

Andy commissioned the boat in England, then two months later the boys and Liza arrived. Duncan had just turned nine, Colin was six and Jamie two. Following a shakedown cruise along the coast, we headed south and the first year went by very successfully. The Mediterranean was ideal for our boys, with short passages, great cultures, interesting food, and sightseeing ashore. We fitted quickly into the routine of schooling on board.

On our return to Gibraltar from Turkey, we increased the lengths of passages to prepare the boys for the Atlantic crossing. Time was starting to run out on our two-year cruising plan, but, we asked ourselves, did we really want to go home? An invitation to join the Tall Ships events to represent Canada in Australia in 1988 to celebrate their bicentenary, a successful Atlantic crossing, and the boys' enthusiasm persuaded us to keep on going.

For the longer Pacific passages we added a Ham/SSB radio, an Aries windvane, a wind generator and a cockpit bimini. We departed Panama for the wonderful nature fix of the Galapagos Islands, then sailed on to French Polynesia, Rarotonga, Tonga, Fiji and New Caledonia, making our Australian landfall in November 1987 at Coffs Harbor, New South Wales.

We loved Australia with its friendly people and exotic birds and animals. The boys did well at school and we, having been given work permits, rebuilt the kitty. We also made several additions to *Bagheera* which included a freezer with holdover plates, solar panels, radar, an electric anchor windlass, and a weatherfax. April 1989 found *Bagheera* heading up the Barrier Reef, then taking part in the Darwin-Ambon race and cruising through Indonesia, Singapore, Malaysia and Thailand.

For a year we ambled across the Indian Ocean, meeting few cruisers and stopping in the Andaman Islands, Sri Lanka, India, the Maldives, Chagos and the Seychelles. Then it was down the East African coast from

Kenya to Madagascar and around the Cape of Good Hope in early 1991. After visits to St. Helena, Fortaleza (Brazil) and French Guyana, we crossed our outgoing track northeast of Barbados, and in Antigua we celebrated the completion of our circumnavigation.

After six years, it was time to go home. The boys wanted to be in regular high schools, and we had to recoup financially. Andy returned to yacht brokerage and formed a new dealership. I started to write cruising books and articles, and to give seminars at the major U.S. boat shows. *Bagheera* sat for too many weekends (when Duncan wasn't using her) at the yacht club dock, although we did manage a trip to the rugged Queen Charlotte Islands and a few weeks of cruising with her every summer, and her mileage continued to mount.

A few years later, we decided we'd earned a sabbatical. We upgraded much of the old gear and added a Profurl in-boom mainsail furling system, a Spectra watermaker, extra solar panels, a second GPS, 12-volt refrigeration, and a cruising chute. A new wind generator was installed during the trip. We left from Vancouver in August to spend the fascinating year cruising 11,500 miles down the Pacific Coast, through Panama, gunkholing Central America and Cuba, then continuing up the U.S. Atlantic Coast to Nova Scotia. Although the plan was to return to Vancouver via the Great Lakes our nephew lured us back to Europe for his wedding. This gave us the excuse to explore more of the Med., including the Middle East, and the Black Sea. Then, after cruising the Moroccan coast to the Canary Islands and Cape Verdes came West Africa with Senegal, 150 inland up the Gambia River and the islands of Guinea Bissau before crossing the Atlantic to Brazil. At this point Andy had to have back surgery so there was no question of rounding the Horn, instead we enjoyed two more years in the Caribbean before deciding that we really should get to know our home cruising ground of the Pacific Northwest. Having been in the world of work and racing we had never done this before - and it is quite magnificent!

About Bagheera

Hull and deck: The hull is hand-laid fiberglass with a massive grid glassed inside. The balsa-cored deck is bonded and bolted to the hull, and all bulkheads are secured for their entire perimeters to the hull and deck. The result is an incredibly strong structure with so little movement that we have never been troubled by leaks or squeaks. The keel is a deep cast-iron fin and the rudder a balanced spade.

In Australia, areas below the waterline were treated in 1988 for osmotic blistering at Beneteau's expense. The hull was painted with Awlgrip at the same time to hide the damage done when a teenager in charge of a fast aluminum runabout tried to take a short-cut through our topsides while we were at anchor. There are wide side decks and a very large anchor locker. The cockpit is large and is protected by a dodger, bimini and side-curtains. A stainless steel scaffold mounted aft carries four elevated solar panels, a wind generator and radar.

Sails and rig: The original Hood genoa furler was replaced in 1998 with a Profurl unit when the new in-boom mainsail system was fitted. We feel the latter is one of the best cruising developments we've seen in recent years, giving us an efficient, fully battened, deeply roached and nicely shaped mainsail that can be reefed or stowed quickly by one of us from the cockpit. There are three furling genoas, a storm jib that hanks on to a removable inner forestay, a new cruising chute with a snuffer, and a very old racing spinnaker. Except for the spinnakers, all sails are of cruising Dacron, which we find long-lasting, reliable and easier to handle and repair than laminated sails. Before heading offshore again, we replaced all standing rigging and the lifelines, as we feel that stainless steel rigging more than 10 years old cannot be relied upon in extreme conditions.

Later we added an electric winch for the main inboom system. What a joy! Now we only have to press a button for the mainsail to go up or down. It can also be used for the genoa furling line and sheets.)

Engine and systems: The standard 50-h.p. Perkins 4-108 has lived up to its reputation for reliability and continued to start instantly and run well. After 10,600 hours it was rebuilt. Except for a rear oil seal, which entailed removing the engine in Fiji to change this $2 part, the only replacements needed were three exhaust elbows. One of the great features of the Beneteau First 38 is the cockpit floor that unbolts, allowing the engine literally to be lifted straight out.

Bagheera has a high-output alternator, an Air Marine wind generator, and 240 watts of solar power to feed five 12-volt deep-cycle batteries that provide 575 amp-hours and 1 designated starting battery. Refrigeration started with a 12-volt system, then an engine-driven holdover-plate arrangement for a freezer that necessitated running the motor once or twice a day. We subsequently replaced this with a Nova-Cool 12-volt unit that has proven excellent for both refrigeration and freezing, even in 90° weather. In addition, it is self-maintaining when we leave the boat to travel inland using solar panel power.

To cope with unreliable diesel quality around the world, we fitted a double Racor filter system ahead of the two standard fuel filters, enabling us to switch filters instantly if the one in use chokes up. We generally use biocide to prevent bacterial contamination.

The Spectra watermaker produces a genuine nine gallons per hour for eight amps, and reliably; it has made life on board infinitely more comfortable. We always have full tanks, take frequent showers, and have no concerns about polluted water. It is quiet, its output is virtually unaffected by temperature changes, and as it draws very little power, it can be run either by solar panels or by the wind generator. Mechanical servicing is minimal because the high-pressure pump has no fast moving parts.

Electronics and navigation: Andy is an ex-navy pilot who likes his gadgets, and we both enjoy good instrumentation. Like most cruisers we continue to add toys and we always have a wish list. Following a lightning strike in Mozambique that destroyed most of the electronics and many of the electrics, we re-equipped the cockpit with Raymarine instruments, and now have their 7000 autopilot and 24-mile LCD radar. We also have a fishfinder, chart plotter with C-Maps, AIS and cockpit VHF radio.

At the chart table, we have another VHF radio and ICOM single side band/ham radio from which, with a Pactor III and laptop, we also send e-mail, get grib files, weather faxes etc: In addition, there is a cockpit instrument repeater and gauges for electrical outputs and consumption.

We carry a 406 MHz EPIRB, two magnetic compasses, one electronic compass, one hand-bearing compass, a recording barograph, two sets of binoculars, a handheld VHF and a powerful searchlight. We have over 300 charts on board, with guides, almanacs, sight-reduction tables, nav-aid and lists, and tables use Nobeltec charting on the laptop.

Safety gear: We replaced our original Beaufort life raft with a Winslow six-person raft packed with food and water . A full range of man-overboard recovery gear goes with us, plus a seven-foot drogue with 400 feet of 5/8-inch nylon, and a collision mat. We find it is prudent to carry two large radar reflectors to avoid the threat of a blind spot from the mast. As we mainly cruise as a couple, there is often only one person on watch, so we have strict rules about using harnesses and jacklines: no one leaves the cockpit to go forward on deck unless the other is there keeping an eye out. Offshore at night we use our masthead tri-color, but in coastal waters we use the conventional bow and stern lights because we feel they are less confusing to others trying to gauge our range and heading.

In addition to our 33-lb. Bruce anchor on 300 feet of 5/16-inch high-test chain, we carry a 45-lb. CQR with 80 feet of 3/8-inch chain and 400 feet of one-inch octoplait nylon, and also a 22-lb. Danforth with chain and line that is used as a kedge, or in a blow in tandem with the Bruce. We find the electric anchor windlass indispensable for the ground tackle, but also to hoist the dinghy on deck and to take a person up the mast (although for these we can also use the cockpit electric winch).

Bagheera is a dry boat, thanks to its moderate displacement and reserve buoyancy in the ends. We love the finger-light steering in all conditions, a sailplan that can be handled by a single not-so-young watchkeeper, and the performance that has allowed us to average more than 150 miles per day on all our ocean crossings. To us, she is the perfect combination of seakindliness, seaworthiness and fun on the ocean along with being a comfortable home when at anchor.

For articles on cruising by **Liza Copeland** see:

Cruising World, Sailing, Blue Water Sailing, SAILNET.COM and *Pacific Yachting.*

APPENDIX D

Glossary of Terms

(Definitions specific to *Comfortable Cruising*)

ABEAM Off one side of the boat

ABOUT To change direction in sailing, when the wind fills the sails from the other side. To come about; change course

ADRIFT Drifting, or broken loose from a mooring. Dragging anchor

AFT At the back of the boat; behind

ALOFT Up above; as up in the rigging or up the mast

ANEMOMETER An instrument for measuring the velocity of the wind

ANTIFOULING Bottom paint, to deter growth of weed, barnacles etc.

ASTERN To go backwards; behind the boat

AUTOPILOT Electro/mechanical steering device for automatic course keeping

BACKS, BACKING When the wind changes in an anti-clockwise direction

BACKSTAY Wire supporting the mast which attaches to back of boat

BAGGYWRINKLE Material on the shrouds, to stop chafe damage to sails, traditionally made out of old rope

BAROMETER An instrument for registering the atmospheric pressure

BATTENS Stiffening pieces usually of fiberglass or plastic, traditionally wood. Used to support the roach of a sail.

BEAM REACH Sailing at about 90' to the wind direction

BEAM Width of a boat at its widest point; 'On the beam' at right angles to the direction of the boat

BEAR AWAY To alter course away from the wind

BEARING The angle between and object and north

BEATING To sail into wind by zig-zagging (tacking) towards it

BEAUFORT SCALE International scale of wind strength, Forces 0-12

BELOW Inside the boat

BERTH A bed; To berth, to come into the dock; A berth, the space in which a boat lies at the dock

BILGE Space under the floor boards

BINNACLE A stand in the cockpit on which the compass in supported

BITTER END The extreme end of a line

BLOCK A pulley

BOAT HOOK A device for catching hold of a ring bolt or grab line in coming alongside a pier or picking up a mooring

BOOM Horizontal spar supporting the bottom of the mainsail

BOOM VANG Tackle from the boom to the deck to keep the boom from lifting (also called a kicking strap)

BOSUN'S CHAIR A chair for going up the mast generally made from wood and canvas and hoisted by a halyard

BOW The front of the boat

BROACH Heading up into wind uncontrollably

BULKHEAD A structural 'wall'which divides the yacht into compartments

BUOY Floating device anchored to the sea's bottom. Used as markers for navigation, automatic weather reporting, enables vessels to tie up, as fishing net markers etc.

BURGEE A triangular flag used to identify a yacht club

CAPSTAN A winchlike drum on a windlass used for hauling in rope

CAST OFF Undo a mooring or towing line

CATAMARAN Boat with two hulls

CHAFE Damage due to abrasion

CHAIN PLATES Hull attachments for standing rigging

CHART Nautical map showing navigational aids, depths, hazards and land forms

CHRONOMETER A highly accurate clock used by navigators

CLEAT Fitting on which to secure a line

'CHUTE Spinnaker

CLEW Aft bottom corner of a sail

CLINKER Lapstrake planked (hull), planks overlapping like clapboards

CLOSE-HAULED Sailing as close to the wind as possible

CLOSE-WINDED A craft capable of sailing very close to the wind

COAMING The raised protection around a cockpit

COCKPIT A recessed part of the deck in which to sit and steer

COMPANIONWAY Entry and stairway to get below

COMPASS An instrument using a pointer which indicates magnetic north

CRADLE A frame used to hold a boat when she is hauled out of the water

CRUISER Any boat having arrangements for living aboard

CUTTER A single masted sailboat in which the mast is set amidships and having split
  headsail rig. (See SLOOP)

DEAD RECKONING (DR) Estimate of the boat's position based on course & speed

DEATH ROLL Side-to-side uncontrollable motion when going downwind

DECKHEAD Underside of the deck (ceiling in a house)

DEPTH SOUNDER An electronic instrument that measures the depth of the water

DEVIATION Angular difference between compass bearing and magnetic bearing caused
  by the effect of iron aboard ship. Effect varies for each point of the compass

DINGHY A small boat or tender

DRAFT Depth of the boat below the waterline

DRAGGING When an anchor slips along the bottom

DROGUE A device trailed behind a boat to create drag

EBB The outgoing tide

ENSIGN A national flag flown on a boat

EPIRB Emergency Position Indicating Radio Beacon

FAIRLEAD A fitting which changes the direction of a sheet or halyard led through it

FATHOM A measurement of depth (1 fathom =6 feet)

FEND OFF To push the boat away from an object so no damage occurs

FENDERS (bumpers)Inflated cylinders used to protect the sides of boat when berthed

FIDDLES Strips of metal or wood to stop objects from sliding e.g. on the stove or table

FLOOD TIDE A rising tide

FLOTSAM Floating debris

FOOT Bottom edge of a sail

FOREDECK Deck at the front of a boat

FOREGUY (downhaul) Line to pull down the spinnaker pole

FORESTAY Wire supporting the mast which is attached to the front of the boat

FORWARD Towards the front or bow

FREEBOARD The height of the hull between the water and the deck

FRONT Leading edge of a moving mass of cold or warm air. Cold fronts are usually
  associated with rain, lightning and squalls. Warm fronts are associated with heavy
  clouds and rain

FURL Mainsail: To drop and lash to the boom. Genoa and some mainsails: To roll around
  an aluminum extrusion which rotates

FURLING GEAR Equipment used to enable furling of the sails

GALLEY Boat kitchen

GANGPLANK A moveable bridge used to get from the dock or pier to a boat or vice versa

GENOA Large foresail (overlaps the mainsail)

GIMBALS A device to enable an object, such as a compass or galley stove, to remain horizontal regardless of the boat's motion

GO ABOUT (to tack) To turn the bow through the wind when sailing

GOOSENECK Hinged fitting which attaches the boom to the mast

GPS (GLOBAL POSITIONING SYSTEM) Position indicating electronic navigational aid

GROUND TACKLE Anchor, chain, etc., used to secure a vessel to the bottom

GUNWALE (gunnel) The upper edge of a ship's side

GUST Sudden increase in wind

GUY Windward spinnaker sheet that attaches to pole

GYBE (Jibe) To change course downwind so that the sails change sides (can be dangerous when unplanned)

GYPSY (wildcat) A revolving sprocket on a windlass which has pockets to engage the links of chain

HALYARD Line for hoisting sails

HANKS Clips for attaching foresail to the forestay

HARD OVER Placement of the wheel, or tiller, when it is put over as far as possible to one side or the other

HATCH An opening through the deck

HAUL To draw a boat or net out of the water

HEAD OF SAIL Top corner of the sail

HEAD UP To luff or turn towards the wind

HEAD(S) Boat toilet

HEAD-TO-WIND When the front of the boat, or bow, points into wind

HEADSAILS Sails that attach forward of the mast

HEADSTAY (forestay) Rigging wire from the bow or foredeck supporting the mast

HEAVING-TO A method of stopping the vessel and allowing it to maintain a comfortable attitude, usually with a reefed mainsail, backed jib and lashed helm

HEEL When boat leans over at an angle (most severe when beating in a strong wind)

HELM To steer; steering device

HOIST Pull up

HULL Main body of the boat

JIB foresail (in front of the mast)

KEDGE A small anchor

KEDGING To move a boat by hauling on a kedge anchor

KEEL Appendage under the hull running fore and aft, needed for vertical stability and to prevent leeway

KETCH A two-masted sailing vessel with smaller aftermast stepped forward of the stern post

L.O.A. Means length over all and refers to the longest measurement of the boat as compared to the length at the waterline

LANYARD A line fastened to an article, such as a pail, whistle, knife, or other small tool, for purpose of securing it

LATITUDE Distance in degrees north or south of the equator

LAZARETTE Storage lockers on deck aft of the steering wheel

LEE CLOTH Length of Canvas secured at the side of a berth to keep occupant in when boat heels or rolls

LEE SHORE Coast onto which the wind is blowing

LEE SIDE, (LEEWARD) Side of the boat away from the direction of the wind

LEECH The trailing edge of a sail (back edge)

LEEWAY Sideways drift

LIFELINE Lines around the boat to stop people falling overboard

LIFERAFT Specially designed inflatable raft with food, water and an EPIRB for use when the yacht has to be abandoned

LIFE RING Floating ring to throw to a person who has fallen overboard

LIMBER HOLES Holes bored horizontally through the frames of the boat near the bottom to allow water in the bilge to drain to the lowest point where it can be pumped out

LINE A term for any rope used aboard a boat

LOCKER A storage compartment on a boat. A chain locker is a compartment where anchor chain is kept. A hanging locker is a closet sufficiently large for hanging of clothing

LOG Measures speed and distance through the water

LOGBOOK, OR THE LOG Regular record of boat's progress with position, speed, weather etc.

LONGITUDE A measurement of distance expressed to degrees East and West of the meridian of Greenwich, England

LUFF Front edge of a sail

LYING A HULL A technique useful in heavy weather, with bare poles and helm lashed such that the vessel lies beam on to the seas

MAINSAIL Large sail attached to aft side of main mast

MAKE FAST To belay or tie a line securely

MARLINSPIKE A pointed wooden or steel instrument used to open up the strands of rope and wire

MAST Vertical spar which supports the sails

MASTHEAD Top of the mast

MILE At sea the nautical mile is one minute of latitude at the equator, or 6,080 feet; used as a measure of distance

MINUTE One 60th of a degree of latitude or longitude; also, one 60th of an hour

MIZZEN The shorter mast aft on a yawl or ketch.Same as mizzenmast

MOOR To secure a boat between two posts, to a dock, or to a buoy

MOTORSAILER A vessel combining the features of both a sailboat and a motorboat

NAVIGABLE Water that is deep enough to permit passage of boats

NAVIGATION LIGHTS Lights used at night. Red faces port (left side) and green faces starboard (right); white faces aft

NEAP TIDES Smaller changes in the height of the tide, occur twice monthly at the half moon (alternate with spring tides)

OARLOCK, OR ROWLOCK Fitting which acts as a pivot point for an oar

OFF THE WIND Sailing on a reach or run

OFFSHORE WIND The wind when it is blowing from or off the shore

ON THE WIND See close-hauled

ONE-DESIGN CLASS A number of sailboats that are built and equipped exactly alike

OUTBOARD Outside the perimeter of the deck; portable engine for a dinghy

OVER STAND To sail beyond an object, such as a buoy

OVER ALL The boat's extreme length. Abbreviated LOA

OVERHAUL To overtake or gain on another vessel at sea. Also to do a complete repair to an engine or boat

PADEYE A fitting on deck used for attaching lines or blocks

PAINTER Bow line by which a small boat is towed or made fast to a mooring

PARALLEL RULES A pair of straight-edges fastened together so that the distance between them may be changed while their edges remain parallel. Used for transferring lines from one part of a chart to another

PAY OUT To let out a line

PILING Vertical timbers or logs driven into the water's bottom to form a support for a dock or to act as a breakwater

PILOT A man qualified and licensed to direct ships in and out of a harbour

PILOTING Coastal navigation

PITCH The up and down motion of a boat about a central axis. Also, the angle of the propeller blades

PLANING When a boat rides on top of the water

PORT CAPTAIN The official at a port who is in charge of all harbor activities

PORT SIDE Left side of the boat when looking forward

PORT TACK When the wind comes on the port side,(sails will be to starboard)

PRAM A small dinghy, usually bluff bowed

PREVENTER Line leading forward which holds the boom at right angles to the boat when going downwind, to prevent a gybe

PULPIT The railings at the bow of a yacht

QUARTER Between astern and abeam (back and middle) of the boat

RACE A very strong tidal current

RADAR Electronic instrument for detecting other vessels, land and storms

RAFT UP Tie alongside another vessel

REACH Sailing with the wind on the beam, the sail is approximate half way out. Can be a close reach, beam reach, or broad reach

REEF A ridge of rocks which is at or near the surface; a portion of sail furled and tied down to reduce the area exposed to the wind

RHUMB LINE A course that crosses all meridians at the same angle

RIG To prepare a boat for sailing; the mast and its supports

RIGGING The gear which supports and controls the spars and the sails such as sheets, shrouds, stays and halyards

RULES OF THE ROAD The international regulations for preventing collisions at sea

RUNNING BACKSTAYS Adjustable lines supporting the back of the mast

RUNNING LIGHTS Lights used at night by vessels to identify type and indicate direction when under way

RUNNING To sail with the wind behind the boat

SAIL TIES Webbing strips used to tie the sails when furled

SAILS Shaped dacron, or other strong material, used to catch the wind and propel the boat through the water

SATELLITE NAVIGATION, OR SAT NAV Electronic device that aids navigation

SCHOONER A sailboat with two or more masts, the aftermost one being of equal or greater height than those ahead

SCOPE The length of mooring or anchor line in use

SEA ANCHOR A drag device, usually canvas, streamed from the bow and used to keep a boat headed into the wind during very heavy weather

SEA COCK A valve attached to a through-hull fitting

SECURE To make fast

SET Trimming a sail for the wind direction; course error due to current; the shape of the sail

SEXTANT An instrument used to aid navigation by measuring altitudes of celestial bodies and hence determining position of the boat

SHACKLE A U-shaped piece of metal with a pin which secures the open end

SHEET A line used to trim a sail

SHIPSHAPE Well-kept, orderly, clean

SHROUDS Wire supports on either side of the mast

SKEG A fixed fin near the stern, often supporting the rudder

SLACK To ease off a line

SLACK WATER The short period of time when the ebb (low) and flood (high) remain stationary before changing direction

SLOOP A single masted sailboat in which the mast is set forward of amidships and usually using a single overlapping headsail

SNUB To check or stop a line

SOLE Floor of the interior of the boat

SPAR Term for masts, booms, spinnaker poles, etc.

SPINNAKER Lightweight, parachute-like sail (usually colorful) used when the wind is aft of the beam

SPINNAKER POLE A boom attached to the mast at one end and the spinnaker at the other, used to support and control the spinnaker

SPLICE To join or finish rope or wire by tucking the strands together, such as short, long, eye and back splice, etc.

SPREADERS Short struts between mast and shrouds to add support to the rig

SPRING LINES Docking lines used to prevent a boat from moving fore and aft

SPRING TIDES Greatest change in the height of the tide, occurs twice monthly at the new and full moons (alternates with neap tides)

STANCHIONS Vertical supports for lifelines

STAND BY An order employed to alert crewmen, or on radio to ask receiver to wait

STANDING RIGGING The shrouds and stays which support the rig

STARBOARD Right side of the vessel when looking forward

STARBOARD TACK Sailing with wind on the starboard (right) side of the boat, (sails will be to port)

STAY Wire supporting the mast fore and aft

STEERAGE WAY Sufficient forward speed to allow rudder control

STERN The back of the boat

STOWING Securing or putting away

STRIKE To lower a sail or flag.

STUFFING BOX A device around a propeller shaft that permits it to revolve freely without letting water into the hull

SWELL Nonbreaking, long, easy waves. The expansion of wood when wet

TACHOMETER An instrument used to display the r.p.m. of an engine

TACK Act of passing the bow through the wind when sailing; the front lower corner of the sail

TACKLE A system of blocks and line to give mechanical advantage

TELL-TALE A short piece of ribbon or wool tied to a shroud or attached to a sail to indicate the flow or direction of the wind

TENDER A small boat employed to go back and forth to the shore from a larger boat or a term used to describe a boat that heels easily

TIDE The rise and fall of the sea level due to gravitational pull of the moon and sun

TOPPING LIFT (uphaul) Lines supporting main boom and spinnaker pole

TOPSIDES That portion of the hull above the water line

TRANSOM Flat part across the back of boat

TRILIGHT A navigation light carried at the masthead combining port, starboard and stem lights.

TRIM Fine tune a sail

TRIMARAN Boat with three hulls

TRISAIL A storm sail used in place of a mainsail.

TROUGH The valley between two waves

TRUE COURSE The actual course relative to true north, or compass course when corrected for deviation and variation

VARIATION The difference in degrees between true and magnetic north

VEER When the wind changes in a clockwise direction

WAKE The eddies and swirls left astern of a boat in motion

WASH The waves made by a boat moving through the water

WATCH A period of duty on board a vessel

WATERLINE Demarkation between portion of hull above water and below

WAY Movement through the water of the boat

WEATHER FAX Instrument for receiving graphic weather charts

WEBBING Woven tape or strapping

WEIGH To raise the anchor

WINCH Round metal drum with detachable handle for winding in lines

WIND GENERATOR Wind driven electricity-producing device

WIND INSTRUMENTS Devices that measure wind speed and determine its direction

WIND VELOCITY Rate of motion of the wind

WINDLASS Mechanical or electrical device to lift anchor and chain

WINDSHIFI'Change in wind direction

WINDVANE device which automatically steers a boat at a pre-set angle to the wind

WINDWARD Direction from which the wind is blowing

WING ON WING Sailing downwind with the genoa and mainsail on opposite sides

YAWL A sailboat similar to a ketch but with smaller aftermast stepped abaft the stem post

SEND A COPY TO A FRIEND!

ORDER through **www.aboutcruising.com**, or at your local book and-marine stores or contact:

Romany Publishing,
3943 West Broadway, Vancouver, B.C. V6R 2C2, CANADA
Tel: 1 (604) 228-8712/ Fax: 1 (604) 228-8779
E-mail: Romany@telus.net

Please send:

☐ *JUST CRUISING* – Europe to Australia $19.95US (S18.95Can)

☐ *STILL CRUISING* – Australia to Asia, Africa and America –
$19.95US (S18.95Can)

☐ *CRUISING FOR COWARDS* – A Practical A –Z for Coastal and
Offshore Sailors $24.95US/Can

☐ *COMFORTABLE CRUISING* – Around North and Central America
$19.95US/Can

☐ DVD – *JUST CRUISING* Based on 'On Board 5 for six', a finalist
in the CANPRO TV Documentary Awards, this video shows the lure of
life afloat around the world, besides giving much practical boating
and travel information. 55 min. $19.95US/Can)

(PLUS $8.00 SHIPPING AND HANDLING)
To:

Name
_____

Address
_____

City _____ Prov/State _____

Postal Code _____ Country _____

☐ Payment enclosed (Sorry, no CODs)
☐ By cheque (made payable to Romany Publishing)
☐ By Credit Card via by tel:/fax:/email

About the Author

Liza is a lifelong sailor. While growing up in England she became an avid racer and has competed in several world championships and offshore events in a variety of classes worldwide. In 1973 she married Andy in the Caribbean aboard the classic yacht *Ticonderoga* and they have since sailed over 140,000 miles together, including a circumnavigation with their three children.

Cruising around North and Central America followed, then they were lured back across the Atlantic for a family wedding. After another seven years in the Mediterranean and Black Sea, West Africa, Brazil, the Caribbean and currently the Pacific Northwest, their Beneteau *Bagheera* has taken them 116,000 miles to 114 countries.

Liza is the award-winning, best-selling author of four cruising books. *Just Cruising* and *Still Cruising* recount their world travels with *Comfortable Cruising* describing their voyage and giving planning information to sail around North and Central America. *Cruising for Cowards* is a current technical and practical A-Z for cruisers whether coastal voyaging or offshore. Liza also writes for a variety of yachting magazines, gives seminars at major boat shows and to a variety of clubs and organizations. When not sailing the oceans of the world, leading cruising groups or touring giving talks on boating and travel, Liza and Andy live in Vancouver, BC where Liza occasionally returns to her former career as an educational psychologist.

Liza is the winner of the Geoff Pack Memorial Award.
Awarded to the person who, by his or her writing, has done most to foster and encourage ocean cruising in small craft and the practice of seamanship.

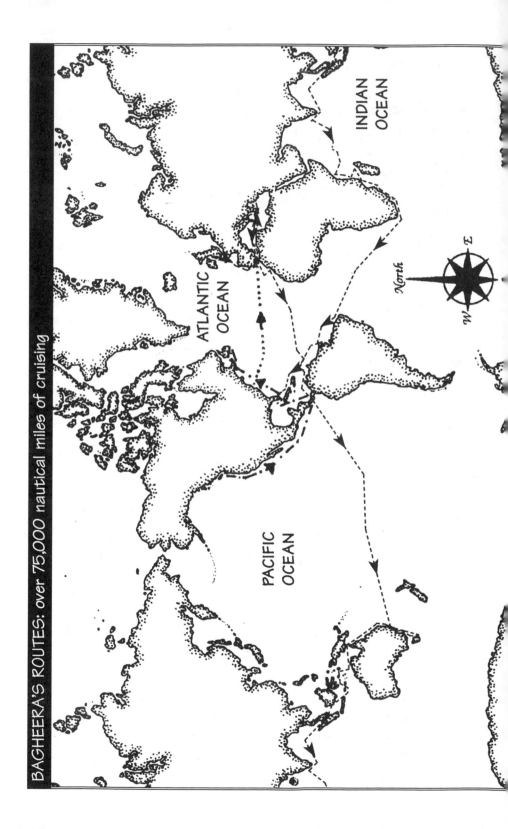

BAGHEERA'S ROUTES: over 75,000 nautical miles of cruising

ATLANTIC OCEAN

INDIAN OCEAN

PACIFIC OCEAN

North

E

W